Lighthouse Hauntings

Lighthouse Hauntings

12 ORIGINAL TALES OF THE SUPERNATURAL

*EDITED BY CHARLES G. WAUGH
& MARTIN H. GREENBERG*

DOWN EAST BOOKS

Cover painting © 2002 by James Sollers
Cover design by Janet L. Patterson
Text layout by Northeast Corner Designs

ISBN 89272-519-2
Library of Congress Control Number: 2002110437
Printed and bound at Versa Press, E. Peoria, Ill.

5   4   3   2   1

Down East Books / Camden, Maine
www.downeastbooks.com
Book orders: 1-800-766-1670

Contents

Introduction

When America was first being explored, lighthouses played a vital role in keeping shipping lanes open on both lakes and oceans. Often a ship would only have that singular beacon of light shining across the vast distance to orient itself and avoid the dangerous cliffs, treacherous reefs, and lurking hijackers that waited to snare the unwary sailing vessel. The lighthouse keeper alone was responsible for dozens of men's lives in an evening. If he failed, the consequences would be tragic.

Because of this idea, and the fact that lighthouse keeping seems a quaint and long-abandoned career with the advent of today's modern shipping equipment and techniques, the light-house and its keeper have become a romanticized stereotype of man against the elements, battling the ocean and weather to bring ships safely to port. People today think of the peaceful solitude, the ocean lapping against the shore as the keeper relaxes after a hard day's work, secure in the knowledge that all is well.

The truth is far different. As these lighthouses were often located on remote coastal peninsulas and small, barren islands, they required a special kind of person to man them. The men and women who kept the lights burning faced a harsh envi-ronment, isolation, and loneliness, especially during the long, dark winters. Storms lasted for days, and even weeks on end, and blizzards and endless snow cut off the lighthouse from the rest of society, leaving the keeper and his family (if he had one) without another soul to talk to for several months. Wrestling with the crude, dangerous equipment for up to twenty-four hours at a time to make sure the light stayed on was part of the job. Yes, it took a hardy breed to survive in the lighthouse—sometimes so hardy that they were loath to leave, even when their time was up.

Recently there has been renewed interest in the history and legends of the lighthouses that played such a prominent maritime role. Along both coasts and all around the Great Lakes, people are rediscovering this exciting time in our past, and finding that some of the men and women who kept the light on have not disappeared with the closing of the lighthouses . . .

A recent documentary explored the various haunted lighthouses around the country, mentioning ones from the rocky coast of Maine to the windswept beaches of Georgia, and the accidents, passions, and sometimes madness that led to terrible tragedy at these lonely outposts of civilization. It seems that lighthouses are an excellent focal point for restless spirits, especially if they were killed accidentally, or, as is often the case, at the hands of another.

We've gathered twelve of today's finest dark fiction writers and asked for stories about these lighthouse hauntings, these spirits from beyond the grave that lurk around a lighthouse like a moth around a flame. From Rick Hautala's chilling tale of a reporter who found much more than he bargained for, to Billie Sue Mosiman's story of jealousy and betrayal at an isolated Florida lighthouse; from a husband who returns from beyond to take care of his family, to a ghost that needs absolution before his final rest; ghosts and specters of all kinds are here. Turn the page and enter the spooky world of lighthouse hauntings.

RICK HAUTALA

The
Nephews

Just like every other Friday night, the Wheelwell—a working-man's bar just up from the docks in Cape Harvest, Maine—was filled with rafts of drifting cigarette smoke. It hung suspended in the air in several clearly defined strata—some charcoal gray, some as blue as the ocean at dawn. Glenn Chadwick had always suspected that on any given night, with a careful analysis of the layers of smoke, you could tell which of the locals was there without even looking or listening for any particular voice. On this chilly late-September night, however, such ruminations were the furthest thing from his mind when he burst through the barroom door a half-hour before closing time.

Perched on stools in their regular places at the brass rail were his buddies, Tony Miller and Jake "Butter" McPherson. Tony nodded and raised his forefinger, which was pretty much the extent of his "glad to see ya" greeting for anyone. Even if he did smile, you never would have seen it behind the thick tangle of his salt-and-pepper beard. Butter, who was clean-shaven, spun around and smiled widely, exposing his single large front tooth, which was stained yellow from nicotine and internal decay. It was the bright yellow color of this damaged

9

tooth that inspired his nickname, "Butter Tooth"—or "Butter" for short.

"Where the hell you been, boy-o?" Butter said, his voice slurring from the numerous beers he no doubt had already consumed. "Marsha was by an hour or so ago, lookin' for ya."

"I'll catch up with her later," Glenn said, waving his hand dismissively. He barely smiled as Shantelle, the barmaid, slid his usual—a twenty-ounce Shipyard—across to him. Glenn noticed that his right hand was shaking a little as he clasped the ice-rimmed glass and raised it to his mouth. The first gulp made him snort and shiver, but it felt good going down.

"What's that you got there?" Tony asked, indicating the black leather carrying case slung over Glenn's shoulder. "You ain't started carryin' a purse around, have ya?"

A few of the locals nearby burst out laughing, but Glenn hardly noticed or cared. Shaking his head from side to side, he eased up onto the vacant barstool next to Butter.

"I've been out to the Nephews," he said. Although he tried to sound casual, he could hear the slight tremor in his voice and wondered if his friends noticed it, too.

"You don't say," Butter replied, raising one gray, bushy eyebrow. Glenn saw Tony's posture stiffen a little as he leaned away from the bar railing and cast a sideways glance at him.

"What the hell you wanna be doin' out there?" Butter asked. "'Specially this time of year."

He took a pack of Luckys from the breast pocket of his denim work shirt, shook one out for himself, then offered one to Glenn. Again, Glenn noticed that his hand was trembling as he slid the cigarette into the corner of his mouth and accepted a light from Butter's Bic butane before he lit his own.

"Remember that writer fella up from Portland who was in here a day or so ago, asking about the lighthouse out on the Nephews?" he said, exhaling noisily.

Both Butter and Tony grunted and nodded.

"Well, he wanted me to take him out there today. I just got back."

Butter inhaled deeply, then tipped his head back and blew a stream of smoke up at the ceiling before responding.

"Wanted to see the haunted lighthouse, huh?" he said with a wide smile. Glenn had always thought Butter would be sensitive about how that big yellow tooth of his looked, but he never seemed to mind. And Butter still did all right with the ladies, which wasn't bad for a suntanned, weathered man in his late fifties.

"You gotta admit," Glenn said, shifting uneasily on the stool, "there's some pretty weird stories about that place."

"And all of it's horse-pucky, if you ask me," Tony said, craning his head around to look Glenn straight in the eye. "There's nothing on that island but a derelict lighthouse and the keeper's old house."

"That's pretty much what I told this guy," Glenn said, noisily exhaling smoke, "but he was determined to see it for himself. He wanted to see if he could spot a ghost or at least hear the music."

"There's no ghosts on that island, and there sure as hell ain't no music," Tony said. "Ain't nothin' there 'cept a couple of old buildings an' rocks covered with seagull shit."

"Yeah, but lemme tell you what happened, 'cause I'm gonna need one or both of you to go back with me in the morning to find him."

Tony groaned as he carefully placed his half-empty glass on the bar, then shifted all the way around so he was looking past Butter and squarely at Glenn.

"Let *me* tell *you* something." Tony's voice was so low Glenn had to strain to hear him above the general noise of the barroom. "The last damned thing we need is another story in some friggin' magazine or newspaper 'bout that lighthouse. All it means is we're gonna get more an' more curiosity seekers pokin' around out there. An' that can only mean more trouble."

"More trouble for you, maybe." Butter turned to Tony and winked. "I'm thinkin' you don't want any more boats around than's necessary so no one will find out how many bales of weed you're bringing in every month."

"Maybe I've got a wife and kids to feed," Tony snapped, "unlike you, you buck-toothed piece of—"

"Hey, hey. Take it easy, there," Glenn said. His whole life, it seemed, he'd been stepping in between Butter and Tony. For two men who swore they were such good friends, and cousins to boot, they sure did argue and insult each other plenty. "Lemme buy the next round. That writer fella paid me an extra fifty to wait around till after dark. That's why I'm so late."

Butter smiled, and Tony nodded slowly as he stroked his gray-flecked beard. Once Shantelle brought the new round, Glenn started to feel at least a little bit fortified. What had happened out on Nephews Island already seemed a bit more remote, a little easier to deal with.

"Tanguay was supposed to ferry this guy over today, but he never showed. Probably went to the fights in Lewiston. Fella's name is Mike—Mike Kimball, I think. Mike somethin' or other. Anyways, he's heard the stories about the lighthouse keeper and his wife. You know, how she was so lonely an' isolated all winter that she made him buy a piano to bring out to the island. Problem was, she only knew how to play one tune, and she played it day an' night, night an' day, till it finally drove the fella nuts. He took an ax to the piano, an' then to her."

"We all know the story, Glennie," Tony said as he raised his beer and took a few noisy swallows. "We don't need to hear it again. But you said you wanted us to go with you in the morning. You mean to say you left that guy out there?"

Again, Glenn shifted uncomfortably on the barstool. His throat felt suddenly dry in spite of the beer. "I didn't exactly *leave* him there. He just never showed up."

"Amounts to pretty much the same thing, don'tcha think?" Butter said as he crushed his cigarette out in the overflowing ashtray at his elbow. Glenn's was smoldering, unnoticed, between his fore- and middle fingers.

"He asked if I wanted to walk over to the lighthouse with him," Glenn went on, "but I figured it was better to stay with the boat. The ocean's still pretty heavy since that storm the other day, an' I didn't wanna get stranded myself."

"But you didn't mind leavin' him, huh?" Tony said.

"I told you, I didn't leave him. He never showed up." Glenn finally noticed that his cigarette had burned out, so he dropped it into the ashtray and continued. "I waited plenty long, an' then I went lookin' for him, but I couldn't find him. I sure as hell wasn't about to stick around all night. I figure either he ain't ever comin' off that island alive, or else he's sacked out someplace, just waiting for dawn."

"He have a cell phone with him?" Butter asked. "I mean, these days, you gotta put some effort into it if you want to be left alone."

In response, Glenn slung the carrying case off his shoulder and placed it carefully onto the bar. A few of the regulars moved closer, no longer trying to mask their interest as Glenn unzipped the black leather case.

"It's in here, 'long with his camcorder, a tape recorder, an' a couple of notebooks. I found all this stuff scattered around outside the lighthouse when I went lookin' for him. Looked kinda like he dropped it in a hurry."

"You really *did* go lookin' for him?" Tony said with a sniffing laugh. "You ain't just sayin' that?"

He was scowling, however, as he picked up the small tape recorder and inspected it for a moment or two. The side of the black casing was scuffed gray, and the small speaker hole in the front was clotted with dirt and turf. He sniffed softly as he placed it down on the bar, then threw back the rest of his beer and slid the empty toward Shantelle, who was standing close by, also listening to Glenn's story.

"'Course I did," Glenn said. "After I told him I wasn't interested in checking out any of the buildings, I told him to make sure he was back by nine o'clock. That's when the tide was up. You know, the dock that used to be there got washed away a couple of winters ago, so I had to run my boat up onto the beach. I was only gonna wait for the tide, 'cause if I missed it at nine o'clock, I wasn't gonna get off there till morning. No way I'm gonna freeze my ass off out there all night."

"Neither time nor tide," Butter said, nodding sagely and smiling to expose his big yellow tooth.

"And he never showed?" Shantelle asked, her dark eyes

narrowing with concern. She, too, knew all of the stories about Nephews Island.

"I hollered and hollered for him, but he never answered. It was dark by then. I got the flashlight from my boat and looked around some, but I never seen hide nor hair."

"You think the ghosts got him? 'S that it?" Tony asked.

Glenn couldn't see it, but he was fairly certain Tony was smirking at him from behind his beard.

"He might've fallen off one of the ledges, for all I know. The door to the lighthouse was open, so he might've gone up to the top where the light used to be, but I didn't see any evidence of him being up there. I didn't see his flashlight or anything."

"Shouldn't you call the Coast Guard?" Shantelle asked. She had taken Tony's empty glass and returned with a full one without asking. Glenn and Butter were still working on their beers.

"If we don't find him tomorrow, I guess we'd better," Glenn said. "The Coast Guard's not too keen about anyone bein' on that island, so I ain't about to admit that I been ferryin' writers out there."

"Good point," Butter said, nodding again, and he was echoed by Tony, saying, "*Damned* good point!"

While he was talking, Glenn was absentmindedly handling the contents of the writer's carrying case. As he looked down at the micro-recorder, he noticed that the tape inside had run about halfway through. He suddenly sat up straight and snapped his fingers.

"Wait a second. He was askin' me all sorts of questions about the island. Tapin' 'em. This is probably the tape."

He inspected the recorder until he found the controls, a small series of indented buttons on the side. After a little experimentation, he found the *rewind* button and pressed it. The tape made a faint hissing sound as it rewound a short way. Then Glenn pressed *play*.

" . . . saying you don't believe in ghosts, or that you just don't believe the stories about this particular lighthouse and island?"

"That's him. That's the writer," Glenn said, addressing no one in particular as the small machine in his hand played back the recorded voice. The barroom had suddenly gone totally quiet as everyone moved closer and listened.

"I'm not sayin' anything either way," Glenn's recorded voice said. "It's just that—when you live and work on the ocean for a livin', you hear all sorts of tales, and you take 'em for what they are, just tales—unless you experience somethin' yourself that you don't understand."

"Are you saying there's no ghosts in the lighthouse or the lightkeeper's house on Nephews Island?"

"I ain't sayin' there is, and I ain't sayin' there ain't," Glenn's recorded voice said.

"Christ! You sound like friggin' Einstein," Tony muttered before quaffing some of his beer. Shantelle and Glenn both glowered at him to keep him silent as the voices continued.

"So, tell me," the recorded voice of the writer said, "have you personally ever had any strange, or what you might call *supernatural*, experiences?"

There was a lengthy pause on the tape, and once it was clear that Glenn wasn't going to answer, the writer continued: "There have been numerous reports from fishermen and sailors passing by Nephews Island, especially late at night, who have heard strains of piano music. Some people have even said that it was a particular song they heard: 'Listen to the Mockingbird.' Have you ever been out here at night and heard anything like that?"

"I'm not usually out this way," Glenn's recorded voice said. "Most of my traps are set south of the harbor."

Butter jumped on his stool and turned to Glenn. "That ain't true," he said. "You have twenty or thirty pots out near the Nephews."

Glenn snapped the recorder off and glared at his friend.

"I wasn't gonna tell him that," he said, fighting back the sudden rush of anger he felt at Butter. "Listen to him. He's grillin' me like I'm some kind of authority or something. I wasn't about to tell him anything."

"But you've heard it," Butter said, pressing. "You know

damned right well you have. You an' me were out that way a coupla summers ago. 'Member? An' we both heard—"

"Nothin'! Least nothin' the guy needed to know about," Glenn said softly, still struggling to control his anger.

Was it anger? Glenn wondered. *Or fear?* Years ago, he and Butter had been out by the Nephews one night, and they had heard and seen—something. The memory of it still sent an icy wave rippling up between his shoulder blades.

But he didn't want to talk about it now, and he certainly didn't want Butter talking about it, so he clicked the recorder on and pressed the *fast forward* button. For a second or two, there was a high-pitched squeal that sounded like a chipmunk on helium. Then Glenn pressed *play* again, and everyone in the bar leaned close to hear more of the recorded writer's voice.

"...not even sure of their names or the names of the lighthouse keeper and his wife—if, in fact, she even lived out on this lonely rock. There are numerous gaps in the historical records from the late eighteen- and early nineteen-hundreds. Of course, it's possible that—"

The writer's voice was suddenly cut off by a loud bang. Most everyone in the bar couldn't help but jump.

"That must've been him, openin' a door," Butter said in a whisper. "Where d'ya think he is?"

"Probably at the front door of the lighthouse," Glenn said, impatiently waving him quiet with one hand while leaning forward. "That's where I found his stuff. Shush."

The tape played back the heavy clump of footsteps on either the front steps or a wooden floor of the lighthouse. They seemed halting, as though the person was hesitant, unsure if he should proceed. Then, with a low, fear-tinged voice, the writer said, "What the hell is that?"

There was another loud banging sound and then several seconds of hissing silence on the tape. Everyone in the bar seemed to be holding their breath as they listened. Glenn was so focused on the tape, waiting to hear the writer's voice again, that he realized he'd been hearing something else for several seconds before he finally let it register.

"Hold on a second," he said.

His hands felt so numb they were tingling as he stopped the machine, pressed *rewind* for a few seconds, then started the tape again.

"Listen," he said, his voice a raw whisper as he raised the small tape recorder and leaned even closer, almost pressing it to his ear.

The sound was so faint that it was almost nonexistent, but Glenn recognized the echoing, tinkling sounds of a piano. It took him a heartbeat or two to acknowledge that the sound was actually on the tape, not coming from the next room or outside. He turned the volume up as high as it would go, but the faint, teasing sound faded away, lost in the static hiss of the otherwise blank tape.

"You hear that?" Glenn asked, his glance leaping from Tony to Butter to Shantelle and back to Tony.

"I didn't hear a damned thing," Butter said. His forehead furrowed with confusion, and he cocked his head to one side, looking like a dog that was listening to a high-frequency whistle that humans can't hear.

"No, no. Listen again," Glenn said.

He rewound the tape and played it again, making sure the volume was turned all the way up. Once again, he heard the writer say, "What the hell was that?"—followed by the loud bang, then silence. Through the tape hiss came the unmistakable sounds of a distant piano, playing "Listen to the Mockingbird."

"Mother of God," Butter said, as he gasped and sat back, letting his shoulders slump. His mouth hung open, exposing his single yellow tooth. His eyes were wide and filled with agitation.

Glenn quickly rewound the tape, and they all listened one more time. This time, everyone in the bar heard the faint strains of the distinctive tune.

"You ain't screwing with us, are you, Glenn?" Shantelle asked. Her eyes were wide, dark pools in the dim barroom light.

Glenn couldn't speak. He could barely shake his head *no*. His fingers were tingling so badly he'd all but lost his sense of touch. He wasn't sure he'd be able to hold onto the tape recorder. A numb, hollow feeling slid open inside his chest, and the cold sensation between his shoulder blades spread like invisible fingers up the back of his neck.

Glenn clicked the tape off and looked around at his friends. They had all heard it, and they were all staring at him as though they expected him to say something profound. But it was Tony who finally spoke up.

"Wanna know what I think?" he said gruffly. Before anyone could draw a breath to speak, he continued. "I think, if you ain't playin' some kinda trick on us here, if this is for real, there's only one thing you can do."

Glenn looked at him, his eyebrows raised in silent query.

"I think you oughtta take that damned tape recorder, zip it back into that carrying case with all that other stuff, put a heavy stone in with it, an' drop it overboard when you go out lobsterin' tomorrow mornin'." Tony raised his hand and pointed a gnarled forefinger at Glenn, shaking it like a schoolteacher who was scolding a child. "'Cause if that tape's for real, there ain't nobody ever gonna see that writer fella alive again. Not on the Nephews an' not anywhere else."

Tony leaned his head back and drained his beer glass with a few deep gulps. After wiping his chin and beard with the flat of his hand, he leaned forward and pinned Glenn with an intense, earnest look.

"That fella drove up here, you say?"

Glenn's throat was so dry he could barely swallow as he nodded and said, "Uh-huh."

"Well, then," Tony said, heaving himself up off the barstool, preparing to leave. "If I was you, while it's still dark, I'd think about drivin' his car out to Nickerson's Quarry and pushin' it off Big Derrick Ledge where it's deepest."

Tony wavered, a little unsteady on his feet as he took a twenty from his wallet and dropped it onto the bar. Before he turned to leave, though, he leaned close to Glenn. His breath was sour with beer and stale with cigarette smoke as he said, "An' I'd also think 'bout movin' them twenty or thirty traps out there by the Nephews."

JANE LINDSKOLD

It Must
Burn

The house was on fire again.

Her heartbeat quickening—despite the nagging insistence from some part of her brain that surely this should be routine by now—Sheila Evans played the stream from the small chemical fire extinguisher over the blaze until it was smothered. Then, before even contemplating the damage, she dragged the ladder over and reset the smoke detectors.

Their shrill nagging whine had dragged her out of bed and sent her running for the attic. Now, as Sheila surveyed the damage—minimal, despite the ferocity of the blaze—she thought blearily that she should feel some gratitude to the little, white flying-saucer–shaped things. All she felt, though, was exhausted annoyance over once again being awakened from a sound sleep.

A prolonged roll of thunder shook the house, jolting Sheila far more than the alarms had done. For the first time since she had been awakened, she became aware of the hiss of rain against the roof, its sheeting against the windowpanes. Judging from the dull rumble in the rain gutters—more audible up here than it would have been elsewhere in the house—the rain had been falling for a while.

Successive rolls of thunder, these shorter and sharper, like the reports of a cannon, finished waking her. Sighing, Sheila thought she might as well call in a report to her insurance company. They weren't going to like this; but then again, neither did she.

At least the smoke alarms had woken her from that horrible dream—the one about the man with the bristling black beard and the empty eyes like pools of death.

When the insurance inspector rang the bell at nine the next morning, Sheila headed for the door knowing she looked like hell.

After the fire, which had been at around three A.M., she hadn't been able to get back to sleep. Hadn't wanted to was closer to the truth, but Sheila didn't like placing herself in the company of those who let nightmares keep them awake. The fire was reason enough. Good reason, sane reason.

No need to think about the man with the beard.

A hot shower had rinsed the smoke's stench and grime from her body, but her thick brown hair, normally so luxuriant that she had to wrestle it into submission with clips and ties, hung limp and stringy as if protesting the lack of sleep. Dark gray smudges beneath her eyes turned their dark blue stormy. Her fair skin was sallow and ashen.

When Sheila had reluctantly accepted that she wasn't going to sleep no matter how much she tossed and turned, she had dressed, then padded down to her living room. There she had spent the remainder of the night curled in her floppy old recliner reading a novel whose "gripping plot" had already vanished from her memory.

Eyes burning with exhaustion, Sheila flung open the door almost defiantly. She knew the man who stood there—she knew every adjuster, inspector, and clerk on In-State's staff by now—and breathed a small sigh of relief. Gary Gonzalez was just about her favorite.

She held out a hand to the short, stocky, red-haired man, wondering for at least the tenth time how someone so obviously of Irish extraction had ended up with Gonzalez for a surname.

"Morning, Gary."

"Good morning, Ms. Evans—Sheila," Gary corrected at her reproving frown. "I heard you've had another fire."

"You heard correctly," she replied with a theatrical sigh, motioning him inside. "Would you like some coffee?"

Gary lifted into view a small bag bearing the logo of a popular local bakery.

"Thanks. I brought chocolate-chip walnut muffins," he said, following her into the kitchen, "though you look as if you could use something more substantial."

Sheila smiled wanly.

"I couldn't sleep after the smoke detectors woke me. I've been up for hours."

"Fire in the attic again?"

"Attic again," she agreed, pouring coffee into two mugs emblazoned with a stencil of Moon Point Lighthouse, the area's one and only tourist attraction. "Same spot, just about the center of the floor, in line with that window."

"But," Gary said, accepting the mug she slid toward him and adding his own sugar and cream, "away from all electrical wiring, pipes, or anything else that could explain the fire."

"Right." Sheila motioned toward the kitchen table. "Why don't we sit and enjoy the muffins during the first part of this interrogation?"

Gary nodded.

"Funny," he said. "When we made out this policy, I remember the estimators insisting on extra coverage for flood and wind and hail—what with you building out here on this rocky point—but we never thought to add extra for fire."

"There was extra coverage for being more than a mile from the fire station," Sheila reminded him with a forced chuckle.

"Well, that's some comfort," he replied with mock relief.

Gary took a moment to get comfortable, arraying his laptop computer in front of him on the scrubbed butcher block of her kitchen table.

"You haven't," he said, in the tone of one invoking a ritual familiar to both participants, "taken to storing anything up in the attic—none of those highly flammable paints or turpentines or solvents or suchlike, of which you are so suspiciously fond?"

Several fires ago, Sheila would have been infuriated by this question. The assumption following the first fire had been that she—a painter by both profession and avocation—had negligently spilled something that had caused the fire. The second most popular assumption had been that oily rags—of which she *did* own an abundance—had been responsible. Her denials had been believed that first time.

After the second fire, though, and again after the third, specialists had been called in. Despite inspecting the area with literally microscopic care, they had found nothing to justify belief in either negligence or arson.

"I may be an artist," Sheila said, an edge to her voice despite her awareness that Gary's question was just routine, "but I'm not an idiot."

"I know. I know," Gary replied soothingly, passing her a muffin. "I have to ask. Between you and me, the main office is hinting that we're paying out too much on this policy…"

Sheila laughed harshly. "I bet they are. How many claims is this? Eight?"

"Nine," Gary corrected, licking crumbs off his fingers before tapping a few lines into his laptop. "If we allow this claim, as I suspect we will."

"I almost didn't call it in," Sheila admitted. "The damage isn't much, just a scorched patch on the flooring and some smoke stains on the beams above. But I knew that if I didn't, and there was something worse later…"

She shrugged.

"You did the right thing," Gary assured her. "In any case, I'm not the main office. Let them worry about the bottom line. Between us, though, I'll admit I'm puzzled as hell. This house is new construction."

"Not even a year old," Sheila agreed.

"And even if there was something wrong with the original materials," Gary continued, "we've replaced just about every board, panel, and chunk of insulation up there."

Sheila nodded. The muffin tasted good, blotting up the acid in her stomach and sweetening her mood. She was relieved that Gary had been the one In-State had sent over. He, at least, believed her. What if she'd had to deal with some officious bureaucrat from the main office?

With a sudden chill, she realized that after the next fire—and she felt certain there would be a next fire—it might not be Gary or Anne or any of the other locals who knew her who would show up at her door. It might be some hotshot trouble-shooter with only the bottom line in mind.

The thought haunted her as they finished the routine questions and trudged up to the attic where Gary inspected the damage, took photos, and made more notes. He included a couple shots of the array of smoke detectors that ringed the attic ceiling—and even extended down into the stairwell.

"It looks like you're being invaded by flying saucers," he said with a chuckle.

Sheila laughed. "That's what I thought earlier. My little fleet."

She grew somber. "I just wish they could do more than warn me. I wish they could stop whatever is causing this."

Gary nodded. "Why don't I put in a recommendation that we pay to install one of those automatic sprinkler systems?"

"Sounds interesting, but wouldn't the risk of water damage be just as bad as what the fire's doing?"

Gary shrugged.

"Water from a sprinkler can't destroy an entire house." He looked her squarely in the eye, though he had to tilt his head back just a bit to do so. "Or kill the woman who lives there."

Sheila felt a sudden weakness in her knees and thrust her hand against the wall for support.

"Somehow," she said, her voice husky, "I'd forgotten about that possibility. I've gotten so that once the fire is out, I just feel annoyed."

"Well, don't forget," Gary said, leading the way down the stairs. "All we need is for you to take a sleeping pill and not be able to wake up when the smoke detectors go off."

"I won't forget," she promised.

He paused at the door.

"Paul Carpenter still okay for the repair work?"

"Great," she answered. "Have him call first, though. I may try and get some sleep."

Maybe the dreams will leave me alone now that the sun's up.

"Do," Gary said, offering her his hand in parting. "Thanks for the coffee."

"And thank you for the muffins."

Sheila stood in the doorway watching Gary drive away. A brush of fur against her ankles announced the return of her cat, the aptly named Big Bopper. The dark marbled tabby meowed demandingly, reminding her he hadn't been fed, his long-furred lion's pouch—as the vet called the belly that drooped to just inches above the floor—swaying slightly as he reared on his back legs to rub against her hand.

"Out all night?" Sheila asked. "Even with the rain? You missed all the excitement, Bopper."

Even as she said the words, she realized she had said them before. Feeling troubled, she scooped up the rumbling cat and carried him inside.

Paul Carpenter was a tall, unobtrusively muscular man with dark skin that resembled expensive oiled leather. He liked to puzzle new acquaintances with the conundrum that he hadn't taken up his profession because of his name; rather, his name had come from his profession.

The solution to this puzzle was that father and grand-fathers before him had all worked with wood, back even—so family legend said—before the Civil War had made them free. Today, people along this part of the coast paid large sums of money for the folk-art sculptures Paul's elderly mother created from driftwood. His daughter was apprenticing with a violin maker.

Paul himself claimed he didn't have an artistic bone in either of his two broad brown hands. As far as Sheila was concerned, the way he could mesh old wood with new and build just about anything was the purest form of art. Paul just guffawed at this and said that what he did was craft, and that an artist like herself should know the difference.

As always, Paul's first order of business upon arrival was crossing the room to see what was on Sheila's easel. He seemed disappointed to find the canvas blank except for a few vague, aimless strokes.

"Not painting anything, Sheila?" he asked.

"Not right yet," she admitted. "I'm too tired. Too stressed."

Paul nodded. "Can't be easy," he said, picking up his tool-box and heading up the stairs, "sleeping nights when you don't know when those smoke detectors will start screaming."

"You know it," she said, following him, then settling herself on the attic floor to watch him work.

There was a drowsy satisfaction to watching Paul go about removing the fire damage. Big Bopper seemed to agree. He stayed curled up in her lap, purring despite the banging and sawing.

"It's funny," Paul said as he checked one of his measurements, "how these fires always start when there's been a storm."

"Do they?"

Sheila bit her lip, trying hard not to remember the other thing that happened along with almost every fire: the dream. The man with his bristling black beard and weatherworn face, each feature as clear as a photograph. All but for the eyes. Those were only shadows, dark as a pit.

"Seems to me they do," Paul went on, his thoughtful tones breaking the nightmare's hold, "least those I've cleaned up after. I remember mopping up the sill whenever I've opened the window to get some air in here."

He gestured toward the window he'd propped open a few moments earlier for just that reason.

"A couple of times I had to replace windowpanes, and those times I'm positive it had rained. Had to worry about letting everything dry out so rot wouldn't set in."

"I wonder if there's a connection," Sheila mused, stroking Bopper along the dark stripe down his spine, grounding herself in the reality of silky fur beneath her fingertips. "Last night I heard the thunder. I remember that."

She grew suddenly excited, anticipating a solution.

"Maybe the fires are started by some sort of unusual lightning strike. Mine is the only house out this way. In fact, now that I think of it, my house is the highest thing around here if you don't count the lighthouse…"

She waved toward where Moon Point's elegant black-and-white-striped conical structure was just visible down the coast.

"Higher, even, since I'm up here and Moon Point is built on slightly lower ground. Maybe my place is somehow drawing the lightning."

Paul's expression was oddly closed.

"Sure is drawing something, Sheila. I'll say that."

She ignored his lack of enthusiasm, sniffing after this neat explanation like a hound dog on a scent.

"Paul, would you take a look up on the roof before you go, and check the lightning rod or whatever it is they use these days?"

"I'll check," Paul agreed. "No problem."

Some note of doubt in his tone nagged at the edge of Sheila's mind, but she was too excited by the thought that a solution might be at hand to care.

Not even Paul's report that he had found nothing wrong with the lightning rod, or her own discovery, after he had left, that the fire inspectors had checked for the same thing several fires back, could diminish her new sense of conviction.

Back issues of the local newspaper were available online. Sheila checked the weather reports and confirmed Paul's vague memory that there had been some type of nasty weather each time the fires had broken out. Even the two daytime fires—anomalies in the general pattern to this point—checked out. On each of those days there had been heavy fog.

Sheila remembered how she'd been home each of those days, cozily painting, enjoying the muted bellow of the foghorn from Moon Point. At that time, all she'd felt had been a sort of unfocused gratitude that chance had kept her in so she'd been able to put out the fires before they could spread.

She was lifting the phone to call Gary and share her findings when a sudden realization chilled her enthusiasm. Thunderstorms—those fit. Thunder was caused by lightning. Lightning could start fires. Fog, though—fog wouldn't cause fires.

Reluctantly Sheila replaced the phone. Further investigation was in order before she could prove a connection.

Even so, she felt a certain degree of relief when she read that the weather report called for clear skies through the end of the week.

The fire nearly made Sheila forget that she was scheduled to take part in an outdoor arts and crafts festival the next day. After Paul left she spent a busy evening getting ready.

She selected a few of her larger paintings—including a nice one of Moon Point Light all wreathed in early morning mist—but mostly she packed a variety of smaller pieces. These were just the things to put in an alcove or line a stairwell or maybe decorate that guest bathroom. Hard experience had taught her that while the big stuff caught the eye, the little stuff lined the pocket.

Lastly, she loaded up a portable easel, her paintbox, and the canvas Paul had chided her for not completing. She still didn't have the least idea what she was going to do with it, but there was nothing like somebody actually painting to make the tourists stop. And if business was bad, well, at least she'd have something to do.

Turned out, she needn't have worried. Not only was business brisk enough to stay interesting without getting annoying, Sheila discovered to her delight that her pitch was right next to that of Paul's mother, Gayfeather Carpenter.

Gayfeather—she insisted on being called by her full name rather than merely Gay—was nothing like her big, oiled-leather son. A petite brown sparrow of a woman with a silvery crown of hair cropped close to her head, she looked too tiny to handle the chunks of twisted wood she shaped with knife and gouge into fantastic creatures or detailed landscapes or scenes right out of dream and nightmare.

From where her own house rested on its rocky point high above the beach, Sheila had seen Gayfeather down below hauling a little red wagon along the beaches, a spotted mongrel dog chasing the waves at her side. The sculptor collected most of her wood that way, claiming that as she walked along the beach the wind and water told her just how to carve each piece.

Sheila liked Gayfeather, liked the way the old woman dressed mostly in practical denim or khaki coveralls, but dressed up for shows by wrapping around her throat a purple feather boa that resembled her namesake flower. Gayfeather had been asked so many times whether she knew the poem about being old and wearing purple that she now kept a copy on display out with her own works.

The two women greeted each other with a quick embrace and exclamations of delight about the clear, bright weather so soon after a storm. They promised to chat after they were set up and kept that promise, too, during a lazy spell mid-morning.

"My Paul tells me you had another fire out at your place," Gayfeather commented, moving her chair to the left front of her booth so that she could chat while keeping an eye on her wares. Not that anything she had on display was small enough to go walking away on its own—it was just habit.

Sheila nodded, wiping her brush clean before switching colors. Inspired by Gayfeather's boa, she'd decided to do a sort of impressionistic piece, a tower with purple-flowered vines creeping up the sides and around its conical height.

"Ninth one," she replied with a sigh that came out more heartfelt than she'd intended. "Not that I mind the chance to visit with Paul, but this is getting real old."

"Older than you might think," Gayfeather said softly. "Those fires."

"What do you mean?" Sheila said sharply. "My house is the first place built out there, and I've been there hardly a year."

"Is that what you think?" Gayfeather said. "Didn't anyone tell you that your land's called Lighthouse Point?"

Sheila dabbed a few flower petals, not sure whether she

was being teased. Gayfeather, however, looked as sober as a judge on the bench.

"The real estate agent told me. Sure," Sheila said slowly. "Isn't that because you can see Moon Point Lighthouse really well from there? That's what Morse said."

"Might be what he said," Gayfeather replied. "Might even be what he thought it meant—no offense to Morse— but he's only been here some five years. He doesn't know all the stories."

"And you?" Sheila tried to laugh.

"I've lived here eighty-three years come Sunday next," Gayfeather said proudly, "and I've heard lots of stories in that time."

"So, tell me," Sheila said, feeling as if the words were being jerked from her, "why my land is called Lighthouse Point."

Gayfeather paused to chat with a couple of tourists who were exclaiming over a polished log carved with an entire town along its length, then took up the thread as if she'd never been interrupted.

"Because that's where the first lighthouse was built, the one before the current one."

"But Moon Point Light is over a hundred years old!" Sheila protested, feeling stupid even as she spoke. "I remember being told that it was built soon after the Civil War."

"Doesn't mean that there wasn't a light before that," Gayfeather said gently. "And there was. You can look it up in the books. They tore it down after Moon Point Light was built. Said it was unstable—something about the pitch. I never quite understood. Moon Point was a better location, too. Easier to get supplies out to or something. Maybe it had to do with the footing. I don't rightly remember."

Sheila nodded.

"Now that you mention it, I think I remember something in one of the tourist pamphlets," she admitted, "but you know how it is when you live somewhere—you never go to the attractions. I must have painted Moon Point Light twenty times, but I think I've only been there once, back when I was trying to decide where I wanted to relocate after my divorce."

She fell silent, her brush making nervous, frantic motions over the canvas.

"I never knew that an old lighthouse stood where my house is now," she added. "Anyhow, what does an old lighthouse have to do with my fires?"

"Well now, Sheila darling," the old woman said. "My Paul tells me that whenever you have a fire, the weather's been particularly ugly. Seems to me that somehow, somewise, that place of yours is trying to send up a light against the storm."

After the show had ended, they went over to a nearby café for something to eat. It was too early for dinner, too late for lunch, so they ordered a sort of makeshift English tea.

Gayfeather wasn't leaving the matter of the lighthouse fires alone, and, as uncomfortable as the subject made her, Sheila didn't want her to. In fact, almost before they'd finished their first pot of Earl Grey, she was telling Gayfeather about the man in her dreams.

"He never says anything. He's just there." Sheila shivered. "To tell you the truth, I'm scared to death of him—more scared of him than of the fires. It's gotten so I'm afraid to sleep at night."

Gayfeather leaned forward, more like an inquisitive sparrow than ever.

"Do you dream of him when there isn't a fire?"

"I..." Sheila frowned. "I don't think so, but sometimes... I feel weird telling you this..."

"Don't. This old lady's seen a few things in her life—"

"Like this?"

"I'm not saying," Gayfeather said, with a peculiar averting gesture. "Let's just say I've seen things a whole lot scarier than some white man in a dream."

Thinking of racist groups like the KKK, of days not so long ago when the two of them wouldn't have been able to have lunch in the same restaurant, much less sit at the same table and share tea from the same pot, Sheila had to agree.

"Sometimes I get the feeling he's roaming about the house—like I've glimpsed him from the corner of my eye."

She straightened, her hand arrested in mid-reach for a miniature blueberry tart.

"Yes?" Gayfeather prompted.

"I think Bopper's seen something, too," Sheila said slowly. "At least there's times when he won't come in the house, not for love or cream. And I was trying to remember this morning, I think, but I'm pretty sure he's never inside when there's been a fire—not even when the weather's been ugly and any smart cat would be inside."

Gayfeather put the blueberry tart into Sheila's hand.

"Cats are knowing that way. So're dogs, come to that. Eat your dessert, honey, while this old lady tells you a story."

"The original lighthouse—the one that stood where your house is now—was called the Cliff End Light after where it stood. It was built some years before the War Between the States. It wasn't nowhere near as pretty as Moon Point. Those smooth, graceful towers—like Moon Point or the one out on Cape Hatteras—they're a more modern style of building.

"Cliff End was built from brick and had eight sides—octagonal, I think they call it…"

Sheila grinned, perfectly certain that Gayfeather knew exactly what *octagonal* meant, but she didn't interrupt.

"—and was fatter at the bottom than at the top. There was a keeper's cottage attached to the tower at the bottom, and a few outbuildings for oil and supplies.

"Now, you're looking at me like, how do I know all this—after all, Moon Point's been in place for over a hundred and twenty years now, and Cliff End gone nearly that long. The answer's simple: there are drawings in the library and a couple over at Town Hall. There're some over at Moon Point, too, for that matter."

Sheila looked properly admonished and topped off both cups of tea. There were some shell-shaped butter cookies on the tray, and she nibbled along the scalloped edge of one.

"Now, Cliff End Light was even more isolated back then than your house is now. The town was smaller—not that it's so big now—so getting a lightkeeper who could handle all the loneliness wasn't easy. After a few false starts the Lighthouse Board found themselves one—a man named Ezra Johns.

"Ezra Johns had been a navy man before some scandal or injury made him tire of the sea. He was North Carolina born and bred, some said coming from money. Others said Ezra just gave himself airs. What was true beyond a doubt was that he was accustomed to having his way and that he could snap out orders like a sure-enough ship's captain. Got so that not many folk cared to visit Ezra Johns, and soon all he saw were just those who were required to bring him supplies, and a few darkies..."

Gayfeather gave a pained twist of her lips that wasn't really a smile.

"...who belonged not to Ezra Johns but more or less to the lighthouse.

"Now, Ezra Johns did get a holiday from his post. Twice a year, when the worst of the weather was thought to be over, someone would be sent out to spell him. During one of these holidays, the War Between the States started. Most of his darkies left him then—the sea being so near was always a temptation, and Ezra's replacement didn't watch 'em as he should. Only one who stayed was an old man who was too poorly to go anywhere. So, when Ezra Johns came back from wherever he went on his holidays, he was more alone than ever.

"Some stories say that's when he started drinking too much. Others say that he'd been drinking too much for years and that's why he left the navy. Me, I doubt that last. Navy's a hard-drinking service—harder drinking back then, even—and I don't think they'd let a man go for being a drunk.

"But I digress. Time passed, and things didn't get better for either Ezra Johns or the South—least the White South. The old slave died. With able-bodied men so hard to come by, no one was sent to relieve Ezra for his holiday. And with the North blockading the shipping lanes, well, the South didn't care nearly so much about keeping the coast safe. Sometimes Southern soldiers would even vandalize a lighthouse—like happened at Cape Lookout—so it couldn't be used by the enemy."

Sheila raised a hand, feeling rather as if she was in school. It was obvious that Gayfeather had boned up on her subject. She wondered just how long the Carpenters had been worrying about the source of her attic fires.

"What about their own ships? Didn't the South care about them?"

Gayfeather laughed.

"Of course they did, but like I said, the South wasn't shipping as much then. Also, temporary lights could be rigged, and there were daymarks, too."

Sheila thought of the black and white stripes on Moon Point Lighthouse and nodded. She'd forgotten that back then most sea traffic went by day when it could.

"But how, you ask, does this bear on one of the great puzzles of the Cliff End Light?" Gayfeather continued. "Even a Northerner like you must have learned how pressed the South got for supplies. A lighthouse lantern—even with a right fine lens—used a lot of oil. Whale oil was popular then, but it was hard to get with the blockade and all. Getting expensive, too, even before the War.

"Despite the shortage of oil, however, and despite Cliff End Light hardly being the most important navigation mark on the North Carolina coast, that light never went out.

"People muttered about that, to be sure. Some said that Ezra Johns was a traitor to the South—that he'd made a deal with the Yankees, who allowed oil for Cliff End through the blockade so's the light would keep burning. Some said he was in league with smugglers running the blockade, smugglers who supplied him with oil.

"But others said," Gayfeather lowered her voice, the note in her voice making Sheila shiver despite the late afternoon autumn sunlight pouring through the café's window, "others said that Ezra Johns had made a deal with the Devil and that the Devil had given him hellfire to keep the light burning."

Sheila stared.

"You can't believe that!"

Gayfeather shrugged and deliberately sipped her tea.

"I'm not saying what I believe. I'm telling you what was

said then. But you're getting antsy, so I'll move along. Just leave it that for whatever reason—and no one ever did find the answer—Cliff End Light never went out.

"After the War, Ezra Johns kept his post for a few years. Then some self-important Yankee from the Lighthouse Board decided that there was no reason that a drunken Southerner should have such a good job. The town was growing then— the rail, you know—and Cliff End didn't seem nearly so isolated. Besides, jobs were hard to come by for some—especially injured veterans.

"Ezra Johns raved, so folks tell it, when the Lighthouse Board gave him the boot. He said he had nothing to live for but keeping the light. The board told him to walk. He offered to stay on at reduced pay. Still they told him to walk.

"Ezra vanished the day his replacement arrived. Everyone thought he'd hopped a rail out of town, but then a week later his body washed ashore. Apparently, he'd committed suicide."

"How awful!" Sheila gasped, thinking for the first time of the grim, bristle-bearded man with something like pity rather than fear.

"Suicide, or being driven to it?" Gayfeather asked, but she didn't wait for an answer. "Ezra Johns's replacement was a Yankee soldier who'd lost an eye in the War. He came here with his wife and two little children. They left within six months. The wife—who was a talker—said they'd seen Ezra Johns about the place, especially in the lamp room at the top of the tower.

"The board brought in other replacements, all Yankees, none knowing anything about the supposed ghost of Cliff End Light—they got real careful about keeping that secret after several more keepers left. None stayed more than six months. Some stayed as little as two. In the end, they brought in a black man—Pen Freedman, he was called.

"Pen was kin to my family—his first name being short for 'Carpenter'—but he had no gift with wood, nor with much else, which was why the board could hire him for a job that, by now, everyone figured was cursed. Pen was desperate and, as he told the tale, that made him hang on. After a while, he

noticed that Ezra did him no harm. In fact, one stormy day
when Pen forgot to light the lantern, he woke from his afternoon nap and found it burning bright as day.

"But the Lighthouse Board had wearied of Cliff End Light
by then. Some say it was just meanness—they didn't like paying a black man a white man's wages, for Pen was canny
enough to insist on that, at least. Whatever the reason, the
board made excuses and started work on Moon Point Lighthouse. When it was built, Pen was fired. Cliff End Light—and
presumably its ghostly keeper—were blown apart.

"And that's how the story rested," Gayfeather concluded,
"at least until a pert Yankee painter with money to spend and
romantic ideas about living on the storm-tossed coast bought
herself a chunk of land and built a new house there. Then Ezra
Johns came back from Hell—or wherever he'd been those
hundred years and more—and started trying to keep his light
burning against the storm."

Sheila knew they must have talked more after Gayfeather
finished her story, but she didn't remember a word of that conversation. She came back to herself about the time she finished
unloading her van.

Bopper was coiling around her ankles, nagging her for a
treat to make up for his abandonment all that day, and as she
poured kibbles into a saucer, she found herself thinking, *Well,
at least I know Ezra Johns's ghost isn't about. Bopper wouldn't be here
if he were.*

Then...

*I wonder where he goes when he's not here. Does he truly go to
Hell, like Gayfeather says? That must be horrible. No wonder he always looks so fierce and angry.*

That night, before she went to bed, Sheila stepped outside and checked the skies. Stars hung bright and clear against
a velvet blackness. Relieved, she went inside and slept
soundly, Bopper purring beside her on the pillow.

But over the next couple of days, Sheila became more and
more nervous. It seemed she couldn't go five minutes without
checking the weather. The slightest gust of wind made her

jump lest it herald a storm. She took to keeping the television tuned to an "all weather, all the time" channel.

When a storm finally blew through, she didn't even bother going to bed, but went up to the attic and sat wrapped in a blanket on the floor. Bopper was nowhere to be found, so she figured that once again Ezra Johns had come back from Hell.

She was dozing—or maybe she wasn't—when a glow of reddish-orange light jerked her awake. The black-bearded man—Ezra Johns, as she now knew him to be—stood in the center of the attic floor.

As in her dreams, he looked as real as any person but for two things: His eye sockets were dark—empty now, she saw, as if the eyes had been plucked out—and his hands were wreathed in flame. He moved those flaming hands as if to kindle a series of lanterns some distance from the floor, and as he worked bits of flame—solid yet viscous, not ephemeral like ordinary fire—dripped onto the attic floor, which began to smolder.

"Don't!" she protested, speaking aloud.

The ghost of Ezra Johns turned those empty sockets toward her.

"Don't," she said again. "You'll burn down the house, and then where will we be? I'll be without a house—because I swear by everything I know that I'll never build a new one here—and you'll be back wherever you've been since Cliff End Light was taken from you."

There must be a light, Ezra Johns said; his voice sounded in her mind, not her ears. *I must keep the light.*

A vision rose in her mind. A dreadful tempest raging offshore from what she knew must be Cliff End. A ship, just glimpsed in the lightning flashes, being driven by the winds.

Ezra Johns stood in his keeper's tower, tending the lanterns. She knew, as he had known then, that he was nearly out of oil. That when the light failed, the ship would lose its bearings and would wreck on the rocks.

The ship might founder in any case, but Ezra Johns was a proud man, and he wouldn't have it wrecked because of his failure to keep the light. He cried out into the empty air, raising his voice against the storm, vowing anything if only he had the means to keep the Cliff End Light ablaze.

And something came in response to his cry, something horrible but full of teasing power. It offered Ezra Johns the means to keep the light ablaze. It would give him hellfire. In return it would take his eyes as a pledge that when the Cliff End Light ceased to burn, then Ezra Johns would go to Hell and dwell forever in damnation.

Proud as he was, Ezra Johns made the deal, and from that moment, the guttering lanterns burned high, bright, and clear. The ship was saved, but no one ever thought to thank the lighthouse keeper.

In the days that followed, Ezra Johns learned to find his way about the lighthouse. He'd lived there alone so long that he knew it well. Since few came to see him, no one learned his secret, for he guarded his blindness as he guarded his lighthouse—with pride and fierce determination.

Then the board took the Cliff End Light from him, and Ezra Johns had neither pride nor determination to guide his sightless way. Trying to make his way down, he missed his step and went over the cliff that had so long been his home. Unnoticed by any, he drowned in the sea.

Hell might have had him then, but Ezra Johns was stubborn even in death. His vow bound him to Cliff End Light, and he tied himself to it, haunting it and tending it until it was destroyed. Then, indeed, did he go to his promised torment.

But the building of the house where Cliff End Light once stood gave Ezra Johns a line by which he could haul himself free of Hell. Not every night—only when the weather was ugly enough to threaten ships would he pull himself out of Hell by that line and once again take up that duty.

Sheila went to Gayfeather's studio the next morning and told her what she'd seen.

"He left then," she concluded, "and I sprayed chemical foam over the little bits of fire he'd dripped on the floor. There wasn't much damage, so I didn't even call In-State. What does it matter, anyhow? Unless I can find a way to come to terms with Ezra Johns, he'll burn my house down. Nothing stops that hellfire. We've seen that already. Even if I sheathed the attic in metal, he'd keep lighting those cursed fires."

Gayfeather nodded.

"You could leave. Go on holiday—visit some artist's colony or university. Take the cat and the things you value. When you return, the house'll be gone. The insurance money will start you toward a new one."

Sheila looked at Gayfeather for a long moment.

"I could. That's true. I even thought of that, but..."

Her voice dropped to a whisper.

"I feel sorry for Ezra Johns. He may have been proud or even drunk when he made that vow, but he's kept it. More than that, he's not resigned to being in Hell, and I don't want to be the second devil to damn him to it."

"What makes you think you should intervene?" Gayfeather asked. Her tone was not critical—rather, it was judicial, as if she were determined that Sheila explain herself to herself.

"I've been thinking about your story," Sheila said, "about how Ezra was able to bind himself to the Cliff End Light after he died, about how he was able to use my house as an anchor. That determination—there's something fine about that. He may have been proud, but he wasn't evil, and I don't want to..."

"Be a devil," Gayfeather said, echoing Sheila's earlier statement. "Still, you can't risk yourself living in that house— not to redeem some ghost. Especially not with that same ghost setting the house afire every time the weather storms."

Sheila shook her head.

"I know, but I was thinking...It sounds crazy, but..."

"Crazier than a ghost keeping a nonexistent lighthouse ablaze with hellfire?" Gayfeather laughed. "Try me, girl."

"What if I build him a lighthouse of his own, right there?"

Gayfeather shook her head. "That is crazy. Let me hear the sense behind it."

Sheila paced as she explained. "First, I thought that painting a picture of Cliff End Light and letting Ezra take it as a substitute would do, but I figure it won't. There are pictures around, as you said."

"Any case," Gayfeather added, "he'd burn it up."

"Then I thought about asking him to move to Moon Point Light," Sheila continued. "But I figure, if that would do, he'd have done it since. Besides, I'd hate to see what his fire would do to a modern, fully automated light."

Gayfeather toyed with her carving tools, following Sheila's restless progress with a thoughtful frown.

"Makes sense when you put it that way. Ezra Johns is stubborn enough to come back from the dead, but from what you and the stories tell of him, he wasn't—isn't—stupid."

Sheila spread her hands wide.

"Building a replica of Cliff End Light is worth a try. Do you or Paul know any bricklayers who would take a strange commission on short notice and accept payment in installments?"

"Fact is," Gayfeather replied, "I think I do. Cousin of sorts, works with Paul sometimes. Care to guess what his name is?"

"Mason?" Sheila laughed, responding to the twinkle in the old woman's eyes.

"Nope. Kowlikowski. He's part Polish, I think."

The building of a miniature lighthouse modeled after the long-gone Cliff End Light attracted only a moderate amount of attention in the area. Sheila was a painter after all, and artists are universally known to be eccentric and impractical.

Building permits were issued allowing her to erect a structure twelve feet high. Sheila couldn't afford much more, even with Paul and Kowlikowski donating their time. They worked as fast as they could, but nonetheless, two more nights passed with Sheila sitting vigil in the attic with a fire extinguisher.

She talked to Ezra Johns both of those nights, telling him what they were doing and how she hoped he'd take up his post in a proper lighthouse once more. The ghost never said a word nor again sent her a vision, but Sheila thought that once, buried in the depths of his black beard bristles, she saw a smile.

As a finishing touch on their brick structure, Sheila traded an ironworker a couple of paintings to craft a gallery-style walkway around the outside of the lantern. A few more paintings bought her the glass panels.

She didn't bother with a real lens or oil or anything like that. Ezra Johns had shown that he was amply able to make a light from nothing at all.

Then all she could do was wait.

As if teasing them, clear weather reigned for more than a week after the lighthouse replica was completed, but at last a major storm was predicted.

Sheila invited Paul and Gayfeather over to her house after dinner that night. Others might have helped with the construction of the lighthouse, but only these two shared the secret of Ezra Johns.

After some debate, they decided to spread out so they would not miss any activity either in the attic or out at the new lighthouse. Sheila would wait in the attic while Paul and Gayfeather took up posts where they could keep the miniature lighthouse in view: Paul in the living room on the ground floor, Gayfeather upstairs in the front bedroom.

"Bopper's vanished again," Sheila said nervously as she mounted the stairs. "I guess that's a good sign."

Paul nodded, and she heard him pull a chair closer to the window.

"I've been wondering why Ezra Johns mostly comes by night," he said.

"Me, too," Sheila replied. "I think I have an answer."

"Oh?"

Sheila raised her voice as she mounted the stairs to the attic.

"I think he can only get that line out of wherever he is when the danger's real. In daytime a lighthouse isn't as necessary. He came, though, when there was a fog."

"Guess he doesn't think much of Moon Point," Paul said with a forced chuckle.

"That isn't his post..." Sheila began.

She might have said more, but even as her gaze came level with the attic room, she saw Ezra Johns taking form. As before, his hands were burning and his eyes were dark. Sheila had a sudden, horrible revelation.

"He's blind!" she said aloud. "He can't see where to go!"

Ezra Johns turned his head toward her and this time she saw his wry grin and knew she understood correctly.

Steeling herself against imagined horrors, she put a hand on the ghost's arm. To her surprise, it felt almost normal. She could feel the rough texture of his cable-knit sweater, but the arm inside it didn't feel quite solid, more as if she was grasping a thick balloon filled with half-frozen jelly.

"This way, sir," she said, taking his elbow. "I'll show you where the lighthouse is."

The ghost said nothing, but let her steer him. As he walked, fire dripped from his hands.

"Paul! Gayfeather!" Sheila called, hearing her voice high and shrill. "I need help! Someone come take the fire extinguisher, and someone bring a metal tray or bowl from the kitchen!"

Gayfeather darted from the front bedroom and had the fire extinguisher in hand almost before Sheila finished shouting. She spared a glance for the ghost, though. If she was afraid, her dark skin hid her blanching. In moments she was efficiently extinguishing what fire had already fallen from Ezra Johns's burning hands.

Paul brought a large steel mixing bowl from the kitchen.

"Hold it under his hands," Sheila told him. "It'll catch the fire for now. Grab a towel to keep from burning your hands."

"What are you doing?" Paul said as he brought a hand towel from the nearest bathroom. His eyes were so wide with astonishment and fear that he looked like a caricature of a frightened black man.

"Ezra's blind, remember?" Sheila said, sharing her revelation. "I'm guiding him out to the lighthouse."

Meanwhile, Ezra Johns said nothing, but he held his

hands up in front of him, rather like a surgeon who had just finished scrubbing for surgery. Paul held the bowl beneath them, and in this fashion they made their slow progress.

Sheila guided the ghost, fancying that his arm grew more solid every moment. Paul held the bowl, his fear swallowed by fascination. Gayfeather trailed behind, extinguishing the gobs of fire slopped from Paul's bowl.

The air heated up around them, and Sheila was certain she could smell her own scorched hair. At last they reached the front door and stepped outside. Rain lashed them and sent steam up from the bowl, but the fire on Ezra Johns's hands continued to burn. Wind tried to push them back, but step by labored step, they made their way to the miniature lighthouse.

Sheila guided Ezra's arm so his hand would brush the brick wall.

"Here's a proper lighthouse," she said. "Go on in. Keep the light, just as you promised."

Before their eyes, the ghost diminished in size, shrinking until he was in scale with the lighthouse. They stepped back, the lashing of the rain forgotten as they stared. Then Ezra Johns went to the door—a door Paul had insisted must work like any other door—and opened it.

The ghost turned then and looked up at them, waving in thanks and farewell. They saw him clearly at that moment, more clearly than they should have been able to do given the night and the raging storm.

Ezra Johns's hands no longer burned. Where before there had been only dark pits, his eyes now glowed like stars.

As the ghost stepped inside, the lantern atop the miniature Cliff End Light flashed brightly—not with the ruddy orange of hellfire, but with the clear, forgiving radiance of Heaven.

BRENDAN DUBOIS

The Tourist
Who Wasn't There

On the dirt path that led to the small dock, Nora Donnelly
turned and gave the mainland group her best tour guide smile.
It was a brisk sunny day in late June on Ivory Island, approx-
imately six miles off the coast of New Hampshire, and this was
her third—and last!—tour group of the day.

"Well," she said, looking at the men and women and two
children clustered together on the small path. "I hope you've
enjoyed your visit to Ivory Island and the Ivory Island lighthouse. Do you have any questions before we head out?"

She maintained her little plastic smile—kept in a back
pocket except for three times a day—and guessed who would
ask a question. There. That confused-looking woman in gray
sweatpants and a black T-shirt commemorating a rock group's
tour last summer. "Uh, I think I do," she said. "I just want to
make sure. Nobody lives here? Nobody operates the lighthouse at all?"

"No, not at all," she said, thinking, boy, guess you missed
the talk coming over on the boat, and the talk during the first
portion of the trail. "The lighthouse was fully automated in
1969, and remains so to this day, under the jurisdiction of the
Coast Guard. However, this whole island is now owned by the
State of New Hampshire, and except for the lighthouse and an

43

outbuilding, this whole area has been designated a nature preserve. Any other questions?"

She gave them a quick second, looked around at their
faces. The dirt path was flanked on both sides by waist-high
brush and other shrubbery. No trees grew on this thin and
rocky soil. Beyond the trail the land rose up, and there was the
gray granite of the Ivory Island lighthouse, and the barely visible roof of a supply shed.

Nora checked her watch. Time to go. She shrugged off her
knapsack and said, "Now, you've been such a good tour group
with me this afternoon, so if you don't mind, I'd like to take
your photo." She bent down, unzipped the bag, and pulled out
a Polaroid instant camera. "Just a little souvenir I like to take
before I bring you back to Cranmore Island."

The group—two men, three women, and a young boy and
girl—clustered together self-consciously as Nora brought up
the camera and took the photo. There was a *click-whir* as the
photo was spat out, and while it developed in her hands, she
counted down the seconds before the three-times-a-day comment came her way. "Hey," one of the heavier men said, grinning, "can we take a picture of you?"

Some of the group members laughed, and she kept her
plastic smile shiny. Very good, she thought. Took only six seconds this time. Was it her fault that her folks' genes gave her
long legs, light brown hair, and a natural set of boobs that
crossed the eyes of most males? She knew the state park uniform of shorts, short-sleeved shirt, and baseball cap—with her
hair pulled through the back in a ponytail—didn't help mat-
ters. Something about a college woman in a uniform...

"No, sir, I'm afraid you can't," she said, artificial smile in-
tact. "As a state employee and proud union member, I'm afraid
it's not allowed in our contract. Now, let's head back, shall
we?"

She put the camera and photo back into her knapsack and
led the group back to the boat, a small open Boston Whaler.
She took out her daily notebook, again noted the number of
people she had picked up at Cranmore Island—seven—and
counted each one again as she passed out the life preservers.

Seven. Okay, girl, she thought. Time to bring 'em back. Seven go out and seven go back.

She shivered a moment as she recalled a story from last summer. A dive group off a reef near Australia had returned from a day of diving. They didn't discover until a day or two later that a married couple had been left behind. Apparently they had gone out with the tour group and were still diving when the boat returned to shore. Nora couldn't imagine a lonelier feeling than to surface and see nothing around you but the wide, empty ocean—to realize with a sick horror that you've been abandoned. Well, nothing like that was going to happen on Nora Donnelly's watch.

"Hey," a small boy piped up. "I'm a good swimmer. Why do I have to wear a life jacket?"

"'Cause it's the rules," she said, tying his on tight. "Even I have to wear one."

He frowned, changed the subject. "What would happen if the engine didn't start? Would we be stuck here all night long?"

"I'd call for help on the radio," she said, untying the lines holding the Boston Whaler to the dock.

"And what if the radio didn't work?" he kept up.

She jumped back in, turned on the engine, throttled back some as the boat began backing away from the dock. "Then I'd use the flare gun to get attention."

"And what if the flare gun didn't work?"

Her forced smile slipped just a bit. "Then I'd ask a young boy to swim over to Cranmore Island and get help, that's what."

The ride over to Cranmore Island took about fifteen minutes, and thankfully, the young boy and the other members of the group kept their yaps shut as she maneuvered through the gentle swells of the Atlantic. Even with no clouds in the sky, the sun didn't feel unbearably hot. Framed by the boat's wake, Ivory Island's empty lighthouse was still keeping guard.

Before her was Cranmore Island, the largest in this grouping of rocky outcroppings called the Isles of Hampton. Cranmore was where the main tour boats came, twice a day during the week, three times a day on the weekend. There was a large, white wooden building once used as a hotel during the Grand Hotel era of tourism in the late 1800s. Now it housed a conference center and religious retreat. A couple of other buildings belonged to the state park system—of which she was a not-so-proud member—and a marine laboratory for the University of New Hampshire.

Three other islands—Anson, Clarke, and Bradbury—were rocky bits of granite studded with some shrubbery. During World War II they had been used as gunnery and bombing ranges for the navy. The sole remaining island—Isaac—belonged to some rich family from New York who came to live in its tiny cottage two weeks every August. Off to starboard was the Atlantic—next landfall, Europe—and off to port about six miles away was the New Hampshire coastline and the channel that led to the state's largest harbor, at Porter. Sea gulls and other marine birds were wheeling overhead, and the ocean boasted its fair share of fishing boats, sailing vessels, and other day-trippers, out looking for rest and relaxation this summer day.

She sighed wistfully as she brought the Whaler into the large dock at Cranmore Island with an expert touch. She loved it here, loved every moment while she was on the water or at Ivory Island—but on Cranmore Island things were bad indeed, and a long summer loomed ahead of her.

The building that housed the state park workers had once been a boardinghouse, when a dozen or so families had actually lived on the island as fishermen and smugglers during the eighteenth and nineteenth centuries. Her room was up near the eaves, and as she went in and dumped the knapsack on her bed, she looked around. What a dump. Tiny window that overlooked the rear of the old hotel; a bed, chair, and tiny desk and bureau. She opened up her knapsack, took out the photo, and thumbtacked it savagely to the wall, joining dozens of others.

"Hey," came a woman's voice.

"Hey, yourself, Grace," she said. "What's up?"

The other woman tour guide for the state—Grace Hollings, a college student like Nora, and about a foot taller and wider than her—ambled in and sat down on the only chair, making it squeak ominously. "Ralph's looking for you."

"Yeah, so what else is new? Story of my life. What's he want?"

Grace giggled. "We both know what he wants. But this time, I think he wants to talk about fuel consumption for the Whaler or some damn thing."

"Uh-huh," she said, looking at the rows and rows of photos. All those goofy smiles, vacant looks. Grace said, "Tell me, why the photos?"

"'Cause when the summer ends and Ralph tries to tell me that I didn't pull my weight, that I didn't do enough work, I'm going to wave all of these photos under his face and show him, that's why," she said.

"You could just show him your log count."

"If the number doesn't match in his favor, then he'll say something stupid about numbers not meaning anything," she said, looking back at Grace. "We know that's how he works."

"Uh-huh," she said, standing up. "And I know how this world works, and for once in my life, I'm not jealous of a body like yours. At least Ralph leaves me alone."

"Lucky you," Nora said.

Grace smiled. "Yeah, you're right. Lucky me."

She left the room and Nora looked back at the photo, at the eight faces looking in her direction. She wondered what it would be like to exchange her life for one of those blank faces on the photo paper. No, she decided, she wouldn't want that, not at all. She wanted to be a historian, wanted to learn and explore and research this tiny little stretch of coastline, and she was going to do it, Ralph Gunning or no Ralph Gunning.

She went back to her knapsack, froze.

Then she went back to the newest photo on the wall. Eight faces. Eight.

Her fingers trembling a bit, she dug out her trip log. Seven.

Seven out and seven back.

So what in hell was going on?

Nora gingerly removed the thumbtack and took the photo down and held it by the window. Okay, she thought. Let's not panic. Two kids, right? Right. Three women, right? Right. Which leaves...

Three men. Not two.

She blinked, stared harder at the photo. She remembered the idiot guy who asked her about getting a photo. Okay, scratch him. Which left the guy on the right and the guy on the left. Both had on dark pants, and one had on a sweatshirt with a hood, and the other, a short brown jacket. Their faces were nondescript, a couple of white guys in their late thirties or so. Okay. Sweatshirt guy—she remembered him, holding the hand of the young boy as they trudged up the path. C'mon, girl, she thought. Think. Where did this guy with the jacket and sorrowful look on his face come from? And how in hell did you miss the count?

A horn blared outside. The tour boat was leaving. Which meant she couldn't run over there and try to match a departing tourist with the face in the photo.

But damn it, seven went over and seven came back!

Which means what?

"Means he's still back there, trespassing," she whispered. "That's what."

Back at the dock, old Roland Cooper—the state's only maintenance man, handyman, and all-around "go to" guy on the island—was in the Boston Whaler coiling up a fuel hose. He had on oil-stained khaki workpants and shirt, and he shaded his eyes with a wrinkled hand as Nora jumped into the bow of the boat. "Going someplace, cutie?" he asked, smiling.

"Yep, going to take her out for a spin, out to Ivory."

Roland frowned, wiped his hands on a greasy rag. "Don't be gone too long. Your boss has been after me over how much gas you've been burning."

"Don't worry, Roland," she said. "I can handle it."

The older man got back up on the dock, still looking troubled. "What should I tell him?"

"Tell him I thought the engine was running rough, and I

wanted to take it out for a test spin without tourists getting in the way," she said, undoing the mooring lines.

Roland shook his head and walked away. "That's what I said last time..."

Back out on the open water, she goosed the engine and let the Boston Whaler do some bouncing as she headed back to Ivory Island. It was nearing dusk, and she knew Ralph was going to be seriously pissed when he found out what she was doing, but so what. That eighth face was beginning to spook her, and she had to settle things before it started really eating at her. A trespasser, that's what he was, for the tour groups from Cranmore Island were the only authorized visitors to Ivory Island. There were signs around its tiny shore announcing that fact, but it was apparent that somebody was out there who didn't belong. And she intended to root him out, because she had a good idea what that fool was up to. It had to be one of two things: either looking for the treasure of Captain Kidd—buried somewhere along the Atlantic Coast from Maine to Long Island—or breaking into the lighthouse and stealing souvenirs or artifacts. Well, that was not going to happen, not with Nora Donnelly around—not to a place that she had grown to love in the few short weeks she had been here.

She slowed down the Whaler and began gingerly skirting the shore of Ivory Island, starting at the small dock that she had left just under an hour ago. She had gotten to know the location of every rock and ridge off the shores of the island, and she motored in as close as she dared to. She was looking for a boat, probably something small, maybe even a dinghy with an outboard on the stern. Yet, as she rounded the island, something was nagging at her. The damn place was too rocky, too rough. The water splashed against sheer walls of rock and tumbled boulders. There was no sandy beach, no opening, no landing place for a boat. Only the dock, which she now found herself back at.

She idled the engine for a moment, just off the dock. The island seemed to beckon to her. Okay, she thought. Maybe somebody was out there, had hung on with her group at the end and gotten his picture taken. What did he do then? Skulk back to hide in the bushes? The only place to moor a boat was at the dock, and while she wasn't bright some days, she knew she couldn't have missed another boat during the tour. So, he still had to be on the island. She eased up the engine a notch and motored in to the dock. Well, if he was still here, she was going to find him, and kick him off. This island may belong to the state, she thought, but during the summer, it belonged to her.

A half-hour later she was taking a break, resting her back against the smooth granite stones that made up the lighthouse. Nothing. Not a damn thing. The island was small enough that it took only fifteen or twenty minutes to explore the dirt-packed paths that cut through the shrubbery. The lighthouse and the sole outbuilding—the lighthouse keeper's residence having burned down years ago—were firmly locked and shuttered. There was no trash, no tent, no firepit. Nothing to show that somebody had been here.

So. Where did that guy come from, the mysterious face in the photo?

She tilted her head to the side, looked up the smooth expanse of stone. She tried to imagine what it must have been like, to be out here months on end—keeping the light and the foghorn operational, feeling that heavy weight of responsibility—knowing that all the ships and cargo vessels and their crews going in and out of Porter Harbor depended on you to make your journey safe. A heavy job.

Still...who was that sad looking fellow in the photo, and where did he go after she took the picture.

"I don't rightly know," she said aloud. She got up, brushed the dirt off her shorts, and went back to the dock.

Heading back to Cranmore Island, she saw a familiar figure standing at the end of the dock, waiting for her, and she had an urge to turn the Whaler around and head away, maybe back to Ivory Island, or even Porter Harbor, if the fuel held up. Ralph Gunning was standing there, dressed in khaki slacks, blue button-down shirt, and a red necktie—probably the only damn necktie on the island—and his expression didn't look happy. Nora made a quick and strategic decision. While apparently idly scratching her chest, she undid another button at the top of her shirt—something the sisterhood would probably frown on, but she had learned earlier about how Ralph's mind worked, and she wasn't opposed to getting him a bit flustered before he started into her.

She came up to the side of the dock, saw Ralph look and then look again at her cleavage. Sleazy guy that he was, he didn't bother to help her moor the boat. No doubt he was showing her that he was in charge, and no doubt, too, he was also trying to catch a free peek as she bent down to tie off the Whaler.

When she bounded up on the dock, he said crisply, "I asked to see you some time ago. Where have you been?"

The lie—like so many others before—came out easily enough. "I thought the engine was running kind of rough. I wanted to test it before I brought out the next crop of tourists."

"I see," he said, his eyes again glancing down to her chest. "My office. Now."

"Sure," she said, and she followed him up to the parks building, knowing that he was probably ticked off that he couldn't walk behind her and take in the view.

Ralph's office was in the best room of the boardinghouse, what had probably been the dining room for the whole building years ago. Nora took a chair without asking. Windows looked over the dock and Ivory Island and its lighthouse. Ralph sat behind his desk and frowned, leafing through a bunch of stapled papers. The walls were bare of pictures, decorations, or anything else vaguely warm and comforting. A tiny bookcase held a collection of state statutes and procedures, bound in three-ring binders, but there were no other kinds of books. Ralph looked up, frowned again.

"Your consumption is way over budget," he said.

"Food or fuel?" she replied, regretting the shot right away, for Ralph didn't rise to the bait, didn't raise his voice at all.

"Fuel consumption," he said calmly. "And you know it. You're pushing us way over budget. Why, Nora?"

"Because I like to test the engine," she said. "You know it's old and needs to be replaced."

"Or is it because you like to run out there on the water by yourself? Go to Ivory Island without tourists? Is that why?"

Of course, she thought. Ivory Island, out there all alone, no tourists, no staff members, nobody. Just find a quiet place in the shrubbery, near the lighthouse, and pretend it's the nineteenth, or even the eighteenth century. Just take in the smell of the salt air and the sights of the seagulls, the rolling swells, the waves breaking upon the barren rocks. Get away from Cranmore Island and a creepy boss who tries to undress you with his eyes every chance he gets.

"No," she said. "That's not why. I don't want the engine dying out there with some mainlanders. It'd be bad publicity for the state."

"Uh-huh," he said. "Well, here's the deal, Nora. Your time here this summer is turning out to be bad publicity for you. You're insubordinate, you're using up our fuel allotment for no good reason, and I should probably let you go...except that at this point in the season, I'd probably have a hard time finding a replacement."

She carefully folded her hands over her bare left knee, clasped her fingers tight. She looked at Ralph, and he looked right back at her. "Well?" he asked.

"Excuse me?"

"You didn't say anything," he said.

Nora took a breath. "I'm sorry. I didn't hear you ask a question."

Ralph's face reddened. "What I'm saying, Nora, is—"

The desk phone rang, making Ralph jump, which pleased Nora but she kept her face impassive. No need to tick him off any more, and part of her felt cold at what he had just said. Fired. Just like that. From her dream job, one that she hoped would eventually lead her into an equally dream career.

"Gunning here," he said. "Oh, hi. Listen, those figures..."

Tom? Tom? This is a lousy connection . . . hold on, I'll use my cell phone."

Ralph hung up and got up from his chair, unhooking the cell phone from his belt. "You stay here. I'll be right back."

"Sure," she said, watching him go outside to the front porch, where he started talking and waving one hand around. Nora turned and looked at his desk. Nice neat piles of letters, folders, and envelopes. Everything nice and straight. She leaned over, saw a red-edged envelope peeking from underneath that day's *Union Leader* newspaper. Okay, so there's one thing askew. She moved the envelope and saw the red letters stamped in one corner.

Personal and Confidential.

She turned. Ralph was still yapping on the phone. Back to the desk and the envelope, a nine-by-twelve brown manila addressed to Ralph was now in her hands. It had already been opened, and the return address was a post office box in Manchester, the state's largest city. For about one second she felt guilty about what she was going to do, but the guilt was quickly replaced by morbid curiosity. She opened it up. What in hell could he be involved with that had anything to do with "Personal and Confidential?"

And in a moment, she had her answer. Nora's throat got tight as she flipped through the documents, the artist's conceptions, the planning that was going into something called Ivory Island Retreat. Words and phrases jumped out at her:

". . . state legislature could be expected to vote to sell Ivory Island to the OTC Development Corporation this fall . . . most votes are already lined up . . ."

". . . construction could start next spring . . . twelve high-concept, high-priced retreat luxury condos . . ."

". . . lighthouse an added feature . . ."

". . . first island manager position would, of course, go to you, Mr. Gunning . . ."

". . . secrecy is of the utmost importance . . ."

She shoved the papers back into the envelope, put it back on his desk. The palms of her hands were quite moist, and she dried them on her shorts just as Ralph came back in and said, "You know, Nora, this could be a good summer for you."

"I'm sure it could be."

Then, the creep came up behind her and gently put his hands on her shoulders. "I've got connections at the university, you know. I know you want to be a historian, and that you need to get some work-study jobs and internships related to the islands and coastal communities." He started rubbing her shoulders. "If you cooperate better, I'm sure we could work something out. But if you don't—well, things could get very difficult for you, Nora. Very difficult indeed."

Nora clenched her fists, kept her voice even. "Is that all, Ralph?"

The rubbing slowly stopped. "For now, Nora. For now."

Late at night she lay in her bunk, dressed in jeans and sweatshirt; when night fell out on these islands, it got cold pretty damn quick. Tonight she was unaware of the chill, though, because she was still burning up inside at what had happened earlier in the afternoon. She couldn't decide what was making her more angry: the not-so-subtle threats from Ralph about her future here on the island and her future at school, or the plans to turn Ivory Island and its lighthouse into a playground for rich people (who now had to go miles off-shore to find a place to dump their money)—plans that Ralph was no doubt shepherding through.

She got up from the bed, restless. No way she was going to sleep, not for a while. She pulled on a short wool jacket and went outside.

In a few minutes, she was on the dock, looking out to-ward the mainland. The lights of Porter and the other coastal towns washed out all save the brightest stars near the horizon, and she folded her arms and hugged herself. Even at this dis-tance she could see the lights of the cars moving along coastal Route 1A. She had a sense of all those crowded, dirty, scrab-bling people over there on the mainland, trying to find a way out here to her islands. She imagined what kind of people would buy condos on Ivory Island—the type who come to a remote area because of its remoteness, and then destroy the very thing that had once attracted them. The brush cut away, the bird nesting areas burnt, trash and sewage and litter...

She turned and looked over at Ivory Island. The lighthouse was doing its automated job, helping to protect the watercraft coming up this way.

But who in hell was going to protect the lighthouse and the island?

She shivered, made to turn back and head off to bed, when she saw the other lights.

Nora stopped, rubbed at her eyes. There. On Ivory Island. Three or four slow-moving yellow lights. Like a little string of beads, moving back and forth.

But nobody went on Ivory Island at night. Nobody.

So, who was there? Her mysterious man from the photo? Or...

Without hesitation, she walked back down the dock and jumped into the Boston Whaler. The keys were locked away in the state parks building, but she felt under the dashboard and pulled out a small magnetic case. A little trick she had pulled off earlier in the season, when Ralph had threatened to take the keys away from her. She put the duplicate key in and then went over to the side, undid the lines, and gently pushed her way off the dock. No need to advertise what was going on. She took an oar and then pushed the boat even further away, and let the current take her out. When she had gone far enough she switched on the engine and, keeping it low, headed over to Ivory Island.

She had a very good idea of who was out there this night. Survey teams, that's what. Sent over at night to check things out, measure out the foundations for Ivory Island Retreat without worrying about a tour group coming through. And her mystery man? Probably a surveyor who got caught out in the open, thought quickly enough to join her group, and then ducked away when everybody started boarding for the return trip to Cranmore Island.

She took a deep breath, boosted the throttle up a bit. Well, guys, she thought. You're in for one big flippin' surprise, 'cause when I get there, it's going to be called trespassing, and that news should do a lot to destroy Mister Personal and Confidential's plans.

As angry as she was at what was going on at the island, a part of her enjoyed being out on the water at night. The stars were so bright and hard looking, it seemed like they were only a mile overhead. The water was dark and forbidding, but also inviting; and before her, the lighthouse was a welcome beacon, save for the intruding lights below it—lights that kept moving from side to side. She slowed the engine as she approached and made sure the running lights were doused. A nighttime approach on a dark dock all by herself was going to be tricky, but she was sure she could pull it off.

And she did. Gauging the current and the movement of the waves, she killed the engine at the right moment, and then leapt out onto the dock with lines in hand. In another minute, the boat was secured; she started going up the dock, flashlight in hand.

Then she stopped. Jeez, girl, take a smart pill, why don't you? You're assuming that there are surveyors out here trespassing. But suppose it's somebody else? Somebody who wouldn't mind having a little encounter with a young college girl, an encounter involving some rough stuff?

"Damn it," she whispered, and went back to the Whaler. Beyond her were the warm and welcoming lights of Cranmore Island, where she was safe but miserable. She shivered, feeling terribly alone. Who was out here on Ivory Island?

Somehow, the burning indignation that got her over here was now drifting away like the smoke from an extinguished campfire. It sure was tempting to just head back to Cranmore. She got back into the Whaler, fumbled around and then pulled out the flare gun. There. In the darkness, it would look like a weapon, and if some guy out here pushed her or came too close, she'd see how he'd like having a burning flare propelled between his legs, just below his favorite piece of real estate.

Climbing back onto the dock, she headed up into the darkness.

After a few minutes of walking, she paused, breathing hard. The lights had disappeared. The only illumination was from the lighthouse, which every few seconds lit up part of the landscape like a recurring flashbulb. But there was nothing, nothing at all. She squatted down, tried to ease her breathing. Something was wrong, and now she realized what it was.

Her boat was the only one on the dock.

So how did this mysterious and so far imaginary survey crew get out here? Parachutes? Okay, maybe they were dropped off, but the boat doing the dropping off, where was it now? Just motoring around in circles? Didn't make sense.

She got up and something grabbed her by the shoulders.

Nora yelped and flailed around, turning on the flashlight. Bones, bare bones . . . and then she took a deep breath, and another. Some bare stalks of a stunted juniper bush, that's all. When she got up, it felt like something had grabbed her. That's it. Girl, she thought, you keep this up, and you'll have a heart attack before you're twenty-one.

She switched off the light and turned back to the trail— and the yellow lights were back.

She paused, and then slowly walked up the trail, the lights now glowing just above a slight rise that led to the lighthouse. All she could hear was the clicking sound of the automated machinery, a few night birds, and the wind. That was it. Then the sound of the birds drifted away. She shivered again. Something was wrong.

She turned around again on the trail, saw the shadows, and her imagination kicked into overdrive. It was like something out there was threatening her, something awful. She swayed in the darkness. Why had she ever come out here? Why? What was so important?

This place, she thought. This whole preserve and the lighthouse and everything else. That's what's important.

She gritted her teeth, switched on the flashlight, and started running up the trail. With the flare gun in her other hand, she headed towards the lights. "State of New Hampshire park police!" she yelled, hoping the intruders wouldn't know that no such agency existed. "You hold on, right there!"

She raced up the rocky path, the flashlight making strange shadows along the brush. The little group of yellow lights retreated, staying just ahead of her flashlight beam, and she continued racing, right past the open area and the lighthouse, heading to the other side of the island. The lights moved fast, so damn fast—and then they blinked out, just like that.

Nora swore, tried to stop, tripped on something, and fell. Things got black quite quickly as she tumbled to the ground. Her legs and back shouted with pain, and she lay still, breathing. The flashlight was still on, just a few feet away. For some reason her face felt cold. She reached out and grabbed the light, and rolled over on her belly, holding the light in front of her.

Illuminating nothingness.

She looked down. Below her was a sharp cliff, falling down to a collection of boulders. Seawater oozed and eddied in and out of the rocks. She rolled over, flashed the light down the trail, tried to see what had tripped her up.

Nothing. The trail was clear and smooth.

She moved the light around. The shrubbery was on either side of the trail, a tangled mass of roots and branches. Hard for anybody to move through if they had to.

Yet the lights had come through here and had disappeared.

She got up, switched off the flashlight, looked up at the stars and then back at the lighthouse—still doing its job, not caring what was going on underneath it—and with her other hand, she squeezed the flare gun tight.

Back at Cranmore, she limped back up to the state parks building, moving slowly, trembling every now and then over what was going on. From the tourist who wasn't there to the strange lights to the mysterious something that had tripped her, something serious was beginning to spook her badly. Not to mention Ralph and that corporation and their plans to destroy that lovely island over there.

About halfway to her bed she stopped, smelled something burning. Pipe tobacco. She looked over at a gazebo on the small lawn next to the old grand hotel. There was an ember of light where someone was smoking, and she felt herself relax some. With the nearest fire department six or seven miles away over the Atlantic Ocean, the mostly wrought iron gazebo was the only place where smoking was allowed, and she walked over and said into the darkness, "Hello, Roland."

"Hello, Nora," said the island's maintenance man. "See you've been out wandering tonight."

"That I have," she said.

"Come up and sit for a bit, why don't you," Roland said.

"I think I will," and she went up into the gazebo and sat in an old Adirondack chair. Roland sat next to her, gently sucking on his pipe. Ivory Island's light was still at work, and the mainland lights were now obscured by a thin bank of fog. There were no mysterious lights dancing around the edge of Ivory Island. Nora cleared her throat and said, "Roland?"

"Mmmm?"

"You've been out here for a while, haven't you?"

"'Bout fifteen years, after I took early retirement from the shipyard. So yeah, I guess I've been out here for a while. Why do you ask?"

She folded her hands in her lap, felt compelled to go on. "This is going to sound crazy and all, but . . . you ever see anything strange out here? Especially at night?"

"'Strange' covers a lot of things, Nora. You want to be more specific?"

"Ever see lights at night? Lights that don't belong? Or people? People who are there one moment, and gone the next?"

Roland didn't say anything, just kept on smoking. Then he took the pipe down and started cleaning out the bowl with a little penknife. "You're talking about Ivory Island. Am I right?"

"Yes."

"Uh-huh," he said. "Might be best just to drop it, Nora."

"I don't want to drop it," she said. "I want to know what's going on."

"You sure?"

There was a tone of warning in his voice that made her hesitate, only for a moment. "Yes," she said. "I'm sure."

Roland sighed. "Tell you what. We can talk about it for a while, but only tonight. You repeat anything, you say anything in the daylight tomorrow, and I'll deny every word. Do you understand?"

"Sure," she said, her hands now getting cold.

"All right. What do you want to know?"

"Ivory Island—is it haunted?" There. The word was out and she felt like a six-year-old, bravely defending the existence of Santa Claus before a skeptical adult.

The scraping sound continued as Roland worked the penknife around the bowl of his pipe. "Well, Nora, let's just get back to what you said earlier. Yeah, I've seen some odd things. And only at Ivory Island. And for no good reason. Lights, for example, like you mentioned. A yellow light that looks like it came from an old oil lamp. Is that what you've been seeing?"

"Yes, tonight," she said. "That's what I saw. And earlier today...I know this sounds nutty, but I gave a tour, and when I took a picture of the group, there was an extra man there. I counted seven out and seven back, but there were eight people in the picture. Roland, what's going on?"

Roland didn't say a word, kept on cleaning his pipe. Nora pressed. "What is it? The ghost of a lighthouse keeper, all these years later? Somebody who died out there? Got murdered?"

The old man refilled his pipe and lit it. Nora saw his face illuminated in the flare of light from the pipe bowl. She looked away, for the man's gaze was nothing like the friendly look she usually got, meeting him on the dock or in the buildings. No, the gaze tonight was that of an old New Englander telling an even older tale—and not sure he should be doing it.

"Edmund Tyler," he said. "Know the name?"

"No, I don't."

"Edmund Tyler," Roland repeated, motioning with his pipe. "He designed the current Ivory Island lighthouse, about a hundred and twenty-five years ago. Years before that, though, when he was a child, right after the Civil War, the old lighthouse there had failed and a boat from Boston had foundered. His parents drowned, and he was orphaned when he was only eight. When he got older, he designed government buildings, especially lighthouses, and he vowed that he would build a lighthouse on Ivory Island that would last forever. Which he did, after a fashion, for he designed one that was more strong, more sturdy, than anything ever built before or since. It was said that he was so obsessed with building the perfect lighthouse that he would work all through the night, planning and sketching by the light of oil lamps, lights that could be seen from Cranmore Island."

Nora suddenly felt quite cold; she brought her legs up and hugged her knees. Roland went on. "But the contractor cheated and skimped, and the lighthouse wasn't built to specifications. Old Edmund Tyler fought and fought to have the place rebuilt, but he was turned down time and time again. Last that was seen of him was when he went over on an open boat to Ivory Island during a storm, to take some additional measurements. He never came back. And, well, that's that."

"No," she said sharply. "There's got to be more. Why am I seeing the lights? Why did I see . . . Jesus, why did I see him?"

Roland took another puff. "You remember our promise?"

"Yes," she said. "Not a word."

"Very well," he said. "Story I heard, growing up, is that he only comes back when the island or the lighthouse is threatened. After the hurricane of '38, the lighthouse keeper and his wife left the island, and word was that there were lights at night, lights that scared them because they moved around so much. During the war, there was a plan to turn part of the island into a bombing range, but that plan was abandoned . . . supposedly because a man was believed to be hiding out there, a man who was often seen but never captured. There were other stories, too. Back in the 1950s and '60s, some of the children of the lighthouse keepers told of a strong but quiet man who saved them from drowning, who saved them from falling off some of the cliffs. It was like he was protecting whoever was protecting his light, his island. So there you go."

"Quite a story," Nora said, squeezing her legs even tighter with her cold arms.

"True, and I'm afraid I have another story for you," Roland said. "Ralph saw you leave with the Boston Whaler tonight."

"Oh," she said.

"Yes," Roland said, "and I believe he means to fire you by the end of the week."

The next day she stayed out of Ralph's way, ran three tours out and three tours back, each time counting and recounting the people. The photos and the count matched, and she could not believe how quickly the day flew by. But with each passing moment, she thought and planned and thought some more.

There. It was early dusk, and after a hurried meal she had gone back to her room and prepared for the evening. She had a wicker basket with a bottle of merlot, some crackers, cheese, and grapes. Nothing fancy, but when the nearest supermarket was an hour's boat ride away, you made do. She looked at herself in the bureau mirror and frowned, sticking her tongue out. She looked awful, tarted up. She had on a pair of tight white dress slacks that she had only worn once, but which did hug her butt pretty close. She had on a blue bikini bathing suit top, and with the judicious use of some tissue, had made her breasts look even larger than they really were. Worn over the top was a short denim jacket, opened. She sighed.

"The things you do for love," she said. And then she picked up the basket and left the room.

God, it was so easy. She knocked on Ralph's office door and walked in; his eyes bugged out, looking over at her. "Um, yes?" he said.

"Ralph? Do you have some time?"

His hands nervously moved some papers around. "Um, well, guess I do."

"Well," she said. "Would you like to go on an evening picnic with me? Just the two of us?"

The man's grin was frightening, it was so wide. "Sure," he said. "Where?"

She smiled back. "Ivory Island."

By the time evening arrived, they'd built a small fire just above the trail, near the dock. After most of the food was gone and half the bottle of wine had been drunk, the score was: six gropes, one back massage, and one sloppy kiss that struck her cheek when she quickly turned her head. Ralph now held her hand tight and was going on about his life, growing up in Portland, Maine, and his leg was slowly rubbing against hers. She felt queasy and the ground was hard against her butt. Her boobs were getting cold and she was wondering what she had set herself up for when the lights came back.

"Ralph, look!" she said, putting some fear into her voice. "What's that?"

Ralph turned, and she managed to free her hand. She agonized for a moment, wondering if she was the only one seeing them, when he said, "What the . . . what kind of lights are those?"

She hated the tone in her voice, but it had to be done: "Ralph! I'm scared! Will you go see what it is? I'll stay here by the fire."

"Sure," he said, getting up. "You hold on."

He grabbed a flashlight and called out, "Hey! You with the lights! Hold on!"

Ralph started jogging up the path and Nora waited, pulling her short coat tight against her, her fingers cold, waiting, waiting, as Ralph and the lights faded from view.

She moved only after she heard his quick scream.

A week later, Nora motored back into the dock at Cranmore after another day of ferrying tourists back and forth to Ivory Island. The day was hot and sunny, and her mood was as bright as the reflection off the waves. As she helped the tourists off the boat—six out and six back, thank you very much—a little girl wearing a plaid jumper and a serious expression on her face said, "Are there any ghosts over there?"

She tied off the bow mooring line and said, "What made you ask that?"

The girl shrugged. "I don't know. I just had a feeling, when I was walking by the waves."

Nora touched the girl on her cheek. "If there are, I'll bet you they are friendly ghosts."

The girl smiled and ran off after her parents. Nora smiled, too, and made the walk back to her room, just enjoying the taste of salt in the air, even enjoying the sight of the gulls weaving around.

Up in her room, Grace Hollings was there, her long and bony legs stretched out before her. She had an envelope in her hands and said, "Time to pay up."

"For what?" Nora asked.

"Fruit basket," she said. "For Ralph. I guess he can eat solid food now, though it'll be weeks before he's walking, and months before he even considers coming back to the island. I guess some of the doctors think he's lucky to be alive."

She dug into her shorts pocket, pulled out a crumpled twenty-dollar bill. "Here. Buy him six."

Grace took the bill and said, "Look, why don't you tell me what really happened out—"

"No."

"I mean, Ralph won't say much, except that he fell, and I just want to know if it's—"

"Grace, no," she said.

Her friend stood up, shrugged. "All right. Thanks for the twenty. Oh, and did you see the *Union Leader* this morning?"

Nora rummaged through her knapsack and pulled out the last tour group photo of the day. "No. What was in it?"

"A wild story about developers who were planning to con the state into selling Ivory Island. Then they were going to build a whole bunch of condos on it. I guess somebody mailed some documents to a columnist for the paper, a writer named Clayton. Everybody's denying everything, but it looks like some people in the legislature want to hold special hearings in a few weeks. Can you believe that?"

Nora took the photo, thumbtacked it to the wall, and then let her eye drift over to the one photo last week that had started everything. The eight-person group when there should have just been seven, where there was an extra face, a man who didn't belong, a man who—

A man whose face was no longer frowning. But was smiling. With the greatest happiness.

"Grace," she said, grinning, turning to look at her. "Some days, I can believe almost anything."

ED GORMAN

Ghost of a
Chance

Pretty much everybody in Colby, Maine, knew why young
Jimmy Tate went to the war over there in Europe that rainy
spring of 1915.

He said it was because it was his patriotic duty—and
maybe there was even a smidge of truth to that—but mostly it
was because of Katie Chandeau, the girl he'd been in love
with since her family had moved next door to his when Jimmy
was but four years old.

Jimmy Tate had two aspirations in life. He wanted to
marry Katie and he wanted to run the lighthouse out at Beacon Point.

Well, as so often happens in life, the young man found
himself disappointed. Both Katie and the lighthouse job went
to another young man named Josh Plummer, the smartest,
handsomest, and most popular young man in the entire
county. This last was with good reason. Even with all his
blessings, Josh managed to be a decent, modest, and genuinely likable young man.

So Jimmy Tate went to war. He'd thought of moving to
Bangor just to get out of town, but that lacked the romantic
resonance of war—manly combat, wine-soaked furtive nights
with elegant French girls, and staring down Old Man Death

day after day. He'd come back here, by God, and sweep her off her feet. That was one scenario he played out constantly in his head, just like the silent pictures he saw at the Odeum on Saturday afternoons. The other scenario was even more simple and dramatic: he'd be shipped home in a flag-draped coffin, and seeing it off-loaded from the train, Katie would realize who she'd loved all along and fling herself on the wooden box, forever destroyed with love-too-late. In some ways, that was an even more pleasing scenario. The only trouble being that he'd have to die in that one.

Abroad, Jimmy liked to joke that when the Germans heard he was in Europe, their whole war effort started collapsing.

And it sure seemed that way. About a week or so after Jimmy landed there, the German fronts started to disintegrate. Within a month, the Huns were even on the run in a few places.

Six months later, along with a half-million other Yanks, Jimmy took part in one of the most important battles of the war, the Meuse-Argonne offensive. The Allied forces did so well that the German surrender seemed imminent.

All around him Jimmy saw the broken bodies and listened to the tortured souls of the men who had survived this war. Europe would never be the same again, nor would the young men who had managed to fight and live.

Jimmy was untouched by it. His fantasy of returning to Colby burned so brightly in his head—a hundred new images a day of Katie in his arms and him working the lighthouse— that he fought the war at one remove. It was never quite real to him, in the same way those silent pictures at the Odeum were never quite real.

In 1918, after six months of traveling Europe and having himself a good time, Jimmy Tate returned, much decorated for his courage, to take his place among the good folks of Colby, Maine.

Here's how things stood when he got back:

Katie and Josh had a beautiful little daughter. And Katie was pregnant with a second child. They lived free of charge in a nice little stone bungalow the government had built them right on the rise of land where the lighthouse stood. They'd even been provided with a Model T for getting back and forth to town.

People used the word "radiant" a lot when they tried to describe Katie; and "nicest young man you'd ever want to know" when they were speaking of Josh.

The first time Jimmy saw Katie, she was pushing her baby girl down sunny Main Street in a baby carriage. She was pleasant enough—and certainly complimentary to him about his bravery in the war—but he could see that she'd forgotten about all the times they'd spent together growing up. He'd taken her to her first dance; and, he was sure, given her her first kiss. Banished now, he was sure, utterly and forever from her memory.

Perhaps worst of all was the simple, undramatic nature of their chance meeting. He'd always imagined that this would be the sort of encounter where she swooned like a movie hero-ine and he—like a granite-faced movie hero—allowed a gleam of tears to show in the corner of his stoic, world-weary eyes. Wasn't he after all a war hero?

But it wasn't like that at all.

The street was noisy with Model T traffic, and passersby were constantly interrupting them to say hello, and the baby cried (and you could smell that she'd pooped recently), and Katie was forever glancing at her smart new wristwatch. God, she was so beautiful.

And it all took less than three or four minutes before she set her sweet hands on the handle of the carriage and began pushing it away.

Three years later, despite a lot of mental planning to move on, Jimmy was living in a boardinghouse and working as a clerk in a hardware store. He played on the town's baseball team; he was a big fan of jazz; he was a right smart Saturday night dancer; and he was known to have broken more than his share of local hearts.

He had a Ford coupe with a rumble seat, and on Sunday

he'd drive out to the Point and look across at the steep promontory where the lighthouse stood, a whitewashed arrow gleaming in the sun, a thousand-pound fog bell as a companion, and so much lore and legend surrounding it that it had inspired tall tales since first being constructed in 1873.

The only job he'd ever wanted.

The only girl he'd ever wanted.

He wasn't what you'd call *un*happy, probably. But he certainly wasn't happy, either. There was an emptiness, was how he expressed it sometimes after several highballs—a hollowness.

A few times, he even ran into Josh Plummer himself.

Josh was always nice and decent, not only because that was his nature, but also because he'd never considered Jimmy a rival. It was clear he didn't know that Jimmy had ever been in love with Katie. They'd just been childhood friends so far as Josh knew. Why wouldn't Josh be friendly to him? And Jimmy, being a decent sort himself, was nice right back.

And so on.

Dances, ball games, ice skating, keeping his roadster running—his life continued on. He wasn't what you'd call inconsolable; he was just—empty somehow.

The accident happened a year later.

Rainy day. November. Icy roads. A Model T skidding out of control. And Josh Plummer, husband and father of two, a guy liked by practically everybody, was dead.

A funeral. A town mourning. A widow weeping. Two sweet little kids not yet old enough to understand.

On one matter, Jimmy moved quickly. He went to the Lighthouse Service and told them why he should be the lightkeeper. He reminded them that he would have applied for the last opening except that he'd been in the war. He reminded them that they'd always seen him as a kid hanging around the lighthouse, learning how it operated, expressing the hope to anybody who'd listen that somebody he'd be in charge of it. His war record, combined with his enthusiasm, got him the job on the spot. They needed somebody. Immediately.

• • •

Eight months later, Jimmy had comfortably settled into the bungalow under the lighthouse. Katie and the kids had moved out almost immediately after the funeral. Sometimes Jimmy felt sad about that, but it was always tempered by the knowledge that he was finally doing what he had wanted to do for so long. And the lighthouse keeper had to live somewhere, right?

One night he had picked up two tickets to a jazz concert in Bangor. He had made a point of calling on Katie under the pretense that he wondered if Josh had ever mentioned this or that about the lighthouse. She took to inviting him to supper on his nights off. There was no hint of romance. Her grief was apparent in every movement of her body, every flick of her eyes. Her grief had aged her. Not terribly, but aged her nonetheless. And her relative poverty didn't help. There'd been no insurance and little savings. Jimmy was always trying to give her money for the food he ate, but she was too proud to take it. So instead he bought the girls endless but practical gifts, mostly school clothes and the like.

Marie and Ella loved him. He discovered to his delight that he had a natural way with children. He had a silly side, and he told great untrue tales of derring-do. He was modest enough to make these stories about others, never himself.

He loved Katie all the more, to be sure. Every part of him ached to hold her and tell her of his feelings, but he knew that she would only skitter away like a frightened fawn. He felt certain that in time—they were like a family already—it would seem natural and not frightening at all for them to be together as man and wife.

One night, when he pulled up to her house for dinner, he saw a new shiny Oldsmobile convertible parked there. He recognized the car at once. It belonged to Bill Jordan, the wealthy and handsome widower who was more tolerated than liked in Colby. The reason was simple. Before his wife had died of the cancer, he'd had a number of mistresses in Bangor, this all coming to light when one of the said mistresses tried to shoot

him one night when she saw him with another lady. All the
Jordan money and influence put together could not stop the
Bangor newspaper, which didn't much like the Jordan mining
family and its power, from running the story.

Bill Jordan wasn't a bad man, Jimmy had always felt,
just an immature one. He was Jimmy's age, and they'd gone
through school together. He wasn't mean; he wasn't even
snobbish. He was just an idler with a fancy for the ladies. And
with his Douglas Fairbanks good looks, they fancied him in
return.

He went up to the door with a sick feeling in his stomach.

"Why, Jimmy. Come in."

Jordan himself greeted Jimmy at the door. And greeted
him in a very relaxed, possessive way—as if this were his own
home and he was the host. He was dressed in an expensive
gray suit and his wavy blond hair was slicked down in big-
city fashion.

While the girls ran to Jimmy, Katie stood in the middle of
the living room. She wore a new dress and looked both elegant and lovely. And just slightly embarrassed, though if you
didn't know her you wouldn't have been able to pick up on it.

Bill Jordan walked to her and slid his arm through hers
and said, "Katie said she didn't want to say anything until
we'd set the date for sure. We're getting married, Jimmy, and
we'd sure like you to be there. We really appreciate everything
you've done for the girls and Katie. Don't we, dear?"

And Katie—still ever so slightly embarrassed—said, "Yes,
we do, Jimmy. We appreciate it very much."

The next night she rode her bike to the lighthouse. At first
he didn't want to let her in. He was angry, hurt. He was afraid
of what he might say. But finally, as he knew he would, he re-
lented, and she followed him up to the tower.

For a little while, they just looked out to the dark sea on
this tranquil, starry night, the lighthouse beacon like the eye
of God in the gloom.

"I wanted to explain."

"You don't owe me anything."

"I know you hate me right now."

"I just can't believe you'd do something like this."

"You only get one night a week off."

"I'm well aware of that."

"So on the nights you didn't come over, Bill did."

"You could've told me."

"I knew how you'd be, Jimmy. I know you—you have feelings for me."

"Not anymore, I don't."

"Oh, Jimmy. I don't want to lose your friendship. I really don't."

"Bill Jordan. I'll bet you don't even love him."

"Don't say things like that."

"Look me right in the eye and tell me you love him."

"That's not fair."

"Isn't it?"

"I love him."

"You're lying. I can see it."

"Think of the girls, Jimmy. Think of what having the Jordan name will mean to them. The schools they'll go to. The society they'll move in."

"So that's it. You're doing this for the girls."

He'd grabbed her arms, harder than he'd intended.

"You think Josh'd want that? You think the girls themselves'd want that? You may not have noticed, Katie, but when we were all having dinner together, we were a family."

For the first time, she began to cry. "Don't say that, Jimmy. Of course, I noticed. And of course I felt—"

And for the very first time since they were youngsters together, he saw love in her eyes. A simplistic way to say it, perhaps, just that one word unadorned—love—but that's what he saw just now, a love that was friendship and trust and care, and at least a sizable smidge of romantic interest, too. He was no Douglas Fairbanks, but he'd do in a pinch.

But then she was gone. He could hear her crying as she descended the winding iron steps she'd climbed so many times when Josh had been alive.

Gone—back to Bill Jordan.

The girls. There was no way he could argue or inveigh against a mother's wish to take proper care of her daughters.

If she'd truly loved Jordan, Jimmy, as the jealous former suitor, could point out the man's many flaws.

But how could he argue against Bill Jordan, the great provider? He'd be a wonderful provider. And how could he argue against Bill Jordan, the man who could give the girls everything? Indeed he could—and would—give the girls everything.

That night in the lighthouse tower, Katie had left much more than the wonderful scent of her perfume behind.

She'd left him crushed and finished...

The first time he heard the voice was two nights later.

The lighthouse had recently become the recipient of a new Fresnel lens. He was proudly inspecting it.

And then the voice said: "You can't let her do it, Jimmy."

Now, most people from time to time suspect they hear voices. They dismiss it as the audio equivalent of a mirage. You're tired; you have a head cold and your ear canals are plugged up; you mistake one sound for another.

Jimmy just shrugged. He'd probably been talking to himself and hadn't been aware of it. Easy to mistake when you're thinking such intense thoughts—as he was about his true love Katie. *You can't let her do it, Jimmy.* Sure, what could be more natural. Muttering aloud to himself.

"Did you hear what I said?"

Right here, Jimmy had to make a quick and very serious decision: He could put that last utterance down to insanity on his part; his sanity was caving in because of his grief. Insanity was not unknown among lighthouse keepers, the isolation and loneliness unhinging them sometimes. Or there really was a disembodied voice with him up here.

He sure didn't want to think of himself as crazy, so he said, tentatively, and with no small amount of embarrassment, "Did I just hear a voice?"

"You sure did, Jimmy. It's me. Josh."

"Josh! But you're dead."

"So I've been told."

"So if you're dead, how can you—?"

"I'm a ghost, Jimmy. There are such things, you know. There isn't a man or a woman who has spent any time in a lighthouse who doesn't believe in ghosts. And ghost ships. And ghost storms. There're a lot of worlds that living folks just don't know anything about."

Jimmy kept looking around. "Where are you?"

"Standing right in front of you, actually."

Jimmy had to make another quick and very serious decision. Should he indulge his insanity—because a part of him believed that he would soon be in the Hastings Clinic, that asylum west of town—and keep on talking as if Josh were in fact standing right here in front of him? Invisible. And dead. Or should he just call for an ambulance and have them cart him off in a straightjacket?

"You can't let her do it."

"You mean Bill Jordan?"

"Sure, I mean Bill Jordan."

"How'd you find out?"

"Well, I pop in every night. Give Katie a goodnight kiss on the cheek and then go down the hall and do the same with the girls. I still love them very much, Jimmy. And I know you do, too. I didn't realize that till after I died. I just figured you'd gotten over her a long time ago. But now I see—well, Katie needs a husband and the girls need a father. And that should be you, not Bill Jordan."

"But I can't stop her. I know she doesn't love him, but she's thinking of the girls."

"Well, she's not thinking clearly. She's worried about money, so worried that she's going through with the first situation that presented itself. I wish I'd been better with money. I should have left her some good life insurance, anyway."

"I don't know how I can stop her, Josh." He paused. "I still can't believe this is a real conversation."

"Oh, it's real, all right, Jimmy. And it's up to the two of us—the two men who love her most—to get her to change her mind and settle down with you."

"I just wish—"

"And I'm wishing the same thing. You think about it, and so will I. I'll be back here tomorrow night about the same time. Maybe one of us will've come up with something by then."

"Josh, wait. I—"

And it was funny, the feeling Jimmy had then. Not only was the phantom voice stilled suddenly, he also felt an *absence*, the kind you feel when someone leaves a room and leaves you alone.

For the first time, Jimmy realized that Josh really had been in the room. Talking. And standing right in front of him.

He spent a long and restless night.

He wasn't sure at first why he drove into town the next day, a Saturday. He usually went in on Mondays, when he did his shopping for the week.

But there was something in his mind—

He was halfway to town before he realized what was going on.

"You're here, aren't you?"

"How'd you know?"

"You aren't real subtle, Josh. 'Go into town. Go into town. Go into town.' After awhile it got to be sort of obvious."

"I paid a visit to Katie this morning. Beautiful autumn morning like this, she's got plans for her and the girls. Figured that might give you an opening."

Katie's plans consisted of a picnic in the park. The occasion was a children's play put on by the library. The girls were still young enough to appreciate things like this, so Katie had packed a picnic basket and off they went.

When the play was over, Katie took the girls and her basket and found a picnic table along the river. The day was sunny, the river blue and true, and the air aflutter with butterflies and birds of all kinds.

Just before he approached their table, Katie went over to talk to a woman she knew. The girls, spotting Jimmy, rushed over.

They each took a hand, and clinging to him, they grinned

and said how they missed him, and those strange imitations he could do—not just wildlife but people around town, too, like old Reverend Tolliver—and gosh, but they missed him.

He hefted them up in his arms and carried them, giggling, back to the picnic table where Katie was waiting.

She usually smiled when she saw him. She wasn't smiling now.

"Girls," she said, "you go ahead and eat."

"Why can't he eat with us, Mom?"

"Because he wasn't invited."

The coldness of her voice obviously startled the girls. They looked at their mother as if she were suddenly a stranger. The girls had often whispered in their moonlit room of how someday Jimmy was likely to become their pop. They loved Jimmy and sensed that their mother did, too.

But if that was the case, why was she acting this way toward him now?

"You girls sit down and eat. Jimmy and I need to talk."

"But we want him to stay," Ella said.

"We miss him, Mom," young Marie said.

"You heard what I said, girls," her voice still as cold as the heart of February. "You sit down there and eat."

She took him along the river. Lovers and fishermen paddled by in canoes and rowboats.

"You have no right to use the girls that way."

"What're you talking about? I love those girls. And they love me. We were just happy to see each other is all."

"Are you telling me you didn't come to the park because you knew we were here?"

He wanted to lie but couldn't. "Well—"

"Whatever you think about my decision to marry Bill Jordan—or whatever I think about it—the girls come first. They're my first responsibility. So I'd appreciate it if you wouldn't make it any harder on me or them—or yourself—by coming around. In time they'll forget you. I know that's not a nice thing to say, but it's the truth. You know how children are."

"How about you, Katie? Will *you* forget me?"

He'd never spoken so boldly to her before.

She softened somewhat—looked, in fact, miserable. "Please, Jimmy, I've tried to explain this. My feelings don't matter. It's the girls I worry about, their future."

She touched his arm, and the sensation sent him soaring. He felt dizzy with the tenderness of this brief moment. "Please. Go on with your life and I'll go on with mine. All right?"

"I love you, Katie."

But she was cold again; and he was banished once more from Eden. "Don't ever say that again to me, Jimmy. Not ever."

Then she turned around and walked away.

Five miserable days and nights, inside and out, the sea storms not half so furious as the storms inside Jimmy. He knew now for sure that she loved him.

Don't ever say that again to me, Jimmy.

As if he'd insulted her.

But she wouldn't have said that if she didn't love him.

He was glad for the loneliness of the lighthouse. Wouldn't want anybody to see him in this condition. So morose.

At least he was useful to somebody. A dozen vessels of a dozen sizes would have smashed up on the jutting rocks if Jimmy hadn't been there to guide them in.

On the sixth day the storms broke. Land and sea were sun-warmed again, and even a few pleasure craft could be seen on the blue waters now that it was safe once more.

When the thought came to him this time, it wasn't put there by a ghost. It was his own idea, and he was going to follow through with it.

The girls would be in school this afternoon. And he knew that Katie would be home working, as she had started to take in laundry in the months since Josh's death.

They would be alone, and he would make her listen to him. He would get her to say she loved him; and he would get her to agree to marry him.

She was hanging sheets on the clotheslines in the back yard when he got there. The smell was clean and fresh and recalled his childhood, his mother hanging her own sheets to dry.

Katie had a wooden clothespin in her mouth when she saw him. She almost swallowed it.

"Oh, Lord, Jimmy. Please don't put me through any more. You gave your word."

"No, I didn't."

He walked up to her, took a couple of clothespins from the pocket on her apron, and helped her finish the laundry.

"I should call the police, Jimmy."

"And what would they arrest me for? Helping you hang sheets?"

"For making things even worse than they need to be. Jimmy—I've made up my mind. And I'm not going to change it. And us together—it's just too painful."

Now that the clothes were all on the line, he took her slender wrists and held them gently together and looked in her eyes. "I want you to tell me you don't love me."

"Why, Jimmy, that's crazy."

"No, it isn't. I just want to hear you say it."

"Jimmy, please, I—"

"C'mon. Say it. And then I won't ever bother you again."

"Jimmy, this is ridiculous."

" 'I don't love you, Jimmy.' C'mon, say it."

"Yes, I'd like to hear her say that, myself."

She glanced over his shoulder. Her cheeks flared with embarrassment. Bill Jordan, jaunty in an expensive blue double-breasted business suit and spanking new necktie, walked into view.

"I don't mean to interrupt," he said. "Katie and I had planned a picnic for the girls down at the shore after school. But I heard voices back here, so I thought I'd see what was going on."

"Jimmy was just—"

"I think I know what Jimmy was just, darling. And because of that, I think it's time that Jimmy and I had a little talk and cleared the air. Mind if we go inside?"

She shook her head silently. Tears formed in her eyes.

"C'mon, Jimmy," Jordan said, sliding a comradely arm around the smaller man's shoulder. "Let's go inside. I left a fine bottle of scotch here for special occasions. And I'd say *this* is a special occasion, wouldn't you?"

They went inside.

Jordan took the bottle down from a kitchen cabinet and poured them each a drink. Jimmy wasn't much of an imbiber but this seemed to be one of those dramatic, manly moments that called for whiskey.

They sat at the kitchen table. The new oilcloth smelled wonderful.

"So you love her, eh, Jimmy?"

"Yes, I do."

"I thought as much. I know you used to." He raised his glass in a toast. Jimmy did likewise. "To the woman we both love."

Jimmy returned the toast. They drank.

"There're two things you should know. She's changed me completely. I haven't seen another woman since I got serious with Katie. And I plan to be completely faithful to her in our marriage. That's the first thing to know."

"I'd kill you if you were ever unfaithful to her."

"That's very strong."

"Maybe—but I also happen to mean it."

Jordan sipped some more scotch. "The second thing is that I plan to put both girls through Vassar. How would that be for a start in life? And I also plan to give each of them a very sizable inheritance when they finish college. And I don't think I have to tell you how I'll set Katie up once we're married. She'll have a perfect life, I promise you that. I'm going to surprise her by building a house for us—a mansion, really. The most splendid mansion in the whole state."

"I see what you're doing."

"Good."

"You're saying I'd have to be a very selfish person to stand in her way."

"Thanks for catching on so quickly."

"And that if I really loved her—the true meaning of love—then I'd stand aside."

"You put it very well."

Jimmy had never felt sadder or more lonely in his life. He wished he were the sort of noble fellow Douglas Fairbanks always played on the silent screen. Fairbanks would step aside instantly to allow Katie the life only Jordan could give her.

But he wasn't.

"I think she loves *me*," he said.

"Perhaps she does, Jimmy. For now, anyway. But if you're the honorable sort—and I think deep down you are—you'll stay away from her and eventually she'll forget you. Believe me, the life I'll give Katie and the girls will take her mind off her past. Including you. And Josh. I'll introduce her into society, and she'll become a very different woman."

And then it was done. Done inside him. And done for good. As much as part of him wanted to fight back, he knew that he couldn't be selfish enough to deny Katie and the girls this opportunity.

Jordan sensed his resignation. "I'd like to give you some money."

"I don't want your damned money."

"I was just trying to be friendly."

"I don't want your friendship, either. I'm not going to pretend I'm happy about this."

"All I want is your word that you'll never contact her again in any way."

"You've got it, Jordan. My word. And I'll keep it."

He was afraid he was going to start crying and he didn't want to give Jordan the pleasure. He stood up, his legs weak as if he were sick.

"I wish you'd reconsider about the money," Jordan said.

"No," Jimmy said. "No money. No money at all."

And then he turned and walked through the little house. Right out the front door to his roadster.

Never again to drive past. Nor stop. Nor even hope.

Never again.

• • •

Harsh winter came soon after.

Jimmy started doubling up on his groceries so he would not have to make as many trips to town. He didn't want to chance seeing Katie. Or the girls. He didn't want to chance seeing anybody.

He had the lighthouse, the brightest dream of his boyhood, and the sometimes comforting isolation of the place, as if it were a world unto itself, some alien planet, and he its sole occupant.

The first snow caused a shipwreck that took seven local lives. The next two snows were bad, but not savage.

Josh's voice wasn't heard, either. Jimmy began to wonder if those strange conversations hadn't actually been a temporary form of derangement. Could he actually have been speaking to a ghost?

Spring was an answered prayer. He was sick of winter by then. He wanted to see living things, to reaffirm the life force that Katie's coming marriage—barely a month away now— had crushed in him.

It was an April dusk when he heard the door open at the bottom of the 141 steps leading to the tower.

A visitor was always a surprise, and almost always a welcome one.

This visitor was an astonishing one.

Katie said, "You're surprised to see me, and I'm even more surprised to be here."

He kept trying to read her face, her voice. Both were oddly expressionless. "I'll go if you want me to."

"That's probably what I should tell you. Go."

"Is that what you want?"

"You know better than that."

She wrung her hands nervously, then took a deep breath and said, "I was asleep last night around midnight. And a voice woke me."

"One of the girls?"

She shook her head. "No. A voice inside my head."

He knew instantly whose voice it had been.

"It told me to go down to a certain address on Clinton Street. I felt as if I was losing my mind. This voice . . . But I went. I couldn't stop the voice from pushing me. So I woke Mrs. Brennan next door, and she watched the girls while I came down there."

Another deep breath. "It's where his mistress lives."

"Jordan's?"

"Yes. She's a new one. Acquired in the last few months. It seems seven months of being faithful—or so he claims, anyway—was about all he could handle. He'd marry me, but have his mistress set up on the side."

He started to say how sorry he was for her. But that would have been a lie.

"So you had it out with him?"

"Oh, yes. Right then and there. I gave him back his engagement ring, and he sent his chauffeur over this morning to pick up all the things he'd left at my house."

"I'm sorry."

"No, you're not, Jimmy. And neither am I. You asked me to tell you I didn't love you, and I couldn't. If you asked me that now, I still couldn't. Because I do love you, and the girls love you, too."

"My God," he said. "Those are the sweetest words I've ever heard." He went to her and took her arms.

She pushed away from him.

"We're going to get married, Jimmy. But it's not the way you imagine it. You have all this sugarcoated nonsense in your head. We're going to be poor, and I'm not the picnic you imagine I am. I'm cranky, stubborn, hot-tempered, and so bossy I used to drive poor Josh crazy. Ask the girls, if you don't believe me."

"I can learn to live with that. I'm no picnic, either. I'm not very practical, and I spend half my time daydreaming. And my feet smell when they sweat. And sometimes for no reason at all, I start bellowing out songs. It's like I need to clear my lungs or something."

"You have a terrible singing voice."

"That's what I mean."

For the first time, she smiled. "Maybe it'll work out, after all."

And then they were in each other's arms.

And she said, "But I want to move slow, Jimmy. You court me, and then we get engaged for a while, and then we get married."

He laughed, "Say, now that you mention it, you *are* kind of bossy, aren't you?"

Long after she was gone that night, while he was tending to the light, Josh said, "I figured Jordan would cheat on her eventually. I just bided my time."

"I figured that was you. You know, telling her to go down to Clinton Street."

"I disguised my voice so she wouldn't know it was me."

"I really appreciate this, Josh."

The disembodied voice laughed. "Just keep that in mind, Jimmy, when she goes and gets cranky on you."

"Bad, huh?"

"You just wait and see."

And then there was that *absence* again. The ghost was gone.

Never to return.

BILLIE SUE MOSIMAN

Dread
Inlet

Barrett Holzworth loved the wild isolation of Dread Inlet despite the fact that the lighthouse was haunted. He had seen the spectres on several occasions. One of them seemed to be Carl, the engineer who had drowned during the building of the lighthouse. Barrett suspected that the ghosts were the reason for the inlet's name. In the beginning he thought the ghosts were no more then pests—if they were real at all. Barrett ignored them until the night when he heard footsteps behind him as he climbed the spiral stairs to the tower. He turned to admonish his wife, thinking she'd followed him. Catherine was always tagging along when he went to check the oil in the lamps. He knew she was lonely, Dread Inlet being as isolated as any place on earth. In fact, he feared his wife's mind was slipping. He often found her talking to herself or weeping into her hands, bereft over some past memory.

But she was beginning to get on his nerves the way she dogged his steps wherever he went. He had commanded her not to come up the stairs to the lighthouse tower. This was his domain, by grace. He'd been hired for the job, and he didn't need interference.

Yet when he turned, a scolding ready on his tongue, Catherine was not there. Someone else was. A haunt. Or rather, a "haint," as his mother would have called it. A lost soul, demented, and wandering old familiar ground.

He thought it must be Carl, the engineer who had drowned during the building of the lighthouse. It could be no one else. He wore a dark blue wool cap with a gold lighthouse insignia on the short front brim. He was always muttering about feet and inches, about brick and mortar, complaining of the terrible weather delaying his project. Although his grumblings were barely discernible, key words could be picked out as Barrett strained to hear.

The first time Barrett had seen the ghost was one early spring night while he was sleeping in bed next to his wife. The lightkeeper's little house at the base of the lighthouse was made of logs, and consisted of one large room with a sleeping loft for their straw mattress. Barrett was awakened by the sound of rain pounding the roof. A norther was blowing in, and he'd have to rise, dress, and check the light in the lighthouse tower. It was during squalls that the ships needed him most.

He had thought the rain had awakened him, but as he opened his eyes and rose up on his elbows, he realized it was a voice that had intruded into his sleep. Someone paced the floor of the cabin below, muttering in consternation.

Barrett slipped from beneath the quilts and took his loaded musket from the corner of the loft. He crept to the ladder and looked down, expecting to see a wild man who had been swept ashore from the inlet during the storm. He might be there to rob and kill them. They had little to take but food, and it was probably starvation that had pushed the intruder through their shuttered windows—as no one could have gotten through the barred door.

What he saw, however, was not a man—of that he was certain. The musket trembled in his hands. He was glad his wife hadn't been aroused. Were she at his side she'd be screaming now, and that would not do.

The person down below was soaked, his clothes hanging from him in dripping shreds as if they'd worn out and fallen apart at the seams. His hair clung to his skull beneath the cap.

His face . . . his face was battered beyond recognition, the flesh torn and gaping and hanging from cheekbone to chin.

It was clear to Barrett that this was no ordinary man. He couldn't be alive; his wounds were far too serious. He faded in and out like fog. For moments he would be as solid as the log walls, and then he'd shimmer and wink out of existence before fading back in again, seemingly solid.

Barrett didn't know what to do. Go down the ladder and confront the haunt? Could a ghost hurt him, he wondered?

Just as he had these thoughts, the man vanished and the room was as empty as it should have been.

Barrett replaced the musket and returned to bed, but not to sleep. In fact, for nights afterward he couldn't sleep, waking with nightmares, a scream escaping his lips.

Twice a year he left Dread Inlet to buy supplies at the trading post on the mainland of Florida. He went earlier than usual after he saw the ghost, explaining to his wife that he wanted to get her some new cloth for sewing and some thread for embroidery. He knew she'd need something to do during the coming winter months and feared locals would buy up everything at the post if he waited.

The real reason he went early, however, was to question the trader about the lighthouse. At that point he hadn't known about the drowned engineer and had no idea who his ghost was or why he would be haunting them.

"His name was Carl Dormaster," the trader said, happy to relate the tale. Barrett had asked if anyone had ever died on the Inlet and Dormaster was his answer. "They say he was obsessed with the lighthouse," the trader continued, a man who enjoyed tale telling, especially the morbid ones. The old man's eyes brightened and he smiled the whole while he spoke. "Before it was completed, he'd had the keeper's dwelling constructed and stayed there at night alone. The crew stayed here, in the settlement, and went out every day by skiff to work, but Carl stayed near his project. He wanted to build the greatest lighthouse on the coast. His father, you see, had died a seaman, run aground on a south Florida coral reef. He didn't want that to happen to anyone along the coast again.

"He made the brick foundation twelve feet deep and forty-five feet in diameter."

"It's not that large at the base," Barrett argued. "Not nearly."

"No, it's just thirty-two at the base, with the walls eight feet thick at the bottom and two feet thick at the top, on the tower. They used one and a quarter million bricks, all of them fired right here. It took them four years to build it."

"So what happened to Dormaster?"

"He almost had the construction complete—that was in 1883. They'd imported the big kerosene lamp for the tower from Paris. A famous French lensmaker finely ground that lens, and it was shipped separately.

"At this time I'm telling you about, though, only the windmill pumphouse needed finishing, to pump water to the cypress water tank. Dormaster wouldn't leave until the windmill was done. He insisted on staying on the inlet even though a hurricane was brewing. All the workers had fled and weren't going back the next day, not with how the wind was up. But Dormaster wouldn't leave, and he threatened to fire the whole crew if they didn't return. He wanted the windmill put up. He wanted the inlet ready for its first lightkeeper before the season turned bad and all the storms blew in."

"So Dormaster drowned that night?" Barrett asked.

"Yessir, he drowned. All they can figger is he went and lost his sanity, what he had left of it. For all four years the workers kept saying he was impossible to work for. He treated them like slaves, going to fisticuffs if they defied him or if he thought their day's work shoddy. Many a man quit in anger and someone else had to be hired. Dormaster was a real tyrant, he was."

"How'd he lose his sanity?"

"Nobody knows what pushed him over, but they think when the hurricane came up and the workers had gone to the inlet, he left the keeper's cabin and went down to the rocky shore. What he thought he was doing, no one knows. Maybe he was defying God. Maybe he was furious that the big storm had come before he was finished, or he thought the winds would take down all his hard work, crumbling the lighthouse to the sea.

"It was four days before the surf calmed enough for the crew to get to Dread Inlet Lighthouse. They found the engineer washed up, swollen and blue-black, his face ripped from his body striking the rock bed and half-eaten by the fish."

Once home again, Barrett thought about the story of Dormaster and decided that it was his personality haunting the lighthouse. The engineer hadn't ever left. That was why they'd had trouble retaining a lighthouse keeper. Barrett was the fifth one hired in as many years. And happy to get the post, he reflected, work being difficult to come by. At least, he'd been happy until now.

So enthralled was he with the trader's history of the lighthouse, Barrett forgot to pick out a bolt of cloth for his wife. When he returned empty-handed, she loosed her tongue on him, and even though he apologized and promised to go back for her, she wouldn't be consoled. She broke down and wept uncontrollably.

He'd known it was chancy to bring a woman to the lighthouse. He had tried to prepare her for the solitude they'd face, explaining the duties he'd be expected to attend to, and she'd been young, a bride almost, having only married him months before. She wanted to go, she said. It would be a magical time for them, all alone, dependent on one another, having no neighbors to bother them.

The reality proved harsher than she'd dreamed. He knew what to expect, having been a lighthouse keeper before for more than a year up the coast in Georgia. He'd given up that post to take his new wife home to Florida where her family resided. He tried to farm with her father for a while, but it didn't suit him. He cared little for the soil and therefore had no gift for crops.

What he cared about was the sea and the safety of the ships that sailed too close to landfall where rocky reefs tore out the ships' bellies and made the vessels founder. Lightkeeping was important work, and although it was poorly paid, the home was free of rent and—most of the time—the view seaward was majestic and awesome, inspiring him to thoughts of the Deity.

He was a religious man, reading his Bible regularly during the long hours in the tower. He'd glance up to watch for a ship and back down again to the Scripture. He believed his wife should be subject to him, just as the Bible said, but she often disobeyed, following when she should stay, staying when she should follow.

To be truthful, Catherine was not a very good wife. Her cleaning was perfunctory, so that it wasn't unusual to find the shelves and mantel in their home covered with a patina of dust. She only swept the floors once a week, and her laundering ability was so poor that his clothes stank of lye and were yellowed or stained. As for her cooking . . . well, he'd lost weight since his marriage, a testament to her undercooked chickens and tough beef stews.

If she were to see a ghost...

If she found out the lighthouse was haunted...

He couldn't tell her, and prayed God Dormaster wouldn't come around when she was awake and might see him.

After a couple of months of seeing the haunt around the place, Barrett came to think of him as a harmless fixture.

If Catherine had never seen him, all would have been well. Barrett didn't think she had seen him, but he'd noticed she wasn't crying as much as she had, and some days she could even be found singing under her breath as she puttered around the cabin—not doing much, as it turned out.

He came to the cabin door one afternoon after doing chores and heard Catherine inside talking to someone. Barrett was about to step indoors and greet their visitor happily, as they never saw anyone. Perhaps one of her family was over from the mainland. It struck him suddenly that he hadn't seen a boat arrive. But then he'd been in the smokehouse, doing some cataloging, and he might not have noticed someone approaching the inlet.

He was just about to lift the door latch when he heard the muttering of a male voice—a voice he knew well. It was the ghost; it was Carl Dormaster. Stunned, his hand frozen on the latch, Barrett stood listening, his mouth falling open.

"Shall we have tea?" Catherine asked in a jolly tone. "I

have some British tea leaves imported from London. I think we should have a pot together."

There came a mumbling Barrett couldn't understand and then his wife said, "I don't think Barrett cares for my tea; nor does he care for my meals. He's a grouchy old thing, don't you think? Until you came along, I thought I'd lose my mind. Worry, worry, worry, that's all my husband can do. What does he worry about? Oh, the ships, of course. He's afraid he won't be on duty and a ship will sail into the inlet, and maybe he has forgotten to light the lamps in the lighthouse. He worries like a little rat over a bit of newspaper. He never has a kind word for me. Oh no, not for me."

Barrett turned away, stricken by the criticism. It was true he worried, but that was part of his job. Didn't she understand? He was responsible for the lives of men. He couldn't forget. He had to haul the oil from the barrels stored in the storehouse up the two hundred and eight steps to the lanterns in the tower. He had to polish the lens and keep it clean. He had to watch the sea for a change in weather, for squalls and storms coming in and bringing with them ships seeking landfall and safety.

What was Catherine doing complaining about him to a . . . a . . . ghost? Didn't she know he wasn't real? How could she serve tea to a man who wasn't really there?

As many times as he'd been disappointed with his wife's lack of housewifely abilities, he had never spoken ill of her to another. He felt betrayed. She must not love him even a little if she could talk about him that way—even if it was to a ghost who wasn't going to go about and spread the complaints.

He returned to the lighthouse and took the spiral stairs to the tower, where he sat in the wooden chair facing the sea, sulking over his wife's little secret. He had prayed that she wouldn't ever see the ghost and get frightened; yet here she was, talking to Dormaster behind his back, making him her own special little friend.

He realized his jealousy was unwarranted, but he was still hurt and couldn't seem to help it. He sat watching the whitecaps along the waves far out into the bay, wishing he were out there sailing away instead of stuck in the tower, trapped with a wife like Catherine. She was probably the greatest mistake he'd made in his life, and now he was stuck with it. She was messy, lazy, prone to fits of weeping, and now she was disloyal to him. How in the world was he going to stand it?

It would drive him mad.

Now, here he was on the stairs, turning to scold his wife but instead facing the ghost, Dormaster. A week had passed since he'd eavesdropped on the teatime conversation between the ghost and Catherine.

"I've come to speak to you of murder. You should get rid of Catherine." Dormaster whispered in a chilly, unearthly voice.

"Why would you want me to get rid of her?" Barrett asked, still sullen and stung by the ghost making himself known to his wife. And his wife enjoying time with him!

"She's untrue, isn't she? She hates you."

Barrett wouldn't listen to such balderdash. He turned his chair a bit so the haunt wasn't in his line of sight. He stared out to sea, ignoring Dormaster.

"I rid myself of my woman when she was untrue," the ghost said quietly.

Barrett turned back in surprise. "You killed your wife?"

"She was a squaw, and I only took her to wed because the Cherokee who had her promised she'd be no trouble."

"You had an Indian wife?"

"A meaner and stingier Indian wife you would never hope to meet," Dormaster said. "She'd wait until I slept, and then she'd pinch me or stick me with thistles. She left pins in my underwear and my pockets and laughed when I stuck myself. She'd hide the salted pork and not give me any, eating on the sly. She was a very bad woman." He had stopped mumbling, wandering as if he didn't see the humans about him. These days he spoke directly to them, holding conversations, the way he had done with Catherine the day Barrett stood listening in.

"So you killed her?" Barrett asked, intrigued.

"I took her out in a dinghy and thumped her on the head

with the paddle, then dropped her over the side. She's out there somewhere . . ." The ghost stood at the glass windows looking out to sea.

"Is that what made you stay on the Inlet the night of the hurricane? Were you watching for her?"

"Oh, I didn't kill her here. It was at another lighthouse up the coast near Saint Augustine. No, I stayed during the storm because I feared the work I'd done here would be ruined."

"But you couldn't have held up the tower by yourself if a great wind came along and toppled it."

"Maybe not, but I'd be here the minute the wind ceased, so I could pick up the pieces."

"What happened the night that you drowned?"

"My Indian wife?"

"Yes?"

"She found me. She must have floated all the way down the coast, looking for me. It took her a year, but she found me that night. She dragged me into the sea. It was her fault, you know. Not mine."

Barrett thought that highly unlikely. Ghosts couldn't drag you into the surf. Dormaster was just bitter and crazy now, going over and over his death on the Inlet. He was as crazy as Catherine.

"If you kill your wife, you'd have to leave the lighthouse," the ghost said as if musing on the mistakes he'd made in life.

"I'm not going to kill my wife."

"Of course you aren't," Dormaster said before he shimmered and disappeared.

"What kind of soup is this?" Barrett asked his wife. He lifted the spoon from his bowl, showing her the carrots and potato bits. "Where's the meat?"

"We've run out. You'll have to go to the mainland again to get more."

"We couldn't have run out. The last I checked, there were two hams and a leg of beef in the smokehouse."

"Go look for yourself, then. I don't have time for your yelling at me day and night."

He didn't yell at her. Not all the time anyway. What was she talking about? He slammed the cabin door as he traipsed outside to the smokehouse. The wind was blowing and a storm was coming in. He'd have to spend the entire night in the tower watching for ships.

He opened the smokehouse door and stood still, looking into the empty gloom. Where was the meat? What could she have possibly done with that much meat? She couldn't have used it up for their meals. He hardly ever got a decent slab of meat in his dinner anymore. She fed him corn mush and brown gravy, claiming she hadn't had time to make something else before it got dark.

He went back to the cabin and began to yell for real. "You must be cooking up the meat and eating it all yourself," he screamed. "Look at you, you're fat as a pig. I bet you've gained fifty pounds since we've been here. Why would you deprive me that way? Am I not your faithful husband? Don't I earn the salary from this job to feed you at all? What's gotten into you? Are you insane?"

She began to cry, denying that she had eaten all the stores. He felt so bad he stomped outside into the gale and went to the lighthouse. He couldn't do a thing with her any longer. No matter what he said, she would cry or argue with him or threaten to leave him high and dry, alone on the inlet.

Dormaster came as soon as he got the lamps lit for the night. "I told you to kill her," he said. "She's a thief, just like my wife was. She's fat and sassy, and you're skinny as a rail."

"You just shut up," Barrett said. "It's all your fault, some way. I know it is. You probably put her up to these things."

"No one had to tempt her. She's greedy and unhappy. Women are like that. Women aren't like us at all."

"Don't connect me to you. I'm not like you. I'm not crazy like you were. Why don't you go to the devil? You're a ghost, don't you understand? You don't belong here."

"This is my lighthouse," the ghost said. "I built it. It's mine."

"Well, you're dead! I'm the lighthouse keeper, not you. You're *dead!*"

"I may be dead, but I'm not hungry and married to a mad-woman."

Barrett grabbed his Bible and began to read, hoping the ghost would go away. If it wasn't Catherine tormenting him, it was a haunt. He never found rest.

"They'll think she drowned accidentally if you throw her in the sea," Dormaster said.

"Go away! Please go away and leave me alone!"

The ghost disappeared and did not return for days. Barrett went in to the mainland and bought more meat and flour and grain and beans. He tried to be nice to his wife, but now she wouldn't let him touch her, scooting away from his hands in bed at night.

"What can I do to make you happy?" he asked, at his wits' end.

"You can leave me alone and not speak to me," she said, turning her back to him.

When the ghost appeared again, as Barrett sat one night in the lighthouse tower, he said, "Now she won't sleep with you. She's cold as a corpse. She might as well be dead."

Barrett took the Bible and began to read, studiously ignoring the torturing spirit. Maybe it was a demon. Maybe it was the devil, come to steal his soul.

"She's eating all the meat again—behind your back," the ghost taunted.

Barrett didn't say a word, but the next morning he went to the smokehouse to check. True enough, the meat he'd just bought was almost gone. She must be stuffing herself every minute he wasn't around. She'd gained more weight and now looked like a ball of butter.

He went to her, pleading softly. "Catherine, this has to stop. You'll make yourself sick. Your heart will give out. You already breathe heavy when you climb the steps to the tower. All this eating is bad for you. And I'm...I'm starving. Why do you do it? Is there nothing I can say to change it?"

She slapped him across the face, taking him by surprise. She walked clear across the cabin, and he thought she was going to take him into her arms and say she was sorry; but instead, she swung her arm wide and slapped him soundly across the cheeks, knocking him from the chair he sat in. He picked himself up and said, "We'll see about this, Catherine. We'll just see about this turn of events."

"Oh, go to your tower and leave me be. I don't care if you ever eat another mouthful at my table."

He could have pointed out that the table was his, as was the food that graced it. The cabin was his as long as he was the lighthouse keeper. The clothes she wore on her back belonged to him. *She* belonged to him.

And he would not be starved while she stuffed herself; he would not be slapped out of his chair in his own home.

"It's time to get rid of her," Dormaster said, blinking into a shaft of gleaming light from the blue sky.

"They'll find out. They'll know I killed her. They'll put me in chains and hang me by the neck until I'm dead."

"They won't know if you drown her in the sea."

That night as he watched the steady lamplight shine out to the dangerous rocky area off the inlet, Barrett thought about Dormaster's advice. No one would question him if she drowned, that was true enough. They'd think she been walking along the rocky shore and been caught by a rogue wave. He'd be careful not to leave bruises or finger marks. The surf banging her against the rocks could explain any bruises that he did accidentally leave on her body. Or she might drift right out to the ocean depths and be eaten to bits by sea creatures. Why should he worry? The haunt was right; a bad woman was worse than no woman at all. A greedy, lazy, abusive woman couldn't be countenanced.

He decided to do it that night. He'd wait until she slept deeply, and then he'd creep into the loft and hold the heavy feather pillow over her face until she stopped breathing. Then he'd take her out in the skiff and drop her over the side. Tomorrow he'd hurry to the mainland and make a report about his wife's drowning. How she'd been walking near the edge when a wave swept in and took her with it, and before he could save her, she'd been pulled under and her body washed out from the inlet.

He'd be rid of her, by grace. He'd be alone on Dread Inlet, free of her ugly, fat face and menacing stare. He'd finally have some peace.

They hauled up Catherine's body in a fisherman's net ten miles down the coast from Dread Inlet. She was already purple and swollen, her face as eaten and disfigured as that of Dormaster's ghost.

At the funeral the mainlanders patted Barrett on the shoulder and the women gave him piteous glances from behind their handkerchiefs. Poor man, they thought, left alone now to live like a hermit at the lighthouse. Poor, poor man, to lose such a young and healthy wife that way.

Barrett played the sorrowful widower until he could get free of the cemetery. As he rowed his skiff to the lighthouse alone, he grinned like a monkey. In the bow sat the haunt of the old engineer, grinning with him. They spoke of what it was like to commit murder and not be held responsible for it; what it was like to be free of wives who meant to drive them crazy.

That night, Barrett cooked himself a whole roast over the fireplace spit until the juices ran clear and the outside was crusted brown and succulent. He carved himself a large serving, doled out several boiled potatoes, and dished up a saucer of peach cobbler given him by one of the mainland mourners.

He ate until his stomach ached. At one point he glared at the empty chair at the table, and with his foot caught the rung and knocked it over onto the floor. Then he laughed, howling with glee that he'd gotten away with it. He could never have made Catherine divorce him, but he'd gotten rid of her nevertheless, and no one was the wiser.

No longer would he half starve. No longer would he live in squalor with a woman who couldn't lift a broom without whining about her workload. No longer would a woman slap him across the face and call him names.

He finished his large meal and pushed away from the table. He washed the dishes and the pans, putting them on the drainboard. He looked around and saw that everything was neat and orderly, just as he liked it, before he left the cabin for the lighthouse. The wind had freshened when he'd come over this afternoon, and he'd smelled rain in it. Before the night was over he expected a storm. He had to check the level of the lantern oil to see if he should haul more up the stairs. He needed to clean the lens and watch the darkened sea.

It was after midnight, while he dozed in his chair, the Bible open on his lap, when he heard a giggle that woke him. He snapped to, thinking he'd been dreaming. It was a female laugh, so he must have been dreaming.

The giggle came again, and he whirled around. In the tower with him stood Dormaster and, at his side, Catherine. She had a hand over her mouth to halt the giggle from escaping again.

"What...what are you doing here?" he asked. He frowned at the engineer and said to him, "What's she doing here? Did you bring her to torment me?"

"She came by herself." Dormaster did not sound happy. "She just showed up. There's nothing I can do about it."

"What do you want?" Barrett asked, rising from the chair and placing the Bible in the seat.

"I want you to throw yourself into the sea," she said, striding close enough that she could have reached out to touch him. "I want you to drown, and the water to fill your evil lungs."

"Well, you won't get that wish," he said. "Now go away and don't come back. This is my lighthouse."

She covered her mouth and giggled again, glancing to the other ghost. She said scornfully to Dormaster, "He thinks he can make me go. Isn't he a funny little man?"

I can make her go, Barrett thought. Dear God in heaven, I must. "Shoo! Get out of here. Go away now. You're just a ghost. You're only a haunt."

"As soon you'll be," she said, advancing again as he backed away.

He saw her hand coming toward his face, flying at him as it had done before when she'd been alive and slapped him. Her hand this time went right through his flesh and he felt only a slight tingle. He looked her in the eye. "I did away with you. You can't steal my food now. You can't hurt me. Go to the devil, woman."

"After you," she said.

That night Barrett argued long and hard with the two ghosts, threatening, begging, praying for them to leave. The storm heightened, wind and rain lashing the lighthouse windows. The sea rose, waves thundering onto the rocky shore and lapping up the brick walls of the tower.

He read the Bible to them. He exhorted them to begone. He screamed and cried and beat his fists against his temples, trying to get them to go, all to no avail.

When morning dawned and the storm had abated, Barrett dragged himself down the long stairs and across the yard to the cabin. He fell into the loft bed, exhausted.

They woke him, trampling through his dreams, showing him visions of their deaths—made him choke on the water that filled lungs, suffocate from feather pillows pressed against airways.

This went on for weeks, the ghosts dogging him day and night, invading both his waking hours and his dreams. Finally, unable to take it anymore, Barrett went to the mainland and sent in his resignation by post. He told the trader he wanted to leave Dread Inlet, but didn't tell him the real reason why. He said he was lonely after his wife's untimely death. He wanted to go home to Georgia and find a different type of employment.

Days before a return post arrived, accepting his resignation, Barrett was found floating face-down near the settlement's pier that jutted out into the bay. They dragged him in with a gaff and buried him next to his wife in the cemetery.

Barrett thought he'd merely gone to sleep. He had no memory of running into the surf, flailing across the waves, trying to escape his tormentors by swimming to sea. All he remembered was that he had a job to do until he was relieved. He had to watch for ships and signal the danger of the reefs. He had to fill the lanterns with oil and polish the lens.

He was surprised to see a stranger in the tower, doing what he'd just come up the spiral stairs to do. He said, "Who are you? I am the lighthouse keeper here."

The man turned fearful eyes on him and in a shaky voice said, "I...I...I was hired to be the keeper."

Barrett didn't understand a word of it.

Not until he saw standing behind the stranger the ghosts of Dormaster and Catherine. He must be dead like them. The stranger could see and hear him, but from the look on his face it was obvious he must look a fright. He reached up to his cheeks and felt the shredded and half-eaten gaps in his flesh. He looked down and saw that his clothes were ragged and wet, seaweed stuck all over him like goose-feather down.

He moaned and turned his back and went down the lighthouse stairs. He stood out in the wind, facing the sea, and wondered how long he'd be penalized for murder. How long he'd be trapped on Dread Inlet.

How long before he could ever rest or find a moment's peace again.

Catherine appeared to his right and Dormaster to his left.

"You tricked me," Barrett said to the engineer.

"Did I?" The ghost gestured to the sea and from out of the waves rose the torn and battered body of an Indian squaw. She came to stand at Dormaster's side. "I suppose I did," he said finally, grimacing at his wife.

"Look at us," Catherine said in the high-pitched, complaining voice he remembered so well. "See what you've done?"

Barrett felt her hand slice through his ghostly face and knew that now and forever she would slap him for his violence and for his failure. He was doomed, and Dread Inlet lighthouse was his home.

It was his home forever.

KRISTINE KATHRYN RUSCH

The Light in Whale Cove

Dan Retsler ripped the packing tape from the tape gun and tossed the thing aside. Useless. Completely useless. He was better off using fingers and teeth to put tape on his boxes. The tape gun jammed and twisted every time he tried to use it.

He sealed the box on his desk, got his finger wrapped in tape, and finally reached across the box to grab the scissors. He managed to cut himself free, then he cursed and tossed the tape in the same direction as the tape gun.

Outside his office, in the front reception area, Lucy swiveled her seat so that she could watch him through the glass window. The police station had once been a retail store and still looked like it. The only office had a large window so that the retail manager could keep an eye on the stock. The last thing Retsler, Whale Rock's police chief for another three weeks, wanted was his staff laughing at his attempts to pack. He stepped over a pile of boxes, walked to the window, and pulled the blinds closed.

Then he sank onto the pile, hearing the cardboard groan beneath his weight. He hated packing almost as much as he hated moving. But he had been excited about the new job and still was, despite the pain-in-the-ass transition.

He was going to be police chief in a Montana town not

much bigger than Whale Rock. Only his new police station had a view of the Bitterroot Mountains, not Highway 101, and the police logs were filled with nothing more severe than shoplifting. It would be a relief to go to a place where the dispatcher hadn't known him since he was in diapers, where the only people who came to town were the occasional hunters instead of hordes of tourists determined to see the Pacific Ocean, and where there were no supernatural occurrences.

Retsler sighed and scanned his office. Maybe he didn't need all this junk. Maybe he'd just leave it for his successor. Jaclyn Tadero was an extremely capable woman who had been hired over his protests. The female city council members had accused him of sexism, but he hadn't opposed Tadero because she was a woman.

He had opposed her because she had never lived in a small town. She had never worked on a small force. She didn't understand the politics or the dynamics, and no matter what the city council said, it was politics and dynamics that made this job work, not experience with high-powered murder investigations.

Outside, the dispatch rang and Lucy answered. He could hear her voice but not what she was saying. Still he strained to catch a word or two. Old habits died hard.

When the murmur of her voice stopped, he stood. He didn't want Lucy to catch him moping. He walked over to the corner to pick up the tape gun. He was trying to shove the tape roll back on it as Lucy pushed open his door.

She had looked the same since he was a little boy, her curly gray hair worn in a short cap over her grandmotherly face. Despite her all-American cuteness, she was ex-military and tough, with a voice so deep that it growled.

"Where's Jaclyn?" she asked.

Retsler shrugged. "Eddie was going to take her to the outlying areas, but that was hours ago. I have no idea where they are now. Why?"

"We just got a call. We got a dead body at the lighthouse."

Retsler set down his tape gun. "I'll take it."

"She needs to go."

He glared at Lucy. "I still have three weeks on the payroll.

No matter what anyone says, I haven't lost my ability to do the job."

"I wasn't questioning your abilities. You just need to take her with you."

This was why he had to leave. Technically Lucy worked for him, but it never turned out that way. She still had an adult's authority over him, as if he were a child instead of a middle-aged man.

"Why do I need to take her along?" Retsler asked.

"Because she has to learn this part of her job now."

"What part?" he asked.

Lucy raised her eyebrows. "You don't know?"

"Obviously not," he said, straining to keep his frustration under control.

"Whale Cove Lighthouse is haunted."

The first winter storm of the season was blowing in. Retsler's car was old and heavy, but not up to the gale-force winds cutting across the highway. Rain came down in horizontal sheets, and his windshield wipers, set on high, barely cleared the water enough for him to see. It was midday but the sky was black.

He hadn't seen a storm like this since the Dee flooded eleven months ago. He had hoped to be gone before the storm season hit, but he had promised to stay and train Tadero, and she hadn't been able to leave the Chicago force until the middle of November. She had driven across the country alone and arrived here on Thanksgiving.

The car slid sideways on the road, and he twisted the wheel to return to his lane. He slowed down. He hadn't been paying enough attention. There was at least three inches of water on the road. At the speed he'd been going, he was probably hydroplaning.

He wondered what Tadero thought of the storm. She had said that nothing could be worse than a Chicago cold snap, but she'd never experienced a winter on the Oregon coast. Winters here usually drove people back to where they had come from, vowing they would never return.

The road dipped. Waves crested over the guardrail, covering his windshield with spray. He slowed down even more. With the spray, the darkness, and the driving rain, he couldn't even see the headland jutting out into the Pacific. Usually, Evergreen Cliff was the most prominent feature of this part of the coast, and the old lighthouse on top of it looked like a beacon, even though its beacon had been dark for nearly half a century.

On a day like this, the light would actually be a blessing.

With some difficulty—surprising, considering he'd grown up here—he found the road that led to the lighthouse. The road had been rebuilt during the summer so that the construction crews would have no trouble getting their heavy vehicles onto Evergreen Cliff.

The lighthouse, which was on the National Register of Historic Places, was being put back into service. After the dedication ceremony on December fifteenth, its light would once again steer ships safely into Whale Rock's harbor.

Apparently it had taken a lot of internal work to get the lighthouse functioning again. And the work wasn't done yet. There was talk among council members that the light wouldn't be ready for the ceremony, only two short weeks away.

Lighthouse Road was even more treacherous than the highway had been. The new asphalt was black and almost impossible to see. He hugged the cliffside as he drove, trying to stay as far from the guardrail on his left as possible.

It was with great relief that he finally reached the visitors' center on the south side of the hill. The center was dark and obviously empty, but a van was parked behind the Dumpster in employee parking. A decrepit one-ton pickup, covered with rust and missing its back fender, was parked haphazardly near the path.

Apparently the coroner, Hamilton Denne, had already arrived.

Retsler pulled up next to the pickup and got out of his car, yanking his dark green rain slicker hood over his head. The rain pelted him, big thick drops made lethal by the wind. His slicker flapped around him and his face was raw within seconds.

He glanced at the path, which wound around the mountainside, and shook his head slightly. He knew the state had paved the path and put a railing along the side, but it still didn't look safe, especially in this weather. But he couldn't turn back now, not after snapping at Lucy and telling her he could still do his job.

The asphalt path looked like wet tar. He stepped on it, clutching the railing attached to the stone side, his hand slipping on the cold metal surface. The wind howled around him, and the surf exploded against the rocks below. The path shook beneath him.

The first storm of the season, and he had to be on a headland, climbing toward the lighthouse. He'd rather be walking through a Montana blizzard right now than be this close to the sea.

Over the whistle of the wind, he thought he heard a voice and a car door. He turned, saw Eddie's police car parked near his and dark shapes at the head of the path. An arm waved at him, probably asking him to wait, but he turned away.

Jaclyn Tadero could learn her business the same way he had learned his—through experience. He wasn't going to coddle her. He didn't want her to get used to him. He was leaving, no matter how she felt about storms or the Oregon coast or haunted lighthouses.

Damn that Lucy, putting that idea in his head.

He rounded the corner and saw the lighthouse ahead. It was an old building, one of the oldest on the Central Coast. It had been a working lighthouse until the 1920s, when the state had finally shut it down. They'd let it rot for years, then the feds declared it an historical site and someone got the bright idea of making the lighthouse a working lighthouse once again.

He made his way up the stone steps to the lighthouse proper, noting a newly built ramp on the side. As if someone in a wheelchair was going to come to this desolate place. But regulations were regulations were regulations.

He ran the last few steps to the main door and pushed it open, resisting the urge to shake himself off like a dog. Water dripping off his slicker might destroy the potential crime scene. He pulled off the slicker and set it near Denne's, on a metal chair near the door. Denne's shoes were also there—loafers, their shine still evident despite the mud and water beading on the leather surface.

Retsler removed his own shoes, a battered pair of tennies, and set them beside Denne's. Then Retsler wiped his hands on his thighs and headed inside.

The base of the lighthouse was wide. Windows facing the sea let in some light, although not enough on a gray day like this one. In the entry were flyers and brochures as well as the standard tourist information, two tables and a chair pushed off to the side, as well as a small booth with a phone and emergency equipment.

Farther inside were the stairs, reinforced metal now, but curving like they had in the original plans, disappearing toward the lighthouse's narrow top.

Voices echoed down them, speaking softly, the words indistinguishable thanks to the overlap of the echo. It almost sounded as if dozens of people were whispering all at once.

A shiver ran down Retsler's back, and he concentrated on the one voice he recognized—Denne's. Retsler went to the base of the stairs and looked up. They curved all the way to the top, but had several landings so that the tourists who visited this place could rest. The light was at the very top on a level all its own. He couldn't see that, only the white-painted metal protecting it.

An arm hung off one of the landings. Shadows indicated Denne's presence and that of at least one other person.

Then the door blew open and a woman stepped in. Jaclyn Tadero, slight, muscular, her hair plastered to her face. Her raincoat was soaked through, as were her jeans and tennis shoes. Her dark eyes met his, daring him to comment.

He looked away.

Eddie staggered in, his rain slicker an almost obscene yellow. He had to push hard to get the door to close, and when it did, he leaned against it.

"Why can't people die on sunny days?" he said.

Tadero glared at him, but Retsler nodded. The levity was necessary, especially given the tension inherent in the situation.

"Where's the body?" Her voice was a rich soprano. It would have been beautiful if it weren't for her accent. Hers was a thick Chicago accent, a mixture of Norwegian consonants and Polish vowels, flat and almost nasal.

It grated on Retsler as much as her glare had.

"Don't know," he said, working at nonchalance. "Just got here myself."

She started forward and he held out a hand to stop her.

"You'll drip on the crime scene."

She cursed and stopped moving. "What do you suggest? I'm soaked."

"Give me a minute," he said. "Let's see how far down the scene extends."

"I thought your crime scene unit was already here. They probably have everything they need."

"The crime scene unit," he said as patiently as he could, "is composed of you, me, Eddie, and the coroner, who is upstairs now. We don't have enough people on the force to do all that fancy work."

He had explained that to her during her interview and had thought she understood. But apparently she hadn't.

"I thought we had use of the state's criminologists."

"We do," he said, "if we request them in time. We have no idea what we're facing here, so I haven't requested anyone. Have you?"

That last was more sarcastic than he wanted it to be. She frowned at him and turned away, wiping at her face with the back of her hand. Eddie was pulling off his rain slicker. He was dry underneath.

Retsler didn't wait for them. He mounted the metal stairs, examining each one before he put his foot down so that he didn't contaminate more than necessary.

"I hope to God that's you, Dan." Denne's voice, stronger this time, floated down to him.

"It's me," Retsler said. "Have you done the stairs?"

"No," Denne said. "I just got here a few minutes ago."

Retsler sighed softly and continued to curve up the circular staircase. As he got closer to Denne's voice, he saw more of the arm, pale and limp, hanging over the edge as if it were reaching for something below.

"You alone?" Retsler asked.

"Clay Emory is with me. He was here when it happened." Denne sounded unflappable as usual. The man was going through a bitter divorce—that truck was his rebellion—and he still seemed cheerful. Even last year, during the worst disaster Retsler had ever experienced, Denne remained calm.

Retsler rounded the last curve before reaching the landing. Emory sat on the next set of stairs going up, his elbows resting on his thighs. He was a big man who had lived in the area all of his life. He wore a Coast Electrics cap over his balding head and light brown work coveralls, stained with grease. His face, normally tan from the western sun, was unnaturally pale.

He didn't even acknowledge Retsler's arrival. Instead, he stared at the body on the landing as if he could will it away.

Retsler looked at the body too. It belonged to a woman. Her face was turned away from him. She had long brown hair, which trailed through the diamond-shaped metal mesh of the landing. Her arm was extended, just as he had noticed from below. The rest of her body was twisted away from the arm, curled in a partial fetal position.

He couldn't immediately tell what killed her.

Denne was crouched by her head, his back to Emory, his camera on the step near his left hand. His bag was open against the wall. He looked dapper as always, even though he had been trying to dress down since he'd separated from his wife. His sweatshirt with its Harvard logo looked pressed, and the white collar of a shirt stuck out from beneath it. His jeans were damp from the storm, but they too looked pressed. Even his bare feet looked manicured.

Retsler's were merely cold.

He stepped on the edge of the landing, not willing to go farther—at least, not yet. "What'd you find?"

Denne gave Retsler a quick, unreadable glance, then looked down. "I'd say she tripped and fell down the stairs."

After all these years, Retsler was familiar with Denne's way of making a point. "Except?"

With a slight movement of his right hand, Denne beckoned Retsler forward. He nodded toward the face.

Retsler caught his breath. It was Pippa Gage. Her features were slack in death, but there were long black markings on each cheek, as if someone had taken a charcoal pencil and drawn lines across her face.

"What's that?" Retsler asked as he crouched beside Denne.

Denne pointed to her clothes. They too were stained with black.

"So what is it?" Retsler asked.

Denne shrugged and was about to answer when someone else spoke.

"I don't think you should be discussing this in front of the witness."

Retsler didn't have to look up to recognize that voice. Jaclyn Tadero had finally made it up the stairs. Still, when he did look up, he made certain his expression was cool. This was his investigation. She was just here to learn.

He would remind her of that when they returned to the station.

She was standing on the top step, hanging tightly to the railing with her left hand. She had pulled her hair away from her face and tucked it into the back of her shirt so that the strands wouldn't drip on the crime scene. She too had removed her shoes. Her mascara had run, making her look like a tired raccoon.

Denne was the one who answered her. "We don't have much of a choice. Even if we asked Clay to go upstairs or down, he'd still hear everything. In case you hadn't noticed, this place has a hell of an echo."

"You know this man?" Her voice was harsh.

Retsler gave her a small smile. "This is a small town, Jaclyn. You'll have to get used to that."

She glared at him. She knew that he had opposed her hire, and she knew he had opposed it because he thought she couldn't handle small-town life.

"Clay Emory," Retsler said, "meet Whale Rock's new police chief as of the first of the year. This is Jaclyn Tadero."

Emory raised his head and touched the bill of his cap, then refocused his attention on Pippa Gage.

"He been like that the whole time?" Retsler asked Denne quietly.

Denne nodded.

"You about done here?"

"Yeah." Denne reached for his camera. "I have the scene photos to shoot, and then I'll be ready to take her to the morgue."

"Your crew is going to have to be very careful," Tadero said. "That storm will wash away a lot of evidence if you don't have the bag sealed right."

Denne's eyes narrowed as he studied her. He didn't seem to like her much either. He watched her as he shouted, "Eddie! You think you can get the bag and gurney from my truck all by yourself?"

Retsler suppressed a smile. Tadero was certainly getting her education this afternoon.

"Not in this wind, Hamilton," Eddie said. "It's going to take at least two of us. And we might be better off without the gurney. A shoulder carry might work better."

Denne tested the body's arm. Rigor hadn't set in yet. "Okay. I'll do a few things before you get to that. If you don't mind bringing the bag."

"If I'd thought of it, I'd've brought it with me," Eddie said. "I don't relish going out there again."

Retsler thought of the steep edge and the slick asphalt. None of them were safe in this kind of storm.

"Go with him," he said to Tadero.

"You heard him," she said. "He can do this."

"I know. But I don't want any of us alone on this headland."

"Why?" she asked. "What do you think happened?"

She was thinking about the body. She had no idea how dangerous these storms were, how the coast killed dozens of tourists every year because they weren't cautious enough when they faced Mother Nature's wrath.

"I think the storm's too severe for anyone to be alone," he said.

She glanced at the window. The wind wasn't even audible. He could feel her reluctance. She was ready to do the hands-on police work. Hell, she'd had five times as much experience with dead bodies as he'd had. He might actually have let her do the work if it weren't for Lucy's comment about the lighthouse being haunted.

He'd ignored comments like that from Lucy twice in the past. Both times, she'd warned him about supernatural creatures in the area, but he hadn't believed her. The first time he ignored a warning, mermaids had killed a friend of his. The second time, he had failed to believe in selkies, and it had cost two people their lives and destroyed most of the trailers along the Dee.

"How long will this storm last?" Tadero asked.

"A day, maybe two. Why?"

She shrugged. "I thought maybe we could wait it out, but it doesn't sound like we can."

"No, we can't," Retsler said.

"Then make sure you get all the evidence you can while you're here." She said that last to Denne, as if he had never worked a crime scene before, and then thumped down the stairs.

Denne rolled his eyes. "Remind me to sit on more committees."

"Wouldn't have made any difference," Retsler said. "Then there would have been two of us who disapproved. Not a majority by a long shot."

Denne nodded and continued his work. Retsler turned his attention to the corpse of an old friend.

What had she been doing here? Pippa Gage had hated heights. The views out of these windows would have paralyzed her. Even if she could have ignored those, the open banisters would have made it impossible for her to miss the distance to the floor below.

He wished dead faces registered their last emotions, like they did in detective novels. He wanted to know how Pippa had been feeling when she died. Or maybe he didn't. Pippa had been a gentle soul who didn't deserve to die in fear.

Retsler looked up at Clay Emory. Emory was still staring at her body, his expression so full of regret that Retsler could almost feel it himself.

"Clay," he said, "you want to tell me what happened?"

Emory didn't move.

"Clay," Denne said.

Then Emory raised his head, like a man who had just come out of a very deep sleep.

"The chief asked you a question."

"Sorry." Emory's voice was deep and slow. Raspier than usual, as if he had a cold or as if he had been talking a lot.

Retsler wasn't going to get anything out of him up here, not with Pippa's body so close. "Come on downstairs. You can tell me what you saw."

Emory's head shook just slightly. Retsler couldn't tell if he didn't want to talk or if he were already answering an unspoken question.

"Come on," Denne said softly. "I'll help you around."

Emory reached behind himself for the banister, hand shaking. He pulled himself up, looking back down on Pippa. This time his head shake was noticeable. "She really is dead, isn't she?"

Retsler realized what he'd heard as hoarseness was actually withheld tears. "Yes," he said.

Denne shot Retsler an uncomfortable glance, then walked over to Emory. Denne extended his gloved hand.

"Come on, Clay," he said. "Let's get you downstairs."

Emory gripped Denne's hand the way a child would grip a parent's. He let Denne lead him around the body, and then, when they reached Retsler, Emory finally moved on his own.

His eyes were swimming with tears. "You know, it's so

weird. One minute you're talking to somebody. You can feel them. You know they're there. Then the next minute—"

His voice broke.

Denne still stood behind him, blocking him from the body. Retsler stepped aside so that Emory could start down the stairs. Emory grabbed the banister and started down, his knuckles white against the metal. Retsler followed and Denne returned to the crime scene to finish the small details he had left.

The light at the base of the stairs seemed dimmer. It took a moment for Retsler to realize that was because the storm was directly overhead. The natural light that came in through the windows above was fading. The artificial light had a greenish-gray quality to it, like institutional lighting—the kind found in big city police stations and the waiting rooms of prisons.

His coat still dripped near the door, his shoes getting soaked beneath it. There were footprints near the exit, probably from Eddie and Tadero.

Retsler grabbed one of the old wooden captain's chairs leaning against the wall and set it in the small alcove behind the stairs. He helped Emory into that chair, then grabbed another for himself.

"What happened up there, Clay?" he asked.

Emory tilted his head back as if he could make the tears recede into his eyes. He sighed, then swiped at his face with the back of his hand.

"I was working," he said after a moment. "Finishing the light. They've all updated everything. It's computerized now. Inside a casing, ready to go. Won't need anyone to babysit it any more. Kinda strange, huh?"

Retsler made a sympathetic sound, but didn't say anything more. Clay Emory was not a talkative man under the best of circumstances. Interrupting him now could possibly stop him permanently.

"We were gonna test it before it got dark because no one's supposed to see the light before the grand opening on the fifteenth. But we had to make sure it worked. The storm was rolling in, and Pippa wanted me to hurry. She was afraid that when the clouds hit, the entire county would see the light shining off the waves."

Retsler nodded, waiting. He still found it surprising that Pippa had been here.

"Pippa, she didn't like the idea of being in the lighthouse when the storm hit." Emory's voice broke again and he brought his head forward, wiping at his eyes some more. "Ah, shit, Dan. I can't do this. I—"

"Take your time," Retsler said.

"But she wouldn't've been here if I hadn't asked her to come. I thought maybe she and me—we were—" Emory stopped all by himself, put his face in his hands, his shoulders shuddering.

Retsler watched him, coming to the realization all on his own. They were having an affair. Amazing how much he knew about this town and yet how little.

He put his hand on Emory's back, felt shudders run through the man. "Just tell me what happened."

"You're not gonna tell Paula, are you?" Paula was Emory's wife.

"Not if I don't have to," Retsler said. "But she might wonder what Pippa was doing here. Everyone knew she was afraid of heights."

"I did that." Emory sat up. He was calm now, as if he'd reached a different state. "I told her she could get past the fears if she just confronted them. We'd been working on it. Places like the path to the lighthouse, then the stairs. She was going to help me finish the light, and then as a reward for staying up so high, we were going to . . ."

His voice trailed off, but the implication was clear.

"Something got in the way?" Retsler asked.

Emory nodded. "Damn light."

"What happened with the light?"

Emory looked at him, eyes flat. "You wouldn't believe me if I told you."

A shiver ran through Retsler. Maybe he wouldn't have five years ago. But he believed most things now. That was one reason he had to leave Whale Rock.

"Try me," Retsler said.

Emory lowered his head and stared at his callused hands. He spoke slowly, measuring his words. "We turned on the light, and for a moment, it was glorious. It worked right. It turned like it was supposed to. It made that little electric hum that meant everything was working properly . . ."

He brought his hands to his face. Retsler didn't move. He figured he had only one chance at this.

"Then—these things—swarmed toward us from the ocean. I saw them coming, under the clouds. Pippa, she said the air had gotten sharp, charged, like it did before a lightning strike. She begged me to turn the light off, and just as I did, the door banged open—"

A bang echoed through the lighthouse, and Retsler jumped. Emory rose out of his chair, his hands before him, as if he were protecting himself.

Retsler turned. It was just Eddie and Tadero, coming back with the bag. They struggled with the door in the wind, pushing it shut. They set the bag on the floor near Retsler's shoes, then pulled off their wet coats. The bag wasn't as wet as they were; someone must have covered it.

"This is normal weather?" Tadero asked, wringing out her hair.

"Welcome to winter," Eddie said.

Retsler watched them, arms crossed. Tadero glanced his way, saw that he was talking with Emory, and her lips thinned. Emory was still standing, his hands before him like a shield.

Eddie called up the stairs, "You ready for the bag, Hamilton?"

"Ready as I can be," Denne said.

"C'mon," Eddie said to Tadero. They hurried past Retsler and started up the stairs.

"It's all right," Retsler said softly, hoping that Emory would take his cue and lower his voice as well. "What happened next?"

"I—I don't know."

"What do you mean?" Retsler asked.

"The door banged open, and Pippa laughed, you know,

nervous, like people do. She said it must have been the wind, and she went down to close it. I told her not to, but she really wanted to go down those stairs, away from being so high, if you know what I mean."

Retsler did. Being startled had probably made Pippa's fear of heights worse.

"She started down the stairs, and then she screamed and then . . ." Emory shook his head.

"And then?" Retsler prompted.

"There was this big crash." Emory was whispering now. "I went down the stairs and I found her. There was nothing I could do. I finally sat on the steps and got my phone out of my pocket and I called—"

His voice broke and tears swam in his eyes again. "How am I gonna tell Paula? And everybody. What am I going to say?"

Retsler hated this part of his job. "I don't know, Clay."

There was clanging above them as Denne bagged the body. Emory closed his eyes, as if that would shut out the sound.

"Come on, Clay," Retsler said. "Let me drive you home."

"I need my van."

"You can come back for it. You're not in any shape to drive."

Emory nodded. Retsler glanced at the stairs. He was surprised to find Tadero looking at him.

"You're not going to let him go, are you?" she asked.

Retsler decided he wasn't even going to dignify her question with an answer. "Meet me at the False Colors. Make sure Eddie and Hamilton come."

"This is not the time to go to a bar."

"Jaclyn," he said, "you're not in Chicago anymore. For the next few weeks, you're doing things my way, or you're not participating at all. Is that clear?"

"Unfortunately," she said, and watched, disapproval evident, as he led Emory to the door.

It was clear from the moment Tadero entered the False

Colors that she had never been inside the restaurant before. Retsler leaned back in his wooden captain's chair and watched her. She ran her hands over the rope banister, and looked up at the skulls above the bar.

The sea chantey on the sound system was something about death and rum. Tadero stopped in front of the black-and-white photographs of wrecked ships lining the walls, made a face, and then looked for Retsler.

He was sitting at their usual table, Lucy studying the menu beside him. Eddie had already arrived, saying that Denne would come as soon as he finished preparing the body.

Tadero had changed out of her wet clothes into a cable-knit sweater and a pair of tight jeans. Her hair was down, curving around her face, softening the angles. From this distance she looked younger than she was, younger and less sure of herself.

For the first time, Retsler wondered why a career detective on the promotion path decided to leave Chicago. He hadn't really thought about how unusual it was before.

She finally saw them and came down the worn wooden steps, walking past the huge fireplace as if it didn't exist. Retsler was amazed. Both he and Eddie had stopped to warm their hands before coming to the table.

"Charming place," Tadero said as she slipped into an empty chair.

"Tourists hate it." Lucy pulled a cigar from her pocket. "So we feel safe here."

Tadero shot her a strange glance. Lucy put the cigar in her mouth and Eddie lit it for her.

"Is this the smoking section?" Tadero asked pointedly.

"It is now," Lucy said.

June, the waitress, handed Tadero a menu, then, behind Tadero's back, raised her eyes in question. Retsler gave her a half smile. "Junie, meet our new police chief as of January."

Tadero looked up in surprise, obviously not used to conversing with waitresses. They gave each other an uncomfortable hello, and then Tadero studied the menu, clearly dismissing June.

"All right, Lucy," Retsler said. "I don't want to wait for Hamilton. Tell me now, so I know what the hell I'm dealing with."

"You really should know the history of Whale Rock by now," Lucy said.

"I'm trying to put it out of my mind," Retsler said.

"So he has more room for the history of Buttfuck, Montana," Eddie said, holding his longneck between his index and middle fingers.

Retsler didn't even try to correct him. Eddie knew the name of Retsler's new town, and still insisted on his crude version. Eddie had made it clear from the very beginning that he was opposed to Retsler's move.

Tadero set her menu down. "What are we talking about?"

"The lighthouse." Lucy puffed her cigar. It had a foul odor. Retsler made a mental note to buy her an expensive box before he left.

"Why would its history be important?" Tadero asked.

"You didn't tell her, did you?" Lucy said.

Retsler shrugged. "Not my place."

Lucy set the cigar on an ashtray shaped like a skull and crossbones. "It is your place. You have to give her the tools to work around here."

"Tools?" Tadero said.

"She'll learn fast enough." Retsler smiled at June, who had returned with his shrimp cocktail. June set the appetizer down, took the other orders, and then left. She knew better than to hang around when the entire police department showed up to talk shop.

"The lighthouse," Lucy said, "is one of the oldest structures on this part of the coast. There've been problems from the beginning."

"What does this have to do with Pippa Gage?" Tadero asked.

"You probably shouldn't have told her to come here," Eddie said to Retsler, then took a swig of his beer.

"She has to learn sometime," Retsler said. "May as well be now."

"Learn what?"

Denne had arrived. He too had changed clothes. He was wearing pressed jeans with a corduroy jacket over a button-down shirt. As he passed the bar, he stopped to order a drink.

"The first lighthouse keeper," Lucy said, as if she hadn't been interrupted, "started a fire his first winter there. It burned the stairs and the interior pretty badly. He died, of course—at least everyone assumes it was him. The body was unrecognizable. His wife saw the flames and smoke pouring out of the lighthouse, but she couldn't do anything. In those days, they were too far away from anywhere."

"So it has a bad history," Tadero said.

"Just listen," Retsler said, even though he doubted she would.

Lucy took a shrimp off Retsler's plate. "About 1890, a group of spiritualists settled Whale Rock. They were told by one of their ghostly guides that this place had a special power."

"No shit," Eddie said.

"They held séances, and mapped out Whale Rock. They used the lighthouse as their base, since no one else would work there, not after that hideous death. They rebuilt the stairs and the light, and kept the ships safe out at sea."

"Spiritualists?" Retsler asked. "I thought that was an East Coast phenomenon."

"Technically, it was," Lucy said. "But there were some groups all over the country."

"And remember," Denne said as he sat down, "Astoria was named after John Jacob Astor. He sent a lot of people here to look after his interests. In those days, there was a strong Eastern contingent on this coast."

"You know this story?" Retsler asked, but without surprise. Denne seemed to know the entire history of the coast.

"Having only heard that last part, I'm not sure," Denne said. "But I have heard that the lighthouse is haunted. At the closed-door meetings about the reopening, there was a lot of discussion about that."

"Excuse me," Tadero said. "People really believe in that crap?"

Everyone at the table stared at her. Retsler remembered
what such disbelief felt like, but dispassionately, the way he
remembered what it felt like to learn his multiplication tables.
But with all this group had been through—the January storm
sparked by a curse placed on the town by a selkie, a curse
Retsler could have prevented; the mermaids that still haunted
the beaches; the seventy-year-old bodies that the sea still
regurgitated from time to time—they had little tolerance for
someone who didn't believe.

At that moment, June brought their meals. She set the
plates down as if they weren't hot at all.

"Come on," Tadero said, breaking the code that no one
spoke about business before June. "You're not telling me you
think ghosts killed her."

"You guys talking about Pippa?" June asked.

News traveled fast in a small town. Only Tadero seemed
surprised that June knew about the death.

"After what happened to those hippies, I'm amazed anyone's allowed in the lighthouse." June continued. "I thought
they were crazy to reopen it. I was with the committee that
wanted to tear the whole thing down and start from scratch."

"Hippies?" Retsler looked at Lucy.

"You should remember that, Dan. You were living here
then."

"I was a little boy. My mother sheltered me from all bad
things," he said. "Unless this was somewhat recent?"

"No," June said. "Nineteen-seventy something. Pretty
ugly. I don't remember the details, just that people couldn't
believe no one warned them."

"Warned them about what?" Eddie asked. He was too
young to remember anything that happened in nineteen-
seventy something.

"Not to have a séance up there," June said. At that moment, a bell dinged in the back and she left.

"You people are crazy," Tadero said.

"Certifiable," Denne said agreeably, and Retsler got a
sense of how the man had survived in that awful marriage for
so long.

"You expect me to believe that a woman died because of ghosts?" Tadero asked.

"No," Denne said. "We expect you to believe she died because she fell down a flight of stairs."

"Because she was pushed," Tadero said. "And what about those marks on her face?"

"What did they look like?" Retsler couldn't resist asking her. He slid the shrimp plate to Lucy and then started in on his crab-stuffed halibut.

"Scorch—" Tadero cut herself off and, to Retsler's surprise, she flushed.

"Go ahead," Eddie said. "It's okay to say scorch marks."

"But that's not possible," Tadero said.

"Wasn't it Sherlock Holmes who said, 'When you eliminate the possible, that leaves only the impossible'?" Denne asked.

"Right," Tadero said, taking a bite from her salmon burger. "We should base this entire investigation on our belief in ghosts and the advice of a fictional character."

"We're so refreshingly small-town, aren't we?" Lucy asked, without a smile on her face. "You can look down your nose so easily at us because we don't have the benefit of your big-city education. Did you ever think that maybe we know Whale Rock better than you do?"

"Did you ever think that crime scene analysis should be about science, not superstition?" Tadero asked.

"The first rule of any investigation," Denne said, with an edge in his voice, "is to examine the evidence without preconceptions. You're assuming that a crime has been committed."

Retsler's halibut was sweet and fresh. He was content to eat it and let the others argue with Tadero for a change.

"The man was alone with her in the lighthouse. They were having an affair, if what Eddie tells me is true. They fight, he gets rough, pushes her, and that's the end of it," Tadero said. "Open and shut."

"Except for the fact that you have no evidence of that," Denne said.

"I haven't looked through the evidence yet," Tadero said.

"First rule of investigation: The eyewitness should be your first suspect."

"If there's something to suspect," Denne said.

"She's young and she's dead, isn't she?" Tadero said. "That's a suspicious death."

Retsler finished the halibut and started on his plank potatoes. He glanced around the restaurant. No one sat close enough to hear the conversation.

"Okay," Denne said. "Let's pretend we like your theory. How'd she get the—what did you call them?—scorch marks?"

"You tell me," Tadero said. "You're the coroner."

"It's your theory," Denne said.

"Well, I can tell you that they weren't caused by a ghostly presence," Tadero said.

"You're sure?" Lucy asked.

"Positive," Tadero said.

"You want to lay some money down on that?" Lucy asked.

Retsler set his fork down. Eddie gave him a small secret grin. Lucy never made a bet she wasn't certain of winning.

Tadero looked at Lucy. "You've got a bet."

"How much?" Lucy asked.

"How much can you afford to lose?"

Lucy grinned. "A lot more than you can."

"I can't believe I'm going to bet on this," Tadero said, almost to herself.

"Neither can I," Retsler said.

She glared at him. "Fifty bucks."

Eddie whistled. Lucy said, "Do you want to make that a hundred?"

Tadero frowned. "No. I'll have enough trouble taking your money as it is."

"Have you thought about how you're going to prove this?" Denne asked her.

"I'm going to solve this crime using science," Tadero said. "Then there won't be any more talk about ghosts on my watch."

Lucy laughed. "I love it when they're young and idealistic," she said, and picked up her cigar.

• • •

After Tadero left, Denne ordered a second Alaskan Amber. "She's going to be a problem," he said.

"Nonsense." Lucy had put out her cigar. "Dan didn't believe for years, and he grew up here. He's done all right."

Retsler said nothing. Now that he believed there were supernatural things that gathered in Whale Rock, he was leaving. His lack of belief, his unwillingness to look at the supernatural—even after he'd learned of its existence—had caused him to make some of the bigger mistakes of his career.

He waved off June's offer of dessert, ordered a cup of decaf, and leaned back in his chair. The room had a chill.

"So," he said to Lucy, "give me the short version of the lighthouse's history."

She sighed. "Near as anyone can figure, the lighthouse itself acts as a type of lightning rod. It draws spirits to it, but only when the light is on."

Retsler felt the threads of disbelief again. "Why when the light is on? Why not all the time?"

"The theory is that it brings souls out of the darkness. They think they're heading toward the light—you know, that death light?—when instead, they're coming for the lighthouse."

"So they're angry when they get here?" Retsler asked.

Lucy shook her head. "They're just lost and confused. The only angry ghost is the lighthouse keeper. He apparently attacks, but in panic, one of the hippies said. Like he was still surrounded by flame and smoke and trying to escape."

"What about those hippies?" Retsler asked.

"They held a séance up there, long after the lighthouse had closed."

"So the light wasn't working?"

"They brought one of their own," Lucy said. "It was a big old oil lamp, like the kind they thought the lighthouse keeper would have used."

Retsler felt his stomach clench. "Then what? A fire?"

"The survivors claimed there was a fire," Lucy said. "They claimed the entire lighthouse was going up in smoke and flames, only there was no evidence of it. Everything was normal inside when investigators came."

"Except . . ." Eddie intoned in a deep, radio announcer voice.

"Except the hippies who died were burned to death."

Retsler wrapped his hands around his mug. The ceramic was hot against his palms.

"The survivors say they tried to call the spirits of the dead from the area. They claimed they saw a lot of lost and sad sailors, and a few other folk they didn't recognize. It was the lighthouse keeper who chased the others away."

"The guy who burned to death."

"Right," Lucy said. "He gave them a warning, which they didn't listen to, and he scorched one boy's face. He didn't go back, that boy. The others did, determined to put the lighthouse keeper's soul to rest."

"And they all died?"

"All but two girls who made it out. They were treated for severe smoke inhalation."

Retsler frowned. "Surely someone thought that was odd."

"Well," Lucy waved, caught June's attention, and mimed drinking a beer. "They might have if it weren't for a few things."

"Like what?" Retsler asked.

June brought Lucy a Rogue ale.

"Like," Lucy said, "the hippies were all tourists, and they had some drugs stashed in their van."

"LSD?" Retsler asked.

"Who knows?" Lucy said.

"Pot mostly." Denne spoke for the first time since Lucy started reciting the story. "But the girls' systems were clean. I had the toxicology tests in my office for the longest time."

"This one interests you?" Retsler asked.

"This one scares me," Denne said. "We're reopening that lighthouse."

Retsler set his chair down on all four of its legs. How had he missed this argument? Probably because he had been spending all spring and summer finding a way out of Whale

Rock. Probably because he felt any part of Whale Rock's future had nothing to do with him.

"So, doc," he said to Denne, "what's your professional opinion? Was Pippa pushed down those stairs?"

"It's kind of hard to tell without a witness, unless there's two large handprints outlined squarely in her back." Denne set his Amber down. "I haven't done the autopsy yet, but I do know that she died of a broken neck. So her injury is consistent with a fall down the stairs."

"Bruising? Any sign of a fight?" Retsler asked.

"Just what you'd expect from a fall," Denne said.

"I went to school with Clay Emory," Eddie said. He was still nursing the same longneck he'd started with. "There's no way he would hurt anyone."

"He was having an affair with her," Retsler said. "And that was news to me. People can surprise you."

"Not Clay. She wasn't his first and she won't be his last. Paula's a—" Eddie lowered his voice so that no one around them would overhear. "—Grade A Number One bitch."

"Eddie," Denne said.

"It's true. She's a real ball-buster, and Clay's had trouble keeping it in his pants since high school."

"But you don't think he killed Pippa."

"Hell, man, have you ever seen Clay in a fight?" Eddie asked.

Retsler shook his head.

"That's my point. He wouldn't hit anyone, not even when we were doing a boxing unit in school. If someone got violent around him, he'd hide his face in his hands and cringe. If someone starts yelling, he leaves the room. I've even seen him take spiders outside instead of smashing them. This is not a man who gets angry and pushes someone down a flight of stairs."

Eddie directed this last toward Denne, as if it were Denne's fault that the accusation was even being made.

"All I said was that the bruises and the neck injury were consistent with a fall," Denne said. "I didn't say he pushed her."

"I hear a 'but' in that sentence," Retsler said.

"I haven't done the official tests yet," Denne said, "but I did some preliminary work. The streaks on Pippa's face are consistent with streaks a person gets when they're in a lot of smoke."

"What does that mean?" Retsler said.

"Think about it," Denne said. "Someone's lit a fire so close to your face that you're feeling the heat. What do you do?"

"Try to put it out," Lucy said.

"And she was panicked because of her fear of heights," Denne said. "She probably waved it away, or pushed it away, and tumbled forward."

Retsler downed the last of his decaf. "Interesting theory, but what are the odds that Clay Emory knows the lighthouse's history?"

"And went to all that trouble to make it look like ghosts killed Pippa?" Lucy asked, her voice rising incredulously.

Retsler shrugged. "He was alone with her all afternoon. He had time."

Denne shook his head. "There was no ash residue, no smell of sulfur, no signs of fire anywhere in that lighthouse. I checked. Besides, the time of death is consistent with Clay's story. The body was still warm when I arrived. You remember, Dan. Rigor hadn't even really started yet."

Retsler did remember the arm hanging limply over the landing. "What about Paula? Any way that she could have been there?"

Eddie shook his head. "She had a shift at Safeway this afternoon. A lot of people saw her."

"We can't just close this one up," Retsler said. "Tadero won't let it ride."

"You can't prove the existence of ghosts," Denne said.

"Why not?" Retsler asked. "All it takes is a scientific method."

"And an open mind." Denne sipped his Amber. "She's missing the second part."

"I missed it once, too," Retsler said.

"What are you going to do?" Lucy asked.

Retsler smiled at her. "Rely on you," he said.

Storm clouds gathered on the horizon, black against a gray sky. The line between the clouds and the ocean was blurred—it was pouring not three miles away.

Retsler stood in front of the lighthouse, the wind tugging at his coat. It had gotten cooler in the last few minutes, and he could smell rain in the air.

"I got a call from the state crime lab this morning." Denne was standing beside him, hands clasped behind his back, staring up at the lighthouse as if he'd never seen it before. "They wanted to know why someone they'd never heard of had requested an autopsy on a case I hadn't even listed as a suspicious death."

"Tadero?" Retsler asked.

Denne nodded. His hair blew across his face, and he pushed at the strands as if they annoyed him.

"Are you sending the body?"

"She has no authority yet," Denne said.

"What did you tell them?"

"That she's new and hungry and won't be chief until January. They understood. They're turning down the request."

Lucy came up beside them, a large bag over her shoulder. She looked small and frail in the wind. "Where's Eddie?"

"Getting Emory," Retsler said.

"Do you really think we should do this?" Denne asked. "They did all sorts of cleansings once the reopening was approved."

"Of the lighthouse." Lucy was standing in the same position Denne had been in, her head tilted back, staring at the top of the massive building before them. "Anyone with a brain can tell the problem comes when the light is lit."

The clouds were swirling in the distance, and the chill had gotten deeper. Retsler pulled his coat tighter.

"Besides," Lucy said, "this place is going to be a spirit magnet for the rest of its days."

"So what are we doing here?" Denne asked.

"That's what I'd like to know." Tadero had come up behind Retsler. Even though he had been expecting her, he jumped.

"You're observing."

"Like hell. You guys are messing with a crime scene."

Retsler smiled. "We're the police, Jaclyn. We're allowed."

At that moment, Eddie and Emory crested the hill. Eddie had one hand on Emory's back, as if propelling him forward.

"What is this?" Tadero asked.

"He's going to show us what he was doing when Pippa died," Retsler said.

"He already gave a statement," Tadero said.

"I still fail to see what we can do that the others haven't," Denne said, referring not to Emory, but the other cleansings.

"The way I see it," Lucy said, "the light will be automated. There will rarely be anyone here when it comes on."

"What are we talking about?" Tadero asked. No one answered her.

"The lighthouse will be open to the public on summer days, but for safety reasons will close any time the light has to go on. So we're only concerned with a few interactions, and only one that could possibly be dangerous."

She didn't have to say which one. Retsler and Denne both knew she was referring to the lighthouse keeper.

"So are we making the same mistake those hippies made?" Denne asked.

"Goodness, no. We're not holding a séance. No one here is that reckless, are we?" Lucy looked at Tadero as if this had all been her idea.

"You people are really and truly crazy," Tadero said.

At that moment, Eddie and Emory reached them. Emory's face was ashen. He looked at Tadero, and Retsler thought he saw fear in Emory's eyes.

"What's she doing here, Dan? You gonna charge me with something?"

So Emory had heard about Tadero's theory of Pippa's death.

"No, Clay," Retsler said. "And even if I did, any good lawyer would throw this afternoon's proceedings out of court."

Tadero sighed and shook her head.

"So what're we doing here?"

"You're going to turn the light on for us."

Emory shook his head. "I quit, didn't you hear? I don't want to go inside this place ever again."

"I know," Retsler said.

"I don't got permission to turn on the light," Emory said. "This is state property. I could get in trouble."

"We have permission," Retsler said.

"To have me do it?"

"They wanted a certified electrician here. The work's not completely done, Clay. We need to be safe."

Emory continued shaking his head. He was backing away. Eddie caught his arm. "I told you what happened. You can't—"

"It's all right," Retsler said. "It'll take ten minutes."

Emory blinked hard. "You don't know what you're risking."

"I think we do, Clay," Lucy said. "Come on."

He looked at her and all the strength seemed to leave him. Apparently Clay Emory, like the rest of Whale Rock, trusted Lucy.

Eddie led Emory inside, followed by Denne and Lucy. As Retsler headed for the door, Tadero kept pace with him.

"Very melodramatic," she said. "Is this show for me?"

"Actually, the others didn't want you here," Retsler said, stating only part of the objection his crew had to the afternoon's proceedings. "Consider your presence to be professional courtesy."

She raised her eyebrows, but followed him inside.

Weak sunlight came through the thick glass windows, reflecting off the newly painted white walls. The light made the interior of the lighthouse a completely different place than it had been during the storm.

Emory and Eddie were already past the landing where Pippa's body had been found. The sound of footsteps on metal stairs echoed in the small space.

Retsler followed. Through the windows on the landing,

he could see the clouds, black in the distance. They had gotten a lot closer.

When he and Tadero reached the top, the others were already gathered around the light. Emory stood to one side, near the control box.

"They haven't got it completely automated yet," he said. "That won't happen until the day after the dedication ceremony."

Lucy had reached inside her bag. She held it against her, one hand inside, the other clutching the bag tightly. The lines on her face seemed deeper than they ever had, and she had lost all of her grandmother-cuteness.

Denne had slipped his hands into his back pockets and was staring out at the storm clouds. Eddie was standing beside Emory as if he didn't trust him to go through with this. Tadero had stopped beside Retsler. He could feel the tension in her body.

"I—I don't think this is smart, Dan," Emory said again.

"Let's just do it," Retsler said. "The way you did the day Pippa died. Keep the timing the same."

Emory took a deep breath and hit a switch. The light hummed. The bulbs lit up and then the light began to rotate, just as it was supposed to. Retsler could feel the vibration through the floor.

The air did feel charged. He glanced at Tadero and saw that strands of her hair had risen as if they were covered with static electricity.

"Dan," Denne said. There was an urgency in his voice.

Retsler followed Denne's gaze and so did Tadero. Shapes had formed over the ocean, small wisps, like fog, all of them scuttling forward. Retsler turned. He saw more wisps coming up the beach from the south.

"What is that?" Tadero asked.

Then the lighthouse door banged open.

"Oh, Jesus," Emory said. He fumbled with the box, punching the switch, trying to shut it off.

"One of us should go down the stairs," Lucy said. She had dropped her bag and was now holding a small vial in her left hand.

"I'll go," Retsler said. "You want me to take that?"

"No." Lucy came up beside him. She held the vial before her as if it were a shield.

Tadero's eyes were wide. "What the hell is this?"

"Don't know yet," Retsler said, but he smelled smoke. Tadero did, too—he could tell from the way her nostrils moved.

"Oh, for God's sake," she said, rolling her eyes. "Let's scare the new recruit."

She started down the stairs without them.

"Jaclyn!" Denne called, but she didn't stop.

Retsler hurried down after Tadero, Lucy beside him.

Flames had formed on the landing. As Tadero got closer, the flames rose up in the shape of a man. He reached toward her, fire blazing off his fingers.

"What the...?" Tadero stopped.

"Back off," Lucy said, but Retsler didn't know if she was talking to Tadero or the fiery shape.

Black smoke filled the air around them. In the space of a few seconds, it got so thick that Retsler could barely see.

"Shut off the damn light!" Denne yelled from upstairs. Eddie cursed.

"I can't get close, Dan," Lucy said.

Tadero backed up the stairs, fumbling for her gun.

Retsler grabbed the vial from Lucy. His eyes stung and he was coughing. "What do I do?"

"Dump it on the flames," she said.

He pulled the cork. The burning man was coming after Tadero, his flames the only light in the smoke.

Retsler tossed the contents at the wall of fire.

"We're helping! We're helping! We're putting you out!" Lucy called.

The liquid hit the flames and they rose up, sparking. Tadero let out a small cry and crouched, protecting her face. Then the flames sucked inward and the smoke vanished. All that was left was a man in severe black clothing, wearing muttonchop whiskers and a confused expression.

"Rest now," Lucy said. "You're free. Go home."

He looked upward, and his body lost definition, becoming fog. It floated through the ceiling and disappeared through the roof.

"Shut off the damn light!" Denne yelled again.

"Move," Eddie said, and Retsler heard clanging. There was a loud click and then the humming stopped.

The door banged again. Closed this time, Retsler guessed, and somehow that relieved him. The feeling of electricity had left the air.

Retsler handed the vial back to Lucy. "What the hell was in here?"

"Holy water," she said.

Retsler started in surprise. "You knew that would work?"

"No," she said and smiled. Her face was streaked with soot. He supposed his was too. "I hoped it would, though."

Retsler shook his head. He hated to think what would have happened if the holy water hadn't worked. The spirit might have vanished anyway, as it had when Emory shut off the light the first time. Or it might have stayed.

He shuddered. He heard the sound of footsteps on the stairs behind him, but didn't turn, knowing it was Denne, Eddie, and Emory.

Tadero was sitting on the stairs. She was covered in black, and clutching her gun. Retsler climbed down to her.

"What the hell was that?" she asked, her voice shaking.

"What Pippa Gage saw before she fell down the stairs."

"I'm supposed to believe that?"

Retsler shrugged. "Believe what you want."

Tadero looked at him. Her eyes were wide, her confidence gone. She seemed as shaken as a rookie at her first arrest.

Retsler took pity on her. He sat down beside her. "You never asked me why I was getting out of here."

"Because the lighthouse is haunted?" The usual bravado was not in her voice.

"Because this isn't the first strange and hard-to-believe thing I've seen in Whale Rock," he said. "Believe it or not, I used to be more skeptical than you are."

"You're leaving because you're afraid of ghosts?" she asked.

Retsler shook his head. "Because I don't handle them well. Because they disturb me on a level that makes me ineffective at my job."

"You don't seem ineffective," she said, and he realized that was the first time she had complimented him.

"Yet," he said.

She nodded, holstered her gun, and looked out the window. The storm clouds had gotten closer, and the waves were large and tipped with white.

"Like ten-year-old crack dealers with guns," she said.

"What?" Retsler asked.

"You never asked me why I gave up a career-track position in Chicago to come here," she said.

"Ten-year-old crack addicts?" he asked.

"With guns," she repeated. "They disturbed me on a level that made me ineffective at my job."

Retsler wasn't sure he knew what to say to that. He'd never seen a crack addict, let alone a ten-year-old brandishing a weapon. "So you'd rather face ghosts?"

She looked at her hands, smudged with black from the smoke. "I'd rather believe this was a prank that you all pulled, but Pippa Gage is dead. To believe this is a prank, I have to believe that you took her death lightly, and I see no evidence of that."

"You called the state crime lab," Denne said, and Retsler heard suppressed fury in his tones.

Tadero nodded. "I was going to prove to you that science was better than superstition."

"But?" Lucy asked.

"My eyes sting from smoke that's not here," Tadero said.

"What are you going to do about the lighthouse?" Emory asked Retsler. "You can't let it open."

Retsler sighed and stood. "It'll be all right, Clay."

"But—"

"But nothing. We got rid of the hostile spirit."

"That won't stop more from coming," Emory said.

"The lighthouse will be empty when the light's on," Retsler said.

"Except if some poor electrician has to fix it." Emory's voice was shaking.

Eddie put his hand on Emory's shoulder. Denne shoved his hands in his pockets. He looked more uncomfortable than Retsler had ever seen him.

"I'll talk to some people," Denne said, "and see what we can do."

"You know better," Emory said. "They should have stopped this thing from the beginning, but they didn't. And now Pippa's dead. More people are going to die here, Dan. You know that."

Retsler did know that, but it wasn't his problem anymore. It was Tadero's.

He reached a hand down to help her up. She took it reluctantly.

"Still willing to stay?" he asked her softly.

"Still planning to leave?" she asked with a touch of the old toughness.

He gazed at the storm clouds hovering just offshore. This storm made him less nervous than the last one had. He was, apparently, coming to terms with the past—and that meant he was ready to move on.

He had needed the experience in the lighthouse to prove to himself that no matter what came his way, he could handle it. He might not be able to solve it, any more than Tadero could stop kids from getting crack or guns, but he could survive whatever was thrown at him.

"Dan?" Denne asked, as if he were waiting for Retsler to respond. "Still plan to leave?"

"Yeah," Retsler said softly, feeling relief for the first time in nearly a year. "Now that I know my successor is up to the job."

MATT COSTELLO & A. J. MATTHEWS

And the Sea Shall Claim Them

The expression *"It was a dark and stormy night"* ran through Derek Townsend's mind as he pulled to a stop in the parking lot of the Rusty Scupper.

He grinned. Might be a cliché . . . but they do occur.

Take tonight, for example. Rain just letting up, but the clouds black as mud and lying low enough to meet what seemed to be a permanent fog bank.

"Dark, stormy, and hot," he muttered as he killed the ignition. He'd thought Maine never got hot.

He swung open the car door, stepped out on the hard-packed gravel, and tilted his head back. No stars—though a sickly July moon had started to cast a faint fluorescent glow through the cloud cover.

Maybe it would burn off.

He smiled at that. *Burn . . . off.*

He stretched his arms over his head and groaned loudly. He knew he sounded like a bear waking up after a long winter's sleep. Tough; he ached.

The drive out to Cape Tumbles—a small coastal town some three hours northeast of Bar Harbor, Maine—had been long and tortuous. The thin, winding ribbon of road hugged the southern edge of the cape close and tight; it had tested Derek's nerves and driving skills. He hated driving anyway.

Every time his headlights swung around a curve, briefly illuminating the vast, dark stretch of ocean and jagged granite rocks off to his right, he felt like he was in free-fall. The sudden drop to his right made his stomach slide up into his chest. Nice feeling . . . like some demented roller-coaster ride.

He looked back at the sky. A bit more moonlight was seeping through.

Derek was damn glad the drive was over. He looked around the parking lot.

Not many vehicles in the Rusty Scupper's parking lot—a handful of battered pickup trucks, some loaded with bait barrels; a Harley or two; a mud-splattered four-by-four; and a rusting white Volvo station wagon.

Nice eclectic group.

Probably half the drinking-age population of town, Derek thought as he walked up to the bar's entrance. He took a deep breath of the air—as close as it was—and pulled the door open.

Inside, the scene was exactly what he had expected. The room thick with cigarette smoke. Small knots of townies ranged along the bar and seated at a few round tables. From the jukebox, Mick Jagger was singing about shuffling on the streets of Manhattan. Manhattan was a world away for these yokels.

It took a few seconds for Derek's eyes to adjust to the dim lighting.

After scanning the room, he had the feeling that the man he was here to meet was the dark hulk seated at the far end of the bar, leaning on both elbows. As Derek started walking toward him, the man turned around and nodded.

"Evenin'," the man said.

The man's deep voice was slurred, but what did he expect? In a backwater coastal town like this, what else could you do but drink yourself into oblivion every night? It's practically a hobby.

"Evenin'," Derek replied with a quick nod of the head. He almost grinned when he noticed how, on this trip to Maine, he had started to adopt a bit of a Down East accent himself. Maybe it was an unconscious tactic to lull the locals . . . make them open up a bit. He'd taken to dropping his *G*s and drag-ging out his *R*s like all of them. "Name's Howie Chadbourne," the hulk said, extending his hand. The man's grip was hard-callused and strong. "Pull up a chair an' have a brew."

Derek nodded, sat down, and asked the waitress for a Geary's ale.

"So, Meg over to the hardware store says you wanna talk about the lighthouse . . . out there on the point," Howie said without preamble. He hooked his thumb over his right shoul-der. Derek took that to be the direction of the lighthouse.

Not the most accurate directional system in the world.

"Uh-huh. I'm writing an article for the *Boston Globe Sunday Magazine*."

Howie snorted. After taking a long pull of beer, he shook his head as though deeply grieved.

"No offense, mista, but we don't 'zactly need no tourist publicity 'round here. Mosta them annoying flatlanders with their credit cards keep way south of here—and that's finest kind with us. You go writin' anything 'bout us, an', far as I can see, all we'll get's more of 'em pokin' 'round here."

He pronounced the last word with two syllables—"he-ah."

Derek nodded sympathetically just as the waitress arrived with his beer. He took a sip; the cold, bitter taste flooded his mouth, so refreshing after the jarring drive.

Before he could say anything, Howie continued.

"We been overfished, overdeveloped, overtouristed and overrun by outsiders—outsiders who don't know an' don't care" (again two oh-so-long syllables: "cay-ah") "that all we want is justa be left alone. Key-rist! Next thing you know they'll hit oil in Damariscotta and be drillin' there!"

"Well—that's exactly what my article is about," Derek said. "You know, about how all along the coast of Maine, de-velopment is ruining the old way of life."

A bit of a lie, that.

That wasn't *really* what his article was about. The truth was, he didn't have a clue what the piece was going to be about. After digging around coastal Maine for the last two weeks, he had—so far—come up with nothing.

"I . . . I don't get it. What's that got to do with the lighthouse?" Howie said. "Meg said you was askin' 'bout haunted Maine, lighthouses and stuff." His eyes rolled a little and he wobbled on the barstool. But then like a harpooner finding his target, he grasped the edge of the bar and righted himself.

Derek took this as his cue to get bold. This guy obviously had nothing to tell him, certainly nothing he hadn't already heard a dozen times already. Besides, what more could one say about Maine lighthouses? Most of them don't work? The little plastic ones make nice souvenirs?

Where was the fresh, exciting angle? There had already been far too many stories and articles. Why add to the list if it wasn't going to be...different, somehow?

This guy Howie was his last pathetic shot.

Maybe it was time to pack it in and head back to Massachusetts. He probably could cobble together something. Hell, all he had to do was read a few back issues of *Up Coast* magazine and he could do some kind of piece in his sleep. No Pulitzer, but the Sunday editor would be appeased.

Howie looked up, suddenly alert. "You know, what I oughta do is take you out there," he said. His deep baritone voice was nearly lost beneath the thump of the jukebox as Queen threatened to "rock you."

"Out where?" Derek asked, already knowing the answer.

"Out ta the lighthouse, 'course...out on Tumbles' Point."

Amazingly, Derek found himself nodding his agreement. A sudden, unexpected surge of excitement hit him. And for some unaccountable reason, he felt like a young kid again, planning to do something he wasn't supposed to. Climbing fences, drinking six packs...

Maybe it was a bad idea. Especially with Captain Howie at the helm.

"Um, isn't the lighthouse off limits?" Derek said, trying to backpedal without being too obvious. He had to be crazy to trust this guy. Nuts to go anywhere this late with someone he'd just met—especially to an off-limits lighthouse.

"Oh sure—Coast Guard don't want anybody out there, but what they don't know won't hurt 'em. 'Sides, how they gonna know we're out there? I can show ya the place. Won't take more'n an hour or so. You game?"

"Why not?" Derek said—even as the little voice in the back of his mind whispered that this was definitely not the brightest idea he'd ever had.

Fifteen minutes later, Derek sat white-knuckled as he rode shotgun with Howie down a winding stretch of dark, deeply rutted dirt road. The headlights of Howie's pickup truck did what they could to push back the foggy night, but the billowy darkness on both sides of the road was as thick as smoke.

"Hey, how much further is it?" Derek asked.

He'd been checking his wristwatch regularly. It seemed as though they had been in the truck for hours, not minutes.

"Just down the road a piece," Howie said. "I prob'ly oughta douse the lights."

"The lights? How can you—"

That was all Derek got out before Howie snapped off the headlights. Darkness closed around the truck like a huge fist. The word *pitch* leapt to mind. After a few seconds, Derek's eyes adjusted, and he could just see the thin, winding stretch of road ahead—at least a few yards of it. The rough gravel looked bone-white in the night. His only hope was that Howie wasn't so drunk that he couldn't even see it.

"So, how long you gonna be up this way?" Howie asked by way of conversation.

"Not long, I guess," Derek said with a shrug he knew was wasted in the darkness. The light from the truck's dashboard wasn't much brighter than a single match. "Couple of weeks, tops. My . . . my wife and I have been having a bit of trouble lately, so I took this assignment just to—you know—get away for a while. Cool off a bit."

"Caught in the ol' trap, huh?" Howie said with a chuckle that seemed to come from somewhere under the truck seat.

"Yeah, well . . . You know how it is. People change."

Derek stretched again, feeling hard knots of tension in his neck and shoulders.

"Boy, don't I ever," Howie said, laughing again as he slowed the truck to a stop.

Derek leaned forward to peer through the thinning fog and saw that, up ahead, the road ended at a barrier, a tall metal gate with a chain-link fence on either side, about ten feet high. The metal mesh didn't shine—probably rusted as hell. One section looked dented, banged in as though something big had rammed into it.

"We—uh—probably shouldn't go any farther than this," Derek said. Howie cut the engine and, snorting loudly, opened his door. The sudden glow of the dome light stung Derek's eyes.

"Aww, come on," Howie said. "You said ya wanted to find out about this place, didn'tcha? So grab the damn flashlight from the glove compartment and get your arse in gear."

Derek's nervousness grew. There had to be a way out of this, but he couldn't think of any. So he did as he was told, all the while wondering—again—why he had let himself be hauled out here by a half-drunk townie.

Actually, Howie seemed to be more than half-drunk. He almost lost his balance and fell as he stepped out onto the roadside and swung the truck door shut.

Great. Auspicious beginning.

The night and the fields out here were alive with the sound of crickets, and from several directions at once there came the hissing roar of night surf. Derek snapped on the light and looked around.

Straight ahead, looming up above the rise of land, he saw the top of the abandoned lighthouse. Its single, white cylindrical tower looked like an ominous pre-NASA rocket ship silhouetted against the now star-dusted sky. Derek suddenly found himself thinking that, whatever the stories about this place, they could be true.

"So, what exactly would happen if the cops caught us out here?" he asked as he directed the beam of light down at his feet and followed Howie over to the gate. The gate wasn't much of a barrier, but the rusted metal was plastered with several "NO TRESPASSING" signs that fluttered in the onshore breeze.

Derek's nostrils sucked in the salt-tinged air. And from somewhere off in the darkness came the faint cry of a seabird.

"Not too much, seein' as how I *am* the cops," Howie said. He exploded into drunken laughter at that one.

"Oh," Derek said. He couldn't help but wonder why he still didn't feel any better about being out here with the local police.

"Whaddya wanta know 'bout this place, anyway?" Howie asked. He reached in behind the metal crossbar, snapped something, and swung the gate open as if opening the gate to his own property.

"Not too sure. Heard some of the legends, myths. What can you tell me?" Derek asked. He'd been looking at Howie, but once again his gaze was drawn to the towering lighthouse up ahead.

At the pointed top, he could see the window where the light used to shoot out, now dark. Maybe it had been boarded over.

"Some folks say the place's haunted, that the ghost of the last keeper" (he pronounced it "keepa") "still lurks 'round out here. They say that he lures other folks into the lighthouse where he kills 'em an' forces their spirits to stay with him, to keep him company."

Howie paused for effect. Looking at him without shining the flashlight into his face, Derek thought he saw the man smiling.

"Just playing with you. But the legend says he hanged himself. That his wife was livin' out here with 'im, but durin' the winter she couldn't take it no more an' went back to her folks in town. He came to the house an' tried to convince her to come back with 'im, but she told 'im no, so he—" Howie finished by clasping his throat with one hand and making a loud gagging sound as though he was being hanged.

"Sure is a lonely stretch of land," Derek said, shivering. "Perfect for a hanging." He continued to swing the flashlight beam back and forth and look around.

The rocky land sported little vegetation other than sea grass and tangled scrub brush and brambles. The land around the lighthouse sloped down with a gentle rounded curve on three sides, ending at the ocean. The surf rose and fell gently, for now at least, on the black water around the jagged rocks.

As they walked side-by-side along the path leading to the

lighthouse, the rushing sound of wind and waves grew steadily louder. Derek could almost imagine voices lost in that breeze.

"Sure is lonely out here. It is that," Howie said. The distant tone in his voice unnerved Derek.

The sound of their footsteps was lost below the whistling wind until they started up the gravel walkway that led past the weather-beaten keeper's house to the lighthouse. The sliding of the stones was audible.

A tight dryness scratched at the back of Derek's throat. As miserable as the place had been, he found himself wishing he was back at the Rusty Scupper, downing another Geary's.

Finally they stopped when they reached the short flight of steps that led up to a narrow porch and the lighthouse door.

"Tall sumbitch, ain't it," Howie said, chuckling again as Derek ran the circle of light up the slanting sides of the tower. The lighthouse's sides angled away with a dizzying perspective. Wind and weather had stripped much of the white paint off, leaving the lighthouse with a chalky appearance.

"We don't have to go in, you know," Derek said, aware of the quaver in his voice. "I'm just glad I saw it." But Howie mounted the stairs to the door and reached for the handle.

He paused, turned, and looked down at Derek from the small landing, a disappointed look on his shadowed features.

"I didn't drive my ass all the way out here for you just to admire the damn architecture," he said. Derek detected what he thought was a hint of . . . a threat. "We'll have a little look around an' see for ourselves if there's a ghost in here or not. That's what you're here for, ain't it? Well, ain't it?"

Not really, Derek wanted to say, but didn't. He wasn't quite sure what he *was* here for. He did know that breaking into an abandoned lighthouse with this inebriated cop certainly wasn't high on his list.

If there was such a thing as a haunted lighthouse, Derek thought, then, boy, this had to be it.

The breeze off the water was warm, but a subtle chill ran up and down Derek's shoulder blades as he watched Howie lift the latch. When it clicked, it sounded like a gun being cocked. Then Howie pushed the door inward. It opened like a huge, dark mouth.

"You sure" (pronounced "shoe-ah") "you're up to this?" Howie asked. There was no mistaking the leering, almost mocking tone of his voice.

Almost against his will, Derek nodded and said, "Sure."

His back was stiff, and he thought his legs might lock up on him as he started up the steps. But Howie had already disappeared into the gaping maw of darkness that was the doorway.

Derek followed.

Suddenly the beam of the flashlight didn't seem anywhere near strong enough. Derek found himself thinking that—even in bright daylight—this place would give him a serious case of the creeps.

Since starting this assignment, he had seen more than his share of lighthouses, both old and new, but this was the first— and only—one that genuinely gave him the willies. And the willies didn't feel good at all.

There was something . . . so *wrong* about the place. He couldn't quite put his finger on it, but there was something off.

"Whew! Smells like somethin' died in here," Howie said, his disembodied voice drifting out from the darkness inside the lighthouse.

Derek was about to ask him what it smelled like when he stuck his head into the doorway and caught the pungent odor himself. Mixed with the damp, closed air of a building long unused was another, far worse smell that Derek couldn't quite place.

It reminded him of garbage that had gone terribly bad— garbage that contained old lobster shells or rotting fish.

"Whew! Jesus!" Derek said, waving a hand in front of his face. He directed the flashlight beam onto the stairs and saw that Howie was already climbing them. Before he started after him, though, Derek shined his flashlight downward and saw something that surprised him. The stairs descended in a curving spiral downward as well as up. The walls below the level of the entry floor were made of concrete, which was covered with thick mold or algae or something.

"Wow! How far does this go down?" Derek called up. He could hear the steady tread of Howie's feet on the metal spiral stairs. The sound receded as he climbed up higher, leaving Derek down below. Alone. Derek started moving.

"Up's where we wanna go," Howie called out.

The sound of footsteps stopped, and Derek knew Howie was waiting for him to catch up. "Helluva view from up he-ah."

Derek started up, but then leaned over and looked down. So strange...the stairwell looked like it plunged straight down into the earth, through the solid granite of the point.

He knew that lighthouses had to be built strong to withstand the ocean's surge during blizzards and hurricanes. But he had never heard of a lighthouse with what looked like this deep a substructure.

And the smell!

If it was coming from anywhere, it came from down there. Maybe the lighthouse builders had to excavate that far down to reach the bedrock. It was strange, all right. And as Derek directed his flashlight beam down the staircase, he almost wanted to go down, rather than up.

"I ain't got all night, ya know," Howie called out.

Sucking in a lungful of the bad-smelling air, Derek shined the light up the stairs and started up again. The air was moist and cloying, but as he mounted the steps, it—and the smell—got at least almost tolerable.

The footsteps of the two men clanged heavily on the metal stairs as they went up. Derek wondered why Howie didn't seem to need a flashlight. The wavering beam from Derek's light wasn't much to go by, even for him.

Was old Howie going all the way up by feel? What if there was a missing stair, like in *Kidnapped*, and Howie plunged to his death—what a loss!

Unless, of course, he dragged Derek down with him as he fell.

"You come out here often?" Derek called out. *For those quiet, meditative times*, he thought to himself, and chuckled silently.

Howie was six or more feet above him on the spiral stair-case. Derek could hear the heavy puffing of his breathing. He hadn't been smoking in the Rusty Scupper, but the man was seriously overweight, and the climb was obviously beginning to take its toll.

"Now an' again," Howie replied, followed by a raspy cough.

"I don't really need to see the top, you know," Derek said. "From the outside, it looked like the windows are all boarded over, anyway. We won't get much of a—"

"Just painted ov-ah. They been scraped off in a few places, and the view's purty nice. Really nice. 'Specially on a night like this."

Derek wanted to ask him what he meant by that. The moon, he had noticed earlier, was playing peekaboo with the clouds. Any view he was going to get would be of a dark ocean and a darker land.

"Not much further," Howie said, panting so heavily now the sound echoed in the well of the lighthouse like something else—something much larger, breathing in the darkness.

At last Howie, then Derek, reached the landing and en-tered the area where the huge lantern had once been. A metal railing ran along the circumference of the tower. The room was thick with junk—discarded beer cans and bottles, wrappers, cigarette butts, and what looked like dried-up, used condoms.

The painted-over windows had spray-painted messages: lovers' initials, logos for several hard rock bands, and assorted obscene epithets.

"Best view of the town's over he-ah," Howie said, leading Derek over to the railing where a large area of the paint had been scraped away. Derek followed him, aware of the sweaty, huffing man next to him in the darkness. It was only when he was close beside Howie that Derek noticed that the man seemed to be giving off the same dank, rotting smell he had caught at the foot of the stairs.

He hadn't really noticed it in the truck on the drive out here, but now it was almost repulsive. Like somehow the stink had attached itself to Howie—recognizing a kindred spirit!

Derek shied away from the "view" so he could catch his breath, but the rotting fish smell seemed to trail after him.

"Say—I could use another brewski. How 'bout you?" Howie asked, his voice sounding raw and dry.

Derek was thinking, great—anything to get the hell out of here and the damp, suffocating stench. Back to the Rusty Scupper—and sanity.

"Why don't you wait here," Howie went on. "I got a coupla cold ones in the truck. I'll go get 'em."

"I'll come with you," Derek said. "Or, let's just go back to the bar. Drinks on me!" The prospect of staying up here— alone—didn't really appeal to him.

"Now, wait a minute—thought you wanted ta see the ghosts that are s'pozed to be here," Howie said. "I made a big effort..."

Was that a mocking tone in his voice now? Derek wondered. He couldn't see the man's face, and he didn't think it would be nice to shine the flashlight onto him. He could only guess what Howie's expression was.

Another, stronger chill hit Derek as he watched the man moving toward the descending staircase.

"Be careful, though . . . Maybe the ghosts come out only when there's just one person up here," Howie said.

"I doubt that." Derek was having a hard enough time keeping his voice steady. "I seriously doubt there's anything up here that isn't human."

Howie laughed out loud at that, and the sound of his laughter made a weird reverberation in the stairwell.

"Are you sure you're not chicken-shit?"

"No." Derek felt a rush of defensiveness. "I just..." He let his voice trail away as he looked around the circular room. It suddenly seemed much larger. The deepest shadows near the ceiling seemed to drip with menace.

"Enjoy the view," Howie said. "Be right back. Won't take me but a coupla minutes to get the brews."

Derek was trapped again. Can't traipse after him. Chicken-shit indeed!

With that, Howie descended the stairs, his feet making heavy clumping sounds that rang on the metal steps and echoed in the dark throat of the building. Derek angled the light in Howie's direction, not shining it directly on him. Howie seemed to sink into the depths of the lighthouse and then disappear from sight.

As soon as he was gone, a muffled silence filled the top room of the lighthouse.

The sounds of Howie descending seemed distant, almost hallucinatory, then...practically nonexistent. And the discomfort Derek felt about being here alone in the dark intensified.

He took a slow breath, held it for a few seconds, and waited, willing his pulse to slow down.

There was nothing to be afraid of, he told himself. He didn't believe in ghosts and the supernatural. It was bull, and any stories about this lighthouse—or any lighthouse—being haunted were just stories and nothing more.

Still, the darkness seemed to press in, rubbing up against him like an unseen animal. He found it difficult to take a deep enough breath—the air was thick and fetid. He sniffed with laughter, trying to calm himself by thinking how ridiculous he was being.

But it didn't work. Without Howie here, he felt exposed, even in the darkness, and vulnerable. If he caught even a slight shifting of motion in the darkness, he was sure he would scream.

Chicken-shit for sure.

From far below, he still heard the faint tread of Howie's feet on the steps. Then the sound stopped. Derek knew he had reached the bottom floor. He wanted to call out to Howie, and tried not to imagine him opening the door and stepping out into the clear, fresh night air.

The dryness in his throat got worse, and he found himself anxious for Howie to return—if only for the relief the beer would bring to his dry throat.

"What's the matter with you?" he whispered in the dark. The sound of his own voice set his nerves even more on edge. Without even thinking, he started for the steps and, directing his flashlight beam down, began to descend. Hell, he had to get out of here.

He was only three or four steps down when he heard the

outside door slam shut. Howie, going out for the beers. The echo filled the darkness like a blast of thunder, and Derek's panic spiked.

He didn't like it here.

Ghosts or not, this place was too creepy. With or without Howie, he didn't want to be here. Not one more second. He had taken only a few more steps down when he heard something else—a loud clanging noise, a rattling of chains—and then gears, the noise so loud it hurt his ears.

"Howie?" he called out. "What the hell—" His voice was pathetically small in the darkness. As he directed his flashlight down, he felt dizzy. He was losing it—big time. The spiral staircase seemed to telescope crazily in and out.

He tightened his grip on the railing so much his arm hurt all the way up to his shoulder.

"Howie? What was that? Howie?"

He heard the fear in his voice, but no longer cared how he sounded. This was all wrong, and he had to get the hell out of here.

The rattling sound stopped, but it was immediately replaced by a loud grinding that sounded like two heavy rocks rubbing against each other. Derek's teeth were on edge as he dashed down the winding staircase as fast as he could without falling, slipping, sliding down the staircase like a rag doll.

He hit the ground floor with a jolt that made his jaw snap painfully. His face was slick with sweat, and his hand was trembling as he grabbed the door and gave it a savage pull.

Almost out—thank God.

He'd expected the old door to open easily, but there was resistance, and it sent an electric jolt of pain through his wrist. Blind with panic, he clenched his hand into a fist and rained several heavy blows against the door. The unyielding wood resounded like a drum.

But beneath that sound he heard a new one that filled the dark interior of the lighthouse.

A sound and a smell.

The nauseating stench of rotting fish and lobster shells

grew so strong Derek dropped to his knees and retched. Pinwheels of bright light zipped like fireworks across his vision. The sound of grinding stones had been replaced by the sound of rushing water.

Trembling with fear, Derek directed his flashlight down into the basement of the lighthouse and saw that a dark gush of water was roaring in. Had some big wave hit? he wondered. He stood there, paralyzed, and watched the water rise, fast, steady...filling the basement.

Panting, Derek looked back at the door and noticed for the first time that the entire door edge was lined with a heavy rubber seal. Like a—like a—gasket.

It wasn't until the water reached his feet, soaking through his sneakers, that he realized what was going on.

The lighthouse was being flooded—with him in it!

He lurched toward the stairway, but as he did, he heard a heavy clang from up above. He didn't need to see it to know that the room at the top of the stairs had been sealed off.

Of course. He was trapped.

The water rose rapidly in the confined space, carrying with it the briny, sick smell of the ocean's dead. Derek moved slowly toward the staircase, knowing he was trapped, but not ready to give up yet.

There had to be a way out.

"Howie, can you hear me? Are you out there?" he shouted. The water was almost up to his waist before he sloshed to the stairs and started up. The chill numbed him and the dampness made him fight to breathe.

The roaring sound of rushing water dropped, but the steady flow continued to rise with such power it swept Derek off the stairs.

He splashed and struggled to stay afloat as a strong current drew him into the center of the narrow circular building. God, no, he thought.

As he floated past the stairs, he made a frantic grab for the railing and caught on for a second but then was quickly yanked away.

"Help! Help me!" he cried.

Was he calling for Howie? No. He realized that was not what he was doing.

He heard his voice echo in the narrow confines of the tower. Could anyone outside hear him?

Only Howie—who had done this to him. Howie, who had brought him here and trapped him on purpose.

But why? Derek wondered, crazy, mad with terror as the water filled the tower. Christ, why go to all the trouble to fill the lighthouse with water and drown him when there would have been so many easier ways to get rid of him? Why not just shoot him, or push him into the ocean? Why go to all this trouble?

The water rose higher and higher, carrying Derek up with it like a human cork, until his head bumped against the bottom of the top floor. It wasn't hard to imagine that, within seconds, the water was going to rise above the floor level, trapping him beneath its surface.

And that would be it.

Derek gripped the metal railing and raised his face as high as he could to catch a breath—a final breath—but then, a miracle happened.

The water stopped rising.

There was a space, no more than three inches between the surface of the water and the floor, but it was enough. Derek could breathe. *He could breathe.* He was just beginning to think he actually might get out of this somehow, when he felt something brush against his leg beneath the surface of the water. It wasn't much. Just a feathery light brushing. It's nothing, Derek tried to convince himself. But then, struggling to remain afloat, the touch came again, this time in several places.

And then something pinched his left thigh just above the knee.

"What the—!" Derek shouted, taking in a mouthful of salty water as he reached down and swatted away whatever it was. A terrifying image suddenly entered his mind, filling him with cold, gripping fear. Before he could ponder it, several more unseen things brushed against him, and this time when they latched on, they pinched him in several locations at once, hard, holding.

Then more, and again, the pinching, the ripping...

Derek screamed so loudly his voice broke, and he sputtered into a violent fit of coughing. He still held the railing and his flashlight with one hand. With the other, he reached down and tried pathetically to swat away the things that had latched onto him.

One dug into his hand. He screamed even louder.

When he brought his hand up, he saw the fat blue claw dug in deep. Then he knew... he had to choke back another scream as tears filled his eyes.

"It's a trap," he whispered, his voice ragged and broken.

Right from the get-go... maybe it had even started back when he first talked with that woman... what was her name? Meg or Marge? At the hardware store. She had set him up, and then Howie had brought him out here to spring the trap.

Derek cried out as more things—begging, pleading, useless things, unseen beneath the dark water—latched onto his body.

And he knew what he was: a piece of bait, like a fish head jammed into a lobster trap to lure in the crustaceans.

That's what this lighthouse was—a huge lobster trap. And he was the bait for what was coming to have him for supper.

Amidst the agony, he understood.

And then he let go of the railing.

JANET BERLINER

Until the
Butterflies

Jenny was fascinated by cycles: birth and death, the waxing
and waning of the moon, tides, the stock market. Her life
seemed to be governed by them.

Like the one she was dealing with now.

She had given birth to two daughters, but found no birth-
ing contained the substance or the pain of finishing one of her
books. These postpartum blues lasted longer, well into the
publishing process. The only way she could get around it to
some degree was to be actively enthusiastic about the next
book before finishing the first. Still, the blues cycle ended in
its own time, when something came along to trigger the end of
one cycle and the beginning of a new one. That unpredictable
"something," the sense that a new and wonderful or just plain
interesting happening was hovering just around the corner.

Even here in intensive care, drugs dulling her senses,
tubes coming out of every orifice and the doctors telling her it
was all over for her, that sense of expectancy kept her fighting.
She had finished ghostwriting a book for a self-proclaimed
psychic just before this episode hit. While Dixie had a magic
touch as a masseuse, her claim to be the recipient of automatic
writings about the origins of Atlantis was tough to believe.
Fortunately, unlike the belief Jenny needed with her own

work, rewriting and translating Dixie's ramblings needed only skill and craft. An exchange of deep body massage twice a week for an equivalent number of hours of translation—which was how she preferred to rationalize it—seemed like a reasonable payment.

If nothing else, it was a clear change of pace, and certainly pleasant compared with the last ghostwriting she'd done—a Mormon Book of Miracles for a prominent and none-too-charming member of the faith. The book was loosely based on his journals. What miracles were missing she had provided. He had paid her well for her skills and her contractual promise of anonymity until death, and as a result thought he owned her. The book was a grand success, but she felt herself well-rid of a client who crossed the street when he saw her coming so that he could take full ownership of the narrative voice, continuity, and plain old grammar she had provided.

It was his book. As far as he was concerned, she did not exist.

Not so Dixie, who sat with her now holding her hand in the hospital room, watching her fade in and out of consciousness. Watching as she had yet another near-death experience.

She was surrounded by brilliant light, floating in warm, viscous fluid. Amniotic. Comforting. She could hear what sounded like the muted ram's horn tones of a shofar. And her mother's voice whispering, *You were born on Yom Kippur, Jenny. The Day of Atonement. A child of God, born to make a difference.*

"You can let go now if you wish." This voice came from somewhere inside her head. It was neither male nor female.

She waited, thinking she would see her life flash before her eyes like pictures in an old family vacation slide show. Instead, she saw a parade of her literary heroes: Fritha holding an injured snow goose in her arms; Anne of Green Gables; Pollyanna; Emma Bovary; Anna Karenina; Miss Brill in her ratty fur, watching other people's children play in the park. She struggled to see herself as a child. The pictures were hazy. Ephemeral. The product more of wishes than reality.

"Would the pain be gone?" she asked, using thought because words were too difficult to form.

"Yes."

"But I have things to do. Sunrises to see. Laughter to hear. Corners to turn."

The voice in her head was silent. Somewhere far in the distance she heard the sound of the Point Piños foghorn, like a familiar voice echoing from her childhood. She opened her eyes.

"Do you hear it?" she asked.

"Hear what?"

"The foghorn."

"There is no foghorn, Jenny," Dixie said. "They've shut down the lighthouse."

"Forever?" Jenny asked, though she had no idea why it mattered.

"Until the butterflies return. They say the lighthouse has chased them away."

Dixie released her hand, walked over to the window, and pulled aside the blind. It was not yet dark outside, but the Monterey fog had rolled in across the Peninsula as it did every day this time of year.

"There," Jenny said. "I heard it again."

"I hear nothing," Dixie said, "But I'm really glad you decided to come back." She reached into the oversized handmade bag she perpetually wore slung over one shoulder, pulled out a worn copy of Paul Gallico's *The Snow Goose*, and placed it on the table beside the hospital bed. "I knew you needed this," she said. "It's a first edition."

The small book, a short story really, was Jenny's favorite from her childhood. She was certain she had never mentioned that to Dixie. She smiled her thanks, wondered briefly how the woman knew so much that seemed unknowable, and fell into a state that was part-dream, part-memory...

Green Point, South Africa. Jenny is thirteen going on thirty-three. She sits alone at an open window, listening to the comforting sound of the Mouille Point foghorn and wondering when it will begin.

"We have to air the place," her mother says, suddenly

cheerful after weeks of depression and daily suicide threats. "I'm going down to put the car in the garage. Be a good girl—open up the windows and doors and get ready for bed."

Jenny wonders where her mother will go this time. She does this a lot. Threatens suicide and disappears, especially after a social event like today's Rosh Hashanah celebration. The girl has done her best to be good. To help. To ignore the dread that is settling in, and pretend she is enjoying the cakes and the company. The *Yiddishkeit*, her grandmother calls it.

Her mother hadn't noticed Jenny's efforts. She never did.

Jenny knows the signs. So does Oma, her grandmother, who is spending the night. She is in the bedroom, listening to the eleven o'clock news on the radio. She calls it the wireless. It is one of her passions. She is the storyteller of the family, the rock who has been there for Jenny between, and often during, her mother's love affairs and four marriages—or is it five? Jenny has lost count.

She cleans up the party debris, puts on her sleep shirt—a coarsely woven hand-me-down from her grandmother's haberdashery—and waits, her shoebox of silkworms on her lap. She had covered the box and the lid with silver foil collected from chocolates. It had taken her a year to find enough. She opens the lid and stares at the first of the cocoons. They are gold and platinum and icy white. Here and there she can see the tiniest hint of aquamarine. One day she will find a loose thread, roll the silk into a ball, and weave herself a silken nightgown that looks like butterfly wings. When she wears it she will be able to lift her arms to the wind and wheel out to sea. Like the Snow Goose.

One day.

The evening fog rolls in, invading the apartment. The clock on the wall ticks on in regular beats, like a metronome playing tympanic counterpoint to the sonorous boom of the foghorn. When three hours have passed, she begins the ritual search: check the garage to make sure her mother hasn't gassed herself; walk through the neighborhood looking for accidents; run down to the cliff, the foghorn growing ever louder. Stand at the edge and look down, not wanting to see a body sprawled at the bottom, yet wishing guiltily that it would be over. If there is no body, Jenny tells herself, she will gather mulberry leaves from the tree near the lighthouse and take them home to her silkworms. That, too, is part of the ritual.

There is no body. Jenny plucks leaves from the tree. Her mother is fine, she tells herself, as she has so many times before. Cold and tired, she places the leaves beside her and huddles against the still sun-warmed wall of the lighthouse. Her mother will know where to find her, she thinks, and falls asleep to the foghorn's lullaby.

"Jenny. I was so worried."

For a moment, in the darkness, Jenny thinks it is her mother. Her anguish dissipated somewhere, somehow. Suddenly, temporarily, more concerned for her daughter than for herself. But the soft smell of white lilac dusting powder mixed with Nivea cream tells her it is her grandmother.

"Thanks God I found you," her grandmother says, losing the edge of her English as she always does in times of stress. Jenny presses herself into the strong stone of the lighthouse wall. Her grandmother stretches out her hand. "Come. Let's go together to home."

"Tell me the story first. You know the one."

Jenny's grandmother sits down on the grass next to her granddaughter. "A bedtime story you want. Some bed you have here." Her movements are awkward. She is getting old.

"Tell me," Jenny insists.

"It was wartime," Oma begins. "Every night in Cape Town there was a blackout. You were a few months old, lying in your crib. Your Daddy was in North Africa. Your mother was in the kitchen—"

"No," Jenny says. "It was you, Oma. Tell it truly."

Her grandmother sighs. "*So soll es sein,*" she says. *So be it.* "Your mother was on night duty at the Castle."

Right, Jenny thinks. *Knight* duty, more likely.

"Her friend, the broadcaster, was on the radio. Morkel van Tonder his name was. A nice man. Handsome, too. I could tell by his voice. I always listened to him. I remember he was talking about Dunkirk, about how men were dying and how every brave man with a boat was out there trying to rescue the living and the wounded from the beach. He told about a crippled man, a lighthouse keeper named Philip Rhayader, who sailed there from the mouth of the Aelder in a small fishing boat with a snow goose perched on the rail. He was interviewing a Commander Keith Brill-Oudener about how he had seen this man rescuing seven troops at a time when..."

She stops speaking. Jenny puts her head on her grandmother's shoulder. "How do you remember all of the names?" she asks.

"I remember everything. I remember it was foggy outside. Usually, the sound of the foghorn put you to sleep, like a lullaby, but they had turned it off, the lighthouse, because of the blackout. You missed the sound and couldn't sleep. Every now and again I heard you whimpering. Once, you cried out loudly. I came to the open door and looked at your crib. I couldn't see much in the darkness, but you seemed to be all right. I was about to turn away when—"

"The foghorn started," Jenny says, taking over the telling. "The strobe from the lighthouse came into the window and lit up the wall behind my crib."

Jenny's grandmother strokes her hair. "As the light hit the wall, I saw a huge spider, such an ugly thing it was, crawling toward you. I screamed, grabbed you out of the crib, and ran next door. The neighbor, a good man from Riga, Latvia, scooped the spider into a jar. The next day he had it tested. It was poisonous. Deadly, they said. When he let me know, I thanked him again. With the few eggs we had, I baked him a cake. I told him how grateful I was that they had turned the lighthouse back on. If it hadn't been for that strobe, I'd never have seen the spider. He said, 'What strobe?' I said, 'From the lighthouse, of course.' He stared at me as if I am *meshugah*. I can still see that look on his face as he said, 'There is a blackout, Frau Abraham.'"

She puts out her hand and touches the wall behind Jenny. "This lighthouse, it saved your life, Jenny. One day you will be required to repay the debt."

Secretly Jenny calls the lighthouse her Light in Shining Armor. She stands up and blows it a kiss.

When they get home, her mother is in bed, asleep. Oma

watches as Jenny puts her ear to her mother's chest, listening to make sure there is a heartbeat.

"She has stolen from you your childhood," her grandmother says.

Jenny nods. Loving her mother and hating her at the same time, she says, "I really am glad she decided to come back."

Jenny did not see Dixie again. She wanted to search for her, to thank her again for being there, and for the gift. Once in a while she searched through *Books in Print* to see if the book about Atlantis had been published, but she didn't look for Dixie, sure that she would make herself visible if she wanted to be found. As always after a hospital stay, everything associated with her health crisis, including Dixie and the ghost-written manuscript, became as much part-dream, part-memory as her near-death experience.

Except for the copy of *The Snow Goose*.

That was real.

She carried it in her handbag the way other people carried around a daily planner. Read, reread, coffee-stained—it contained, for Jenny, the meaning of life. She thought of writing to thank its author and tell him of the gossamer nightgown she had never woven for herself. She didn't, too afraid that he would not understand. That he would think it a childish thing to say.

Jenny's publisher wanted her to write a memoir. She agreed, put the advance in the bank, then found that she was not strong enough yet for full immersion in writing about a childhood that she had mostly allowed to escape her consciousness. It was too emotionally demanding a project. Instead, she got herself a few assignments with *Monterey Life*. The pay wasn't much, but it was enough to cover the rent for the rest of the year on the small house she had leased in Pacific Grove without having to tap into the advance, something she never liked to do until she was actively involved in the project.

This arrangement gave Jenny plenty of time to think. So much that she found herself all too often in heavy sweater and windbreaker, walking the beach in Asilomar, dwelling on some part of her childhood. While her route automatically took her to the lighthouse and back again, her thoughts traveled to her relationship with her mother, a topic that generally left her feeling insecure and guilty for fully loving her best only when the two of them were apart.

She reminded herself that she was an independent adult, a writer with a not inconsiderable body of work, but the guilt stuck with her like a leech on the leg of a dog. Early one morning, hoping to ease her guilt, she called Berlin and spoke to her mother on the phone. Her mother had lived there since '61. Ever a magnet for drama, she had become a repatriated Berliner the day before the Wall went up, and found herself caught on the wrong side. By the time Jenny-the-rescuer had reached Berlin, her mother was free again. Jenny arrived from Tempelhof Airport to find her, feisty as ever, in the process of changing the locks on her Kantstrasse apartment to keep out her latest lover. Now eighty-one and more than ever filled with piss-and-vinegar, she said, "Give me a list of the people you hate, and I'll take care of them. What are they going to do to me? Sentence me to death?"

She laughed, the tinkling giggle of a young woman, and Jenny laid their past to rest.

That day, the day Jenny forgave her mother, she came across the last letter she'd received from her beloved grandmother.

> Mine darling Jenny,
> I have had a good life but Dayenu. It is enough. I
> have completed the circles of my life. Wherever I am,
> I will love you and watch over you. Do not ever forget to repay your debts and always tell stories. I
> hope some day you find the child you lost.
>   Your Oma

Jenny had begged her doctors to let her fly to South Africa. "I need to do this," she'd said. "I have to say goodbye. I must close my circles there."

They were adamant. She could not so much as contemplate flying, they'd told her. Her immune system was too depleted to withstand the onslaught of recycled germs in the plane; and if that didn't get her, the altitude would.

Sitting in the gingham-and-lace living room of the cottage in Pacific Grove with the letter in her hand, Jenny swore she could smell lilac and Nivea cream...and love. Haunted by her grandmother's words, she remembered the foghorn that had called out to her when she was in intensive care here, on the peninsula. She went to the Pacific Grove Natural History Museum and read everything she could find about the Point Piños Lighthouse.

What she found was enough for a really great article, but none of it held any clues as to why there should be any connection between it and her, unless she counted the fact that Robert Louis Stevenson—another of her other favorite writers—visited the lighthouse and wrote of "...the light keeper playing the piano, making models and bows and arrows, studying dawn and sunrise in amateur oil painting."

For the rest, there was nothing mysterious, nothing to indicate a foghorn that could blow of its own volition. The Cape Cod–style bungalow was built in 1855. The first keeper, an Englishman named Charles Layton, was killed while serving in a sheriff's posse that was trying to find a famous outlaw. His wife, Charlotte, and their four young children were left destitute. Fortunately, she was paid a thousand dollars a year to take over Charles's job. Nothing strange there, or in the fact that, in 1883, one Emily Fish—who loved entertaining and was known as the "Socialite Keeper"—became the next woman keeper of Point Piños.

She took notes and returned the books and articles to the historian.

"Did you find what you needed?"

"Not really. Maybe there's something I'm missing."

That was when she remembered what Dixie had said about the foghorn. "*Until the butterflies return. They say the lighthouse has chased them away.*"

On a whim, she took out a new stack, this time about the monarch butterflies, which had, in the past, come to Point Piños en masse each fall.

"They won't be coming this year," the historian said, seeing Jenny's reading choices. "Too much spraying has killed the milkweed. They live on it, you know. Maybe they won't ever come back. If the tourists stop coming, we'll lose our funding for the lighthouse. It will become expendable like the rest of us oldies."

Suddenly Jenny understood. The foghorns of her life had led her to this place so that she would call the monarchs back to Point Piños. Now what she needed to know, she thought wryly, was how she was supposed to accomplish this feat.

The next morning, before the fog had quite lifted, she walked along Sunset Drive until she reached Asilomar Avenue and the shelter of Point Piños lighthouse. There, hoping to find the inspiration she needed, she reread *The Snow Goose*. When she was done, she knocked at the door of the keeper's residence. No one answered. She peered through a few small windows, hoisting herself up to them with some difficulty.

The place seemed to be deserted.

She stared at the building and the grounds around it.

The structure of the building itself was very different from the one in Green Point, but the setting bore an eerie resemblance to Mouille Point and the Cape at the tip of Africa. The weather patterns were almost identical, as were the flora and fauna—only instead of mulberry trees, there were pines; instead of silkworms there was the annual anticipation of the monarchs' stop on their short life-cycle. If she could bring them back, maybe some of her own cycles, begun ten thousand miles away, could also be closed at last.

But how?

Jenny didn't have a clue. What she did have was conviction. She felt a sense that—like the name of an old tune or of an actor once familiar—the solution would come to her as soon as she stopped looking.

That was Labor Day.

By late September, as Rosh Hashanah and Yom Kippur approached, she had developed an observable pattern. She was comfortable with it, content to sit out of the breeze, against the wall of the lighthouse, with her books and her portable computer. By now, she had read everything she could about the monarch butterfly.

The monarchs, Jenny had learned, though huge by butter-fly standards, each weigh only half a gram. They habitually traveled thousands of miles, all the way from Canada, where they spent the summer, to Mexico, where they commonly wintered.

Or here, where they gathered each September and October.

As the month drew to a close, Jenny's hopes dwindled. She had thought that by some magic the monarchs would sense her presence. That one morning she would be greeted by the sight of Monterey pines blanketed in orange and black.

Every day, she was disappointed.

Then came the morning of Rosh Hashanah. The day of the Jewish New Year.

Jenny is alone on the grass, half-asleep in the late-September sunlight.

"I can show you how to bring them here."

The voice is sweet and young, like Jenny's long ago.

In all of the weeks she has been coming to the lighthouse, no one has so much as smiled at Jenny. Now, a young girl, about thirteen she guesses, sits down on the grass next to her. She is quite beautiful. Her eyes are the color of rich, green olives, her face golden, her dress white as snow and made of the purest of silk ninon. Around her neck and ankles she wears fine bands of platinum. As she speaks, she moves her hands with the grace of flight.

"Most of them die on the way, you know," the girl says. "It's really their children who come back. But they won't come this year, the monarchs. Or next year. Not if we don't help them."

"And how exactly do we do that?" Jenny asks.

The girl leaves for a moment. She returns holding an over-sized shoebox covered with aluminum foil. There are holes poked in the lid. She hands the box to Jenny and says, "They need a lot of sunshine."

Like children, Jenny thinks, removing the lid. The scent of lilac assails her senses, bringing with it the presence of her Oma. She looks inside the box and finds a crowd of brilliantly colored, nectar-bearing blooms. She recognizes them as the milkweed she saw illustrated at the natural history museum. Here and there she can see small clusters of eggs. In one corner there is a caterpillar, in another three cocoons.

When she looks up, the girl is dancing away, arms raised as if she is readying herself for flight.

Jenny would have thought it all a dream, were it not for the shoebox. For the next twelve days, she carried it to Point Piños and followed the sun. She watered the flowers and protected the box and its contents. By the eve of Yom Kippur, nothing had changed. Nor had she seen the girl again.

Tired and disappointed, Jenny packed up early. She could smell the fog coming in, for the first time since Labor Day. She got home well before sundown, closed the shoebox, and placed it on the step at her front door. Inside, she stared out the window toward Point Piños, thinking that soon, in the synagogue, the rabbi and cantor and congregation would be singing *Kol Nidre*. The prayer for the dead. For her grandmother. She wondered if it was permitted to pray for the dying heart of a lighthouse.

Crying softly, she opened her front door. She picked up the shoebox, flung her coat around her shoulders, and walked through the fog toward Point Piños. Though she had walked those streets many times, the fog confused her. Then a small ray of setting sun broke through the clouds, and she heard it— the deep, mournful sound of the foghorn blending with the sharper tones of the shofar. "Jenny," they sang. "*Jenny.*"

She followed the sound to Point Piños. Standing at the top of the cliff, in the glow of the sun's last ray, she opened the shoebox. Atop the milkweed lay one quivering black and orange butterfly.

The ninon girl floated out of the fog. "Put it on the tree, and the others will come," she said.

Jenny did the girl's bidding. "For you, Oma," she said, faintly. Through the fog she heard the shofar. And the lighthouse, thanking her. She turned to thank the girl but could not find her.

Eyes closed, she looked inward—and saw the child—and knew she had been given the strength to begin her memoir.

YVONNE NAVARRO

A Beacon
Shall I Shine

"The light's on again. I can see it from here."

Did Gary even look up from his evening newspaper? Renee couldn't tell, but she didn't dare take her gaze from that faraway twinkle of light. When he didn't answer, she inhaled slowly, willing herself to stay calm. Surely he couldn't be *that* unfeeling—perhaps he hadn't heard her. He was an intense man, and intense people tended to lose themselves in things, focus all their concentration on the task at hand. Reading the newspaper, for instance.

Or blocking out the truth.

Renee repeated herself, louder this time. "I said the light's on ag—"

"I heard you." Her husband's voice was sharp. "And the time before that. Last night, wasn't it?"

Surprised, Renee's eyes widened and she was glad she was still facing the window. She didn't want Gary to know how amazed she was that there was still any fight left in him. She could see his reflection in the glass, bisected by the thin wood separating the panes. For once he had put down his paper, but that was small comfort when she realized he did so only because tonight he was spoiling for a fight. The image in the glass, dimmed by the darkness outside, erased the lines in his face and made him look younger, gave an illusion of warmth to the cold box that had once been their serene New England–style home.

"Don't you think we should check on it?" she asked. Her fingers squeezed the aged windowsill, cold and splinters sinking into her flesh and helping her to stay grounded.

His voice was even harsher. "Like we did the last time, and the time before that?"

Now who was repeating himself? "But—"

"*No.*"

Renee turned and looked at him, leaving behind the gentle deception of the windowpane's reflection. "Then I'll go alone."

"You do that." Her husband stood suddenly, spilling the newspaper onto the floor, then ignoring the untidy pile. "What's the difference? You've acted like you've been alone ever since . . . ever since . . ." Instead of finishing, he spun and stalked out of the room. A few seconds later she heard him in the kitchen, knew what he was doing by the sound of the cabinet door slamming, the whoosh of the freezer as it opened and closed, the clink of ice cubes. Tonight was Friday—did that mean vodka? He had never left her to deal with these questions by herself before, never *abandoned* her. Why did he sound so bitter tonight? Why—

Of course.

Renee spun and stared out the window again, her eyes straining to penetrate the night. There, just over the tree line— yes, the glow from the top of the lighthouse was still there. It shouldn't be—for God's sake, she wasn't crazy. With the closing of the seldom-used shipping lane at the mouth of their small bay almost five years ago, the Coast Guard had discontinued maintenance of the old lighthouse. The lamp itself had been broken out by vandals, the reflectors were rusted and bent, the whole thing was beyond repair—pieces missing and the housing smashed for nearly a year now. And yet—

There it was.

The light.

Shining.

Beckoning.

Why do you stay with him? Unbidden, her sister's voice replayed through her mind, the whispered words insistent and well-meaning. *You waste your life for security, when love is the only thing a woman really needs to keep her warm. Love—the real thing— would make your heart and soul fly, Renee.*

Such sweet intentions, but where had the love Larissa sought taken her? No one knew for certain, but Renee was convinced that it was love gone bad that had sent Larissa to the rocks on the cliffs below the lighthouse—falling, not flying. Whatever love had done for her sister, the wintry air currents of Lake Erie had refused to carry her slight weight that blustery late evening—

One year ago tonight.

At least the foghorn had stopped, the diaphone mechanism pulled out by the Coast Guard and relocated a month after Larissa's death. No doubt it now sent its lonely, drawn-out moan from some other coastline location. Thank God—Gary had always hated it, and although she and Larissa had loved it for years, Renee didn't think she could have withstood that ghostly sound night after night now that Larissa was dead.

She went to the hall closet and pulled out her coat, scarf, and hat, made sure her heaviest gloves were in the pockets. How odd that Gary might remember that dark anniversary, odder still that if he had, he'd neglected to mention it to her. Or perhaps it wasn't strange at all—obviously, he hadn't wanted to remind her. But how could she not remember the night her twin had plunged to her death?

Love is like a beacon, Renee. You see it shining through everything that you are, everything you can ever be. It's like you feel the light inside you, spinning around and around as it tries to get out and show the world how you feel. It's a radiance that reveals the truth to everyone else in your life—there's nothing and no one who can hide from it.

That was Larissa, ever the romantic, the unpublished young romance novelist living—no, *dying*—the latest of her own unfinished novels.

Bundled into her winter garb, Renee stepped outside and quietly closed the front door behind her. The late November wind slapped snow against her cheekbones and bit into the skin of her face, but the cold on the outside was nothing compared to the arctic emptiness she felt inside. Half of her had been shattered on the snow-dusted boulders below the lighthouse one year ago tonight, half of her was just ... *gone*. Gary, the sole child of doting parents, could never understand the bond that had existed between Renee and Larissa. He was too far removed from how they had grown up with little beyond their love for each other when their existence had become hell at age nine in a state-run orphanage, after their parents were killed in a car accident. Alike in so many ways, sharing movements and thoughts, Renee and Larissa were still so different in others.

You waste your life for security...

Renee climbed into her small Toyota and started it, then backed out of the driveway without bothering to wait for the engine to warm. The cold of the vinyl seat bled into the backs of her thighs despite her wool slacks and the heavy coat. It reminded her of many things, none of them pleasant ... like the dozens of times she had felt the cushions of a vinyl couch against her unwilling flesh, the dirty way it smelled when her face was pressed against it to keep her from screaming. After what she and Larissa had endured, especially when they'd hit their mid-teen years and begun to blossom, was it so wrong to want a little security and safety in your life, even if you had to trade a piece of yourself to get it?

She scowled as she steered the car along the road that led to the lighthouse. The darkness was cut here and there by the building snow and the holiday lights of the houses along the way—small, blinking pools of festive lights leaking onto the slick two-lane blacktop like bait, promises of brightness, love, and laughter that would never be. What, Renee wondered, would it be like to have a life like that, filled with the things her sister had always dreamed about? She wouldn't know. A sworn atheist, Gary didn't believe in things such as Christmas trees and holiday gifts; her husband worked his five days a week, fifty weeks a year, and the only time he stayed home on a so-called holiday was if the building that housed his law office was literally closed. He worked out twice a week, paid his taxes, and followed politics, but he didn't believe in giving to charity, having children, or mouthing useless sentiments like *I love you.*

But that was all right with Renee. Gary gave her all the things the terrified, abused girl inside her had yearned for—a warm house with plenty of food, stability, the knowledge that when she went to bed at night the occasional sex she endured would be at a minimum pain-free, at a maximum passionless, and that suited her just fine. And if the breath of the man who shared her sheets was often tinged with alcohol ... well, that was a small thing indeed to weather.

It's like you feel the light inside *you...It's a radiance that reveals the truth...*

She'd never felt any such thing. But she'd damned sure felt its *loss,* the chunk of herself and her soul that had been ripped away with Larissa's death.

"As near as we can figure, ma'am, she jumped, or maybe she slipped. There's no evidence that anyone else was up there with her. We'll call it death by misadventure, and we'll be keeping our options open. You give us a call if you hear anything."

Jumped? Slipped? "I don't believe that," Renee whispered. Her breath fogged in front of her; she had forgotten to turn on the heater. "I *won't.*" Since Larissa's death, Renee had called Sheriff Rylan's office at least a half dozen times and reported the light; each time she'd felt more and more like they thought she was crying wolf. When Rylan had not so gently pointed out that she was the only person who ever saw the glow, she'd finally stopped.

And then the turnoff to the lighthouse was there, the faded sign barely a smudge along the unlit side of the road and the five-mile trip past in a slice of time so thin it might have been a heartbeat. Renee slowed and steered the car carefully into the narrow drive, feeling the snow-packed ruts beneath the tires and praying she wouldn't get stuck. Another mile in the darkness and there was the lighthouse, sprouting from the ground like a gray monolith, pitted stone blackened on one side by the weather, mottled green on the other by the damp lake moss over the last two centuries. She pulled off to the side and got out, surrendering to the icy, moisture-filled air that swirled around her. She knew Gary was right, that it couldn't be so, but when she craned her neck and looked up—

There, far above, the beacon broke through the darkness and swept the turbulent lake water to the north beyond their small bay. She'd once read in the local newspaper that on a clear night, the beam could be seen for twenty-two miles, but that bad weather could cut that to barely half a mile. Tonight, despite the blowing snow and all logic, the light had cut through the darkness and made it to her home six miles away.

Like the beam at the top, the lock on the door at the tower's base had succumbed to rust and vandals, leaving the entrance closed but not locked, swinging slightly askew on bent and decaying hinges. The smell that washed over Renee when she pushed through was heavy with dead fish and age, and something else that was familiar and bittersweet ... Jean Naté, Larissa's favorite scent.

For a moment, Renee simply stood there and didn't question the whys and hows, just drank in the scent and let it carry her back to the too-seldom happier times that she and her sister had shared. Then she oriented herself in the near darkness and found the staircase, sliding her gloved hand along the rail as she began the long climb.

How many times had she done this over the past year? Ten? Twenty? Whatever the number, she knew the upward route by heart, even knew the exact number of stairs—two hundred forty-eight—that would take her to the top where she could step outside in the wind and water-spray and study the spot from which Larissa had plunged to her death. The feel of the stairs beneath her shoes was solid and comforting, markers of her progress: stair seventy-two was crumbling a bit on the left; in the daylight, you could see the quarter-inch crack that ran all the way to the back of the hundred and forty-fourth riser, the halfway point. Two-thirds of the way she was, as expected, breathless but not defeated—never that—and straining to make the top. By the time she did, her heart was pounding, half in exertion, half in anticipation.

Had Larissa felt that same way a year ago?

Up here the wind alternated in its moods. One moment it could be calm, almost caressing, its touch like the hands of a lover grown cold but still gentle and considerate; an instant later, it might turn hard and angry, giving pain with every windswept strike and bringing back recollections of winter nights in the orphanage, a thousand things best left unremembered. Renee ignored the old thoughts and stepped onto the upper walkway, fingers gripping the railing against the gusts that wanted to pry loose her determined hold. Her coat and hair were soaked in only seconds, longer than it took for her to realize that it was dark up here. Where was the welcoming beacon she'd seen only a short while ago?

Disappointment razored through Renee and she ground her teeth and stared at the water. This was no different from all the other times, running to the lighthouse in the middle of the night in search of... what? Larissa's ghost, perhaps? Some unseen essence that would tell her the truth about what had happened that storm-soaked night the police suggested her twin had ended her own life.

Spread out for as far as she could discern, the lake rippled in the winter wind like a strangely beckoning sea of oil. The air twining around her suddenly calmed, and Renee pulled her gaze from the lake's surface back to the shoreline, where the water rushed to meet the boulders at the base of the lighthouse. Every wave that pounded apart reminded her of the way her heart had felt in the forever time since her sister had died.

She turned to make her way back to the staircase door, then started when she saw headlights winding their way up the lighthouse drive. From up here they looked like pinpricks of yellow in the night, a useless attempt to break the hold the darkness had on everything. Who could it be—who would be crazy enough to come up here on a night like this?

The question made Renee laugh. She had, of course, so why not someone else? Perhaps it was her husband, some misplaced smidgen of concern muddling up through the liquor. Or teenagers—it wasn't the most pleasant of places to make out, but with a couple of heavyweight sleeping bags and a camping stove, Renee supposed a couple might do all right. Or—and this one made her laugh more bitterly—maybe it was the killer, come to celebrate the anniversary of the dreadful crime.

Frowning, Renee stood at the railing and watched the car crawl the rest of the way up the drive, following the slow progress of its headlights. Closer now, the blowing snow made the car's lights soft and golden, but did they bring with them good ... or bad? The answer would come within minutes, but Renee felt no fear; tonight, of all nights, she would learn once and for all the truth behind this, even if it meant facing whoever had taken that thing that was most precious to her. The car pulled up next to hers, then the driver cut the lights and the darkness reasserted itself, ensuring that she couldn't see well enough to recognize the model, easily swallowing the short-lived glow of the auto's interior light.

The person moved from the car toward the lighthouse's entrance, a blacker shadow than the rest that occasionally slid into a silhouette against the rock-strewn snow. Renee waited, one hand on the rusty railing, watching and forgetting about the cold and the snow and the wind, the elements fading in the face of her curiosity and need for closure. In fact, she felt almost warm, suffused by peace and the certainty that tonight, at last, the blank spot inside her would be filled.

The wind stopped, shrouding her with a silence that was completely out of place. After a long while, Renee heard footsteps, then labored breathing as the unknown person made it up the last of the climb and stepped to the galley door. For a moment she couldn't see anything, couldn't hear anything in the quiet, couldn't *breathe*. Then disappointment hit her again—it was only Gary, standing a few feet away, sweaty and angry and, no doubt, waiting for her to explain herself. So much of their marriage had been like that, him always wanting an explanation of her behavior—why did she do the things she did, why did she and Larissa spend so much time together, why did she love Larissa so much?

Staring at him, at the scowl on his face and the way his gloveless fingers opened and closed in a useless effort to generate warmth, the reasoning behind their disagreements suddenly sank in. Incredible as it sounded, it was *jealousy*—Gary's envy of the love Renee had carried for her twin and could never duplicate for him. The sorry truth of the matter was that she *didn't* love him. She never had. But she *had* chosen him, and she would treat him as right as she could, forever. What love she might have felt toward a man, any man, had been beaten and raped out of her as a young teenager; what she had left of true affection had been and would always remain reserved only for that other half of her own heart, soul, and flesh—Larissa.

She thought back over the months since her twin's death, over the years of her marriage before that. His jealousy had been an unspoken, unacknowledged thing—they'd never known exactly what it was, and so had never outright fought about it. Besides, a good battle required two, and Renee would only duck and slip, ward off his verbal attacks and icy treatment with a blandness and unfailing tolerance that she only now realized had done nothing but infuriate him more.

"What are you doing up here?" Gary finally demanded. He sounded angrier than she had ever heard him. "Why do you keep coming *back?*"

"Because I want to know why she died." The answer slipped from Renee's mouth before she realized the words were in her head. "And I won't stop, *ever*, until I find out."

Gary's face crumpled, and for the first time in their marriage Renee thought she was going to see him cry. "But it isn't supposed to be like that," he said pleadingly. He stretched his hand toward her. "When people—family members—pass away, you're supposed to move on, to turn to the ones left behind for support."

Renee stared at him, then her mouth twisted, and the laughter that spilled out sounded as though it came from a stranger. Perhaps it was the wind, picking up again and swirling around her, yet still not cold—something in it made her feel wild, free—giving her for the first time the ability to speak the truth. After all these years, what could he, what *would* he, do to her anyway? What had he *ever* done?

"Support? From whom—you?" Her hair lifted on the air and fanned across her face and she shook her head to clear her eyes. "There is no support in your world, Gary. There's no *me* in it. There's only you and your work, and your nightly round of drinks. Support comes from love, and if you have any of that, it's focused only on having the things in your life be just perfect, exactly the way you want them. Your house, your office, your *wife*. You don't 'support' me, and you certainly don't *love* me. I'm just a neat little robot who helps your little slice of existence function the way you and the rest of society thinks the average American family ought to."

Gary's face went shock-white. "I can't believe you'd talk to me like this," he said incredulously. "Like I'm some sort of flunky, like I don't have any feelings. I've given you *everything*—"

Renee shook her head, and the movement was enough to cut off whatever else he was struggling to say. "No, you haven't." Her voice was gentle, but still easily heard. "You've *starved* me, Gary." She thumped the center of her chest with one gloved hand and the hollow sound seemed to hang between them for a long, strange moment. "In here."

Her husband's expression was grim. "What are you saying, Renee? That you don't want me anymore? That you don't want our life?" His lips bent into an ugly sneer. "You can't just walk out on me, you know. You have nothing else—no place to go, no money, no family. Hell, if it wasn't for me, you'd be nothing right now—probably a waitress flipping hash in some cheap diner." Gary's eyes were pools of scorn. "You were never much to begin with—*I* made you everything you are now."

His cruelty should have made her angry, but all Renee could do was look at him with pity. "So I'm...a possession of yours. That's been it all along, hasn't it? Except you could never quite get it all, could you? There was always a part of me that you couldn't claim."

"The part you gave to Larissa," Gary said. Renee nearly took a step back at the venom in his tone. "The best part, I think."

"You were—you still are—jealous." She squeezed her

eyes shut briefly. "Even now that she's gone, you can't accept how close we were. You never could. You just didn't say so."

"I thought it would die with her."

Renee's eyes flew open and she gasped when she saw her husband standing right in front of her. Somehow he had crossed the ten feet between the door to the gallery and her position at the railing without making a sound. He stepped closer yet, and she felt the rust-covered metal shake beneath her gloves as he crowded her against it.

"I knew she was coming up here that evening," Gary said. His alcohol-scented breath misted Renee's face and he reached to either side of her, effectively pinning her in place. "The night before, while you were in the shower, I read the manuscript she gave you, right up to the end of what she'd written." He shook his head ruefully. "Another one of her ridiculous romantic fantasies. She was always into the personal research thing. I knew she'd come up here."

"Wait a minute." Renee frowned. "I don't—"

"I only wanted to ask her to leave," Gary said. He sounded sad, absurdly apologetic and desperate for her to understand. "See, she was... *stopping* you from being my wife, from being what you were supposed to be. Her constant talk about finding true love, and forever, and those stupid books she was always working on—I knew it would eat at you, make you think there should be more. I was already giving you everything I could, but instead of giving me everything in return, you gave the best part of yourself to *her*."

Something horrible and cold, far more frigid than the wintry air surrounding her, slid into Renee's mind and her eyes widened. "Wait a minute," she said. "Gary, where *were* you that evening? You said you were at work, you were *always* at work—"

Her husband looked off to the side, his gaze skimming the far-off swells of the lake. "She was standing almost exactly where you are now," he said dreamily. "I was just trying to...talk to her. That's the only reason I came up here, to make her understand how she was messing up everything between us." He pulled his gaze away from the water and shook his head. "It just got all out of control or something. One second we were arguing and the next..." His voice trailed away and he couldn't look at her.

For a long moment the world and the universe just stopped. Her brain put all the pieces together—the closeness she'd had with Larissa, and her sister's passion for life; the way Gary had always found that same exuberance overwhelming. Her husband's sly jealousy of anything that could have made Renee aware of an existence beyond their home and the simplified life he provided for her.

"You pushed her."

The accusation hung between them, irretrievable words that now spoken would change everything—what they had been, what they were, and most certainly what they would become.

"She fell," Gary said quickly. Too quickly, a statement made on the defensive, a shallow, automatic denial of guilt. "It was an accident."

Rage poured through Renee, as icy and black as the waters of Lake Erie pounding against the rocky shore below. "You bastard," she hissed. "An accident? *You killed my sister!*"

Gary reached for her. "Renee—"

She swiped at his outstretched fingers. "Don't touch me—don't you *ever* put your hands on me again!"

Gary gaped at her, caught completely by surprise. "Wait," he finally managed. "You don't mean that. What—"

"I don't *mean* it? What did you expect—that I would say 'Oh, that's okay, I know you didn't mean it'?" She glared at him. "Not a chance—I'll see you rot in jail for the rest of your life, you—murderer!"

The wooden planks of the circular gallery were slick with snow and ice, but Gary again moved quickly enough to surprise her. His cold fingers dug brutally into her shoulders as he lurched forward and yanked her against his chest. "Don't be absurd, Renee." His voice was calm, as if they were having nothing more serious than a dinner conversation. "I told you— it was an accident. Accidents should be...forgiven. You leave them in the past and move on, pick up your life where it was, and sometimes even improve it. Now that you know what really happened to Larissa, that's what we can finally do. Move on."

"I'm moving on, all right." Renee wrenched herself out of his grip. "As far away from *you* as I can get!"

Gary staggered backward as though she'd slapped him, then his expression turned ugly. "You'd *leave* me, Renee? After all I've done to keep you? I don't think so." He pitched forward and grabbed her again, pulling her away from the railing and back toward the door that led downstairs. "Just come on home. You'll come to your senses soon enough."

She fought against his hold, but Gary was stronger than he looked, his frame full of sinewy muscle. "Stop it!" she cried. "Let me go!"

"You don't mean that." He was panting with exertion but he still sounded absolutely certain. "You—"

The foghorn wail was sudden and huge, outright painful. It blasted through his words like a hammer of sound, and his hands flew up and clapped over his ears. Renee didn't stop to ponder how or why the horn could blow when the diaphone was gone; instead, she ran in the opposite direction, her footing treacherous along the snow-covered surface of the gallery. He would come after her for sure—he was already refocusing— but if she could get to the door before he did, she might be able to slam it shut and lock him out. Then she could go for the sheriff and tell him what Gary had admitted.

Her husband was about a quarter of the way behind her when Renee glanced over the railing and saw the lights of a car far below, someone else negotiating the rutted drive up to the lighthouse. The unexpected sight made her stumble and she almost went down, her heartbeat clanging as one of her feet slid between the walkway and the metal supports of the railing, kicking momentarily at nothing but snow-blown space. She clawed her way upright again, acutely aware of the safety net of time that she'd lost—Gary was only a few feet away now, and his expression was ugly and dark, the revealing portrait of a terrifying inner personality she'd never guessed existed. Somehow she picked up enough speed on the dangerous

gallery surface to hurl herself through the door; she twisted
and threw her weight against the aging wood, felt it slam shut
and the knob catch. Another precious second and her fingers,
half-numb with cold, closed around the old-fashioned bar on
the back side of the door, and Renee slid it across and into the
bracket on the doorframe.

"Renee, open this door! Please—just let me talk to you!"

The absent foghorn was still going, competing with Gary's
voice and making it sound like a faraway howl, the drowning
cry of a hopeless animal. Renee stared at the door as Gary
banged on it, seeing but not registering in the shadowed interior the way dust filtered down around the locking brackets
with each of her husband's blows. On the other side of the
wood, Gary's cries took on an enraged edge and the pounding
increased; finally, it crept into her stunned brain that the left
bracket was loosening, and it wouldn't be long before it gave
out entirely.

She spun and headed for the stairs, stumbling downward
in the near blackness, much too frenzied to count and keep
track of her progress. It was impossible but the foghorn was
still going, like a huge, living animal whose bellow over-
powered the life-sounds of everything around it. Gary's shouting faded in her ears as she made her awkward descent, then
her breath caught in her throat as another sound drifted up the
staircase from below. Belatedly, she recalled the headlights
she'd glimpsed. Who—

Without warning a beam of light spilled around the turn,
blinding her. She flailed and nearly fell, felt a hand close
around her upper arm and steady her, then let go.

"Mrs. Peters? What are you doing up here?" Sheriff Rylan's weather-beaten face stared at her from a few feet away,
washed by the spillover of a small flashlight.

"I—" Renee started to answer, then realized she couldn't
find the words. A crash from above blotted out her second
attempt—her husband had finally managed to batter his way
through the galley door.

"Who's up there?" the sheriff demanded. "What the hell's
going on?"

"I-It's G-Gary," Renee said. Her teeth were chattering and she didn't know if the cause was cold or fear. "H-He f-followed me up h-here, and we argued." She ground her teeth, determined to stop her jaw from shaking. "He told me he was up here with Larissa the night she died. I think he...pushed her over the railing."

The sheriff scowled and his gaze flicked past her as Gary's footsteps thumped overhead. They could hear him yelling as he headed toward them, but couldn't make out the words.

"Stay here," Rylan ordered as he edged around her. "Jesus, where the hell is this noise coming from?"

"I don't know," Renee answered. "I thought the mechanism was gone."

"It is," Rylan said grimly. "I just wish it would stop."

And then, as though something unseen had registered his request, the sound abruptly cut off. For a moment, Renee's ears rang, vibrating with the sudden absence of the overbearing noise that had filled them only a second before. Then—

"Renee—damn it, come back here!"

Gary's furious voice blasted through the silence, making them both jump. The sheriff's ruddy scowl deepened and he started to climb, staying light and quiet on his feet as her husband's heavy, frenzied footsteps thudded down to meet him. But before the lawman had gone up five risers—

A stream of hot brilliance filled the stairwell.

Sheriff Rylan back-stepped into Renee, and they both nearly fell as she lost her balance. The railing groaned but held under their combined weight when she clutched at it. Somewhere in the darkness above Gary cried out in surprise, then cursed angrily.

"What the fu—"

His profanity ended in a half-choke, half-scream, a sound that, even though she now feared her husband, made Renee shudder on his behalf.

"G-Gary?" she called timidly. "Gary?"

His footing regained, the policeman tried to shield his eyes and peer up the stairwell. It was like trying to look directly at double suns. "Mr. Peters, this is Sheriff Rylan," he shouted. "Why don't you come on down here and let's figure out what's going on."

No answer.

"Mr. Peters, please don't make this any more difficult than it already is," Rylan called. "Otherwise I'm going to have to come up after you, and that really isn't the way to handle this."

And still—no answer.

The sheriff's right hand slipped to the holster at his side, and a flick of his finger undid its strap. Renee gaped at him when he eased his .38 free of the leather. "Wait—is that really necessary, Sheriff? Gary doesn't have a gun, he's never—"

The sheriff's implacable gaze briefly fixed on her. "No offense, ma'am, but your husband's acting a lot different tonight than you or I ever expected. He might yet have a surprise or two waiting for us."

Rylan turned his back and began to climb, his broad form nearly blotted out by the brightness in front of him. Renee hesitated, then followed, shrugging aside his earlier instructions. Surely Gary would calm down when he saw the sheriff, and especially when he saw the gun. Surely they could bring this whole ugly thing—the death of Larissa included—to a close.

And just like that—

—the light went out.

"Shit," Rylan said.

Renee heard him fumbling for the flashlight he'd clipped back to his belt. "Mr. Peters?"

As before, no answer. In fact, there was no sound at all— no creak of the wooden stairs, no soft footfall—not so much as a sigh from the wind that usually pushed its way through a thousand cracks and drafty spots in the two-hundred-year-old lighthouse. Nothing.

The sheriff cursed again, then clicked on his flashlight. Its glow seemed weak and pathetic after the radiance that had surrounded them only seconds before. "First the foghorn, now the lantern," Rylan grumbled. "What the hell else is going to happen in this place?" Without waiting for an answer, Rylan hurried up the stairs and Renee followed, her heartbeat tripping in her temples, her breathing shortened by terror and the freezing air. Had Gary slipped on the stairs and injured himself? Or would the policeman find her husband waiting just around the next turn, some stray piece of wood or iron held high and guaranteed to buy him only a bullet?

And so they climbed—

Higher.

Higher still.

But no Gary.

Until they stood in front of the decimated door to the gallery. Up here sound had returned, and the lake wind wailed around them, lifting their hair and frosting their cheeks as the sheriff played his flashlight beam through the opening. He stepped outside cautiously, shoulders hunched and weapon held ready, but the dim glow of his light found nothing. Even the footprints of Renee's earlier meeting with her husband were gone, erased by the blowing snow and ice crystals. Rylan turned and inspected the lantern in the center, but what he found was no different than what had been there for months: broken glass and twisted remains of metal, too many pieces missing for anything but rust to come of the mechanism.

The sheriff swiftly walked the circumference of the small gallery. She cautiously followed him, casting frightened glances behind her, but they found nothing. Renee thought Gary might have faced them and ducked through the door when they were on the other side, but Rylan pointed to a thin buildup of clean, unbroken snow on the surface of the fallen door—evidence that no one had touched it since the two of them had come through searching for her husband.

"I'm sorry, Mrs. Peters," Rylan finally said. He walked to the railing and peered down, but it was impossible to confirm anything beyond the fact that all three cars—hers, Gary's, and the patrol car—were still parked at the base of the lighthouse. "He didn't get past us, so he must've gone over. There's no other explanation." For the first time since Renee had met up with him on the inside stairs, the policeman's expression softened a bit. "You might want to stay in the lighthouse until I can find the...uh, find him and get him covered up."

Get him covered up? For a second she didn't understand,

then Renee realized what he meant. Rylan thought Gary was dead, and if he'd gone over the railing, that was a given—her husband's body would be as shattered on the boulders below as Larissa's had been a year ago. She'd been told the damage was too great, so she'd never seen her sister's broken corpse. Now the man who had done that, her own husband, had shared Larissa's fate.

"I want to see him for myself," Renee heard herself say. For a maniacal moment, she almost smiled, but common sense stepped in and held her mouth in a grim line. The sheriff, with his no-nonsense mind and sense of justice, might be hard-pressed to understand a happy expression, given the circumstances.

"It'll be damned ugly," was all Rylan said, but at the bottom he gestured for her to follow him outside as he began a careful search of the jagged ground surrounding the base of the lighthouse.

But as they had on the gallery far above, Renee and Sheriff Rylan found...

Absolutely nothing.

They searched again, and again. Sheriff Rylan radioed for backup, and then he and his men combed the rocks and the shoreline. They continued their hunt through the night, and on into the cold light of the early morning.

Nothing.

Finally, Renee went home.

And she waited while the sheriff and his crew kept up their search throughout that day, and the day after that, and the day after that.

But her husband's body was never found. And the beacon from the lighthouse never shone again.

NINA KIRIKI HOFFMAN

Gone

She had a name from a madrigal, and I met her in my name-sake, the reeds.

We were both in our second year at college, and we'd both gone to feed stale bread to the ducks at the bird sanctuary when we should have been studying for midterms. I'd seen the back of her head in our History and Philosophy of Education in America class—she always sat near the front, and I liked to lurk in the back row. Her hair color was a bright yellow-orange I knew must come from a kit, but it appealed to me anyway, so I spent time studying her. I'd watched her profile, seen her laugh, knew her eyes were wide and sea-gray. I knew her last name was Hardesty; the professor called on her a lot, and she always answered questions well.

It wasn't until that Saturday on the edge of the bird sanctuary that I discovered her first name was Amaryllis. Other people called her Maryl, but I never did. Sometimes I called her Ama, sometimes Ryllis, and sometimes her full name. I never tired of finding new ways to talk to her. She had a one-sided smile that let me know she liked the joke. She used it even when I was serious, which was another thing I loved about her.

We discovered much common ground. We played music

and sang together. For a while we sang folk songs every Saturday night in a coffeehouse; I played guitar, and she played the fiddle. We moved in together a month after we met, and married a month after we moved in together.

She was crossing the street to come to me when the car hit her. We'd planned a special date to celebrate our tenth anniversary. We left our eight-year-old daughter Samantha with a babysitter, snuck out in separate cars, parked the cars and walked toward each other on opposite sides of the street. We pretended we were meeting by mistake, as though we'd just glimpsed each other across the street and had to rush together. We never reached each other.

A month after Amaryllis died, the high school where I taught music and Amaryllis had taught history let out for the summer. On the last day of term, my friend Nick Allen, who coached boys' sports, said, "Reed, you've been running on autopilot since your wife died. Snap out of it."

We were in the teachers' lounge. Someone had left the window open. The early summer air felt soft. I looked out toward the lawn. There were daisies in the manicured grass, the pink-edged ox-eye daisies that Amaryllis had made into chains for Samantha to wear like haloes when she was four.

Nick shook my shoulder. "Stop it."

I stared at him.

He frowned. "Stop it, Reed. Stop it with the blank eyes. Say something."

I had been able to talk with music, enough to keep the students going till the end of the term, anyway. I could conduct. I could instruct. I could test. Normal conversation was still beyond me.

I dredged up some words. "It's not something I can turn off."

"You have to do something. Have you noticed how thin Sam looks lately?"

I blinked. I hadn't noticed Sam. What I had noticed about Sam was that she was being very good, very quiet, didn't ask for anything. She made it okay for me to ignore her. I made a sack lunch for her every morning and made sure she ate breakfast. We both came straight home from school, me an hour or so later than Sam. Before dinner we did homework, often in the kitchen together. Dinner—takeout, McDonald's, microwave things, nothing like the dinners Amaryllis had concocted—we ate together. After dinner, we watched TV. The upright piano against the wall, where we used to gather with Ama after dinner to make music, stood shut and silent. Sometimes Sam leaned against me on the couch and I put my arm around her.

She probably had a great big empty hole in her chest like the one I had. I hadn't even noticed.

"You should get away," Nick said. "Go somewhere you never went with Maryl."

"It's creepy," Sam said.

I squinted at the house. It sparkled in the bright June sunlight, the roof red, the walls white with light green trim. White lace curtains graced every window. Once the assistant lightkeepers' duplex for the Bodega Head Lighthouse on the Oregon coast, the house had been turned into a bed and breakfast by the Forest Service.

A white picket fence surrounded the stretch of velvet lawn, keeping nonpaying visitors away. Green plastic Adirondack chairs stood scattered across the front porch, perfect perches for looking out to sea.

Farther up the headland, through a gap in the trees, Bodega Head Lighthouse stood, a clean white pillar surmounted by the glass-sided chamber that held the light, capped with a red roof. Its beacon flashed even in daylight.

I glanced around. Sam and I stood, suitcases in hand, on a gravel drive in front of the fence. Our car was parked in a lot beyond some trees. Behind the house rose the heavily forested headland. The house was perched above a steep, wooded slope. On the beach below, waves marched in to shore, and tourists who had paid three dollars for day-use permits parked their cars and wandered the beach, or followed trails up to the lighthouse.

Amaryllis and I had never come here. We had explored

other Oregon coast spots together, but we'd never stopped at Bodega.

I glanced back at the house and frowned. "What's creepy about it?" I asked my daughter.

She wrinkled her nose, then sucked on her bottom lip. "It's just—" She stared up at the third-story windows. Her shoulders rose and fell.

I waited, but she didn't say anything else.

Should we give up on this expedition, go back to the car? Drive home in silence, the way we had driven here? Hole up in our respective rooms at home and think about what we missed most?

Sam looked so small and lost. She had shadows under her eyes, and her pale hair was lank; the gold had drained from it, leaving it the flat color of unpulled taffy.

"Let's look inside," I said. We had a reservation for Thursday through Monday for two of the three guest rooms, courtesy of my buddy Nick and his wife Joan, who had made plans eight months earlier to come here with their teenage daughter for the start of summer vacation. I had known Nick was right, that I needed to snap out of my grief somehow and take care of Sam, but I hadn't been able to think what to do next. Somewhere under the dead surface of my mind, I knew I owed Nick a lot. Maybe later I'd be able to figure out how to repay him. I couldn't focus on much at the moment.

Sam shrugged. We lifted the latch on the gate and walked past the signs on the fence that told the day-trippers to leave the residents alone. We crossed the porch and knocked on the right-hand glass-paned front door, the one with a stained-glass sign above it that said, "Manager."

After a couple of minutes a woman came to the door. She was plump, and might have looked pleasant if she'd smiled, but she frowned at us. "Yes?"

"We have a reservation?" I said. I couldn't even state it; I had to ask.

She frowned more deeply. "Are you the Allens? I thought there would be three of you."

"Nick Allen said we could take their place. He gave me his

confirmation number. I'm Reed Wilcox, and this is my daughter, Samantha."

Her face smoothed. As I had suspected, her smile was wide and friendly. "Oh. Sorry. I thought you were tourists. Sometimes they come up on the porch in spite of the signs. Hi. I'm Lucy Travis. My husband Ike and I manage the place." She held out her hand.

For a few seconds I stared at it. Her smile melted. Then I remembered, and shook her hand. "Sorry," I said. "Sam and I are both pretty tired."

"Ah." She stood back. "Come on in. I'll get you set up here, and then maybe you can rest."

We stumbled up the stairs after her, and she showed us into two spacious bedrooms furnished in Victorian style, side by side. One room had a view of the lighthouse, and the other looked out at the dark forest behind the house.

Sam stepped on the braided rag rug in the middle of the lighthouse-view room, then glanced back at me.

"Okay?" I asked.

She shrugged. Her shoulders sagged.

Someplace Amaryllis had never been. It was a start. "You take this room," I said.

She blinked, nodded, and set her suitcase on a chest of drawers. I went into the other room, set my suitcase down on the floor, and stood, staring at the dark spruce trees out the window.

"Mr. Wilcox?"

I shook my head, then turned to glance at Mrs. Travis. I had forgotten she was there.

"Bathroom you and your daughter are sharing is through this door," she said. "This other door goes to the third guest room, but it's not reserved this weekend, so it's locked. There's a public kitchen area downstairs where you can fix yourself instant cocoa or coffee or tea. There's one of those little fridges for your groceries.

"This house used to be two houses, mirror images of each other, so we have two of everything, except we took down the wall between the two dining rooms. You're welcome to use the dining set on this side of the house, and this side's front parlor. Ike and I have the other suite, up the other set of stairs, and we have our own kitchen. That's where we'll fix your breakfast, so you can come in there in the morning, but the rest of the time, it's off-limits. The doors to the private areas on the caretaker side of the house are shut; we prefer to keep it that way."

"Thank you."

She seemed taken aback. "Will you be all right?" she asked after a moment. "There's extra blankets and pillows on the shelf in the closet."

"We'll be fine."

"You're on your own for lunch and dinner, though you're welcome to eat at the dining table, like I say, providing you bring your own food. I'll fix you breakfast tomorrow. Hope you like eggs and pancakes."

"We'll be fine," I said again. "Thank you."

Her smile crumbled. She handed me two labeled keys, shook her head, and left, her footsteps heavy on the stairs.

I don't know how long I stood there. No thoughts entered my head.

Sam grabbed my hand, and I blinked. It seemed to me that the light had shifted on the trees outside. I glanced at my daughter.

"I'm hungry," she said.

I locked our rooms and we left, driving thirteen miles to town where we found a chowderhouse.

I watched Sam eat. One piece of cheese toast and half a bowl of chowder—not enough. My own bowl of chowder had disappeared, I assumed into me, though I couldn't remember eating it. "Come on, honey. Eat some more."

Sam frowned at me and pushed her bowl away.

"Something wrong with it?" I asked.

"I've had enough."

I couldn't remember what Amaryllis had done to get Sam to eat. Was it ever a problem before? Sam had always been skinny, but now she looked gaunt. "Want some dessert?"

"I'm not hungry anymore."

I wasn't sure what to do. I couldn't force-feed an eight-year-old. Maybe she really had had enough. How much fuel did such a small body need? I signaled for the check.

"Let's go shopping," I said after I paid for our meal.

We went to a supermarket, and I bought things. Sam didn't say what she wanted, even when I asked her questions. I watched her eyes and bought anything I saw her glance at. We drove back to the lightkeepers' house and I put the groceries away, then filled a kettle and set it on a burner. I made two cups of instant cocoa and tried to remember how to talk.

I brought Sam her cocoa. "Hey, is this place still creepy?"

She had plopped down in one of the armchairs in the front parlor that faced the big front window. From here one saw the mouth of the river where it spilled into the sea, the arched highway bridge over it, and the forested slope of the coastline across from us, with the road climbing it. A tall yard light had gone on as twilight deepened, but I could still see the foamy lace on the waves below as they flung themselves on the beach. Light flashed through the gap in the trees toward the west, the lighthouse's beacon warning even land-going ships that they were approaching a border between one world and another.

"Sure is." She sipped the cocoa. I sat in a chair beside her and stared at the view. "Don't you feel it, Dad?"

"Feel what?"

"It looks nice on top, but there's something crawly underneath."

I studied my daughter's profile. Her eye glowed pearly sea-gray in the westering light. "Do you want to leave?" I asked.

She studied me for a long moment, then shook her head.

I cupped my hands around my cocoa mug, but I couldn't feel the heat. Ever since Amaryllis's death, my fingers had been icy.

Samantha got a pennywhistle out of her pack and played a verse of "Greensleeves." Each note sliced into me. Amaryllis and Sam and I had played a lot of music together—it was one of our evening rituals—and "Greensleeves" was the last tune we had practiced the night before the accident.

"Did you bring your whistle, Dad?" Sam asked me.

"No." I no longer did anything I had done with Amaryllis. At school I had started practicing clarinet. I had played clarinet in high school marching band, before I had met Amaryllis, but I hadn't picked one up again until recently.

"I brought two." Sam rummaged in her pack. "Play with me."

"No!" I couldn't bear it.

Sam's sea-gray eyes widened, and she flinched as though I had struck her. She dropped her whistle into her pack, where it clanged against something.

We sat without moving.

I got up. "I think I saw some cards on the bookshelf."

We spent the evening playing rummy at the dining room table, and went up to bed early. After I turned out my bedside light, I stared at the ceiling and wondered what we were doing here. It was a beautiful place. We still had nothing to say to each other. I didn't know how to take care of my daughter.

I needed a plan. It was so hard to think. My mind kept turning, turning, back to that moment when Amaryllis died; I had been stuck there ever since. Horrible in that bright stop-time way, to see something so close, so inevitable; I couldn't fight it or forget it.

Something scraped across the ceiling, then scraped again.

A chill brushed me.

It was nothing. Maybe a tree branch against the side of the house.

There weren't any trees near the house.

Whish. Whish. Someone was sweeping above me.

I rolled my head and glanced at the clock. It was only about ten-thirty. Still, an odd time to do housework.

A faint tinkle, as of glass chips scattering before a broom.

Did Mrs. Travis really have to do housework right now?

I lay under an excellent down quilt and debated whether I wanted to get up, put on a robe, and figure out how to get to the attic so I could ask Mrs. Travis to sweep tomorrow. The bed had been so cold when I crawled into it, and it was warming now. If I got up and left its comfort, how long before it would warm again?

Was I even going to sleep? I hadn't had a deep sleep in weeks. If I wasn't going to sleep anyway, maybe I shouldn't let a little noise disturb me. I could turn the light on, read one of the books I'd found on a shelf downstairs and brought up to the room.

I reached toward the lamp switch, and the sweeping stopped.

Sometime later, I woke with a start.

"Daddy?"

Samantha's voice sounded low and uncertain, and came from the direction of the doorway.

"What is it, honey?"

"I heard a noise."

I tried to get my bearings. Where were we? It trickled back to me. The lightkeepers' house on the Oregon coast.

I had been asleep. That surprised me.

"Daddy?"

"Yes?"

"Can I come in?"

This time I didn't miss the note of fear. I sat up and switched on the light. "Of course, Sam."

She rushed across the room and jumped onto the bed, curled against me. "There's something in this house," she whispered.

"Of course there is. There's us. There's Mrs. Travis. Maybe even a Mr. Travis around somewhere. Didn't she mention a Mr. Travis when we first got here?"

"There's something else." She clung to my arm. "I'm scared to go back in my room, Daddy."

Sam had grown out of night frights two years earlier. The first time Ryllis and I woke up to hear Sam screaming in her room, we pulled on our robes and went in together to comfort her. When she saw us, she thought we were monsters, and screamed even louder. It took a couple hours to calm her down.

She screamed again the next night, and we went in to her. Ryllis was wonderful with her; no matter how tired she was when she went to bed, if Sam screamed, Ryllis was ready to comfort her. I did my best to imitate my wife, to forget my own problems and desires and just be there for Sam. In time I got better at it.

Then Sam had stopped screaming.

Ryllis once mentioned, after we'd turned out the lights, that she sort of missed it. I thought she was nuts. I thought about it all day.

As Sam grew older and needed us less, I realized what Ryllis had meant. There was something sweet about having someone depend on you.

"Baby, you wrap up in my quilt. I'll go get yours from your room. You can sleep in here."

"Thanks, Dad."

I lifted the quilt so Sam could slide under, then slipped out into the frigid air. Goosebumps rose on my arms and legs. I was wearing a comfortable pair of briefs and nothing else. I grabbed my robe and put it on, then padded across the hall to Sam's room.

The floor was even colder in her room than it had been in mine. I heard a faint sound and stood, trying to decipher it. A murmur? A croon? The mutter of water in pipes? A radio playing half a house away?

A lullaby. A voice, humming a thread of melody. My hair rose and prickled at the sound, even though it was pleasant.

I snatched the quilt off Sam's bed, strode back into the hall, and closed the door of her room. I paused a moment and listened, but I didn't hear anything.

Sam had curled up in the center of my bed and already dropped off to sleep. Fortunately the bed was full-size. I wrapped Sam tighter in the quilt and edged her over to the side, then wrapped up in the second quilt and lay beside her. I decided to leave the light on in case she woke up and wondered where she was.

Or maybe in case I did.

The sound of her slow breaths comforted me. I drifted off to sleep.

"So," said Mrs. Travis, as she set a mug of coffee in front of me, "did you hear anything strange last night?"

I rubbed grit out of my eyes. "Pardon me?" I had slept better than I had since Amaryllis died. Still, I needed that coffee.

"Any manifestations?"

"Manifestations? Of what?" Sam asked.

"Did our gray lady visit you?"

I drank coffee. Unpleasant suspicions pricked my mind. "Are you saying this place is haunted?"

"One of its chief draws," Mrs. Travis said. A door slammed somewhere above. "That'll be Ike. How do you like your eggs?"

"There's a ghost here?" Sam asked.

"You didn't know? Your friend didn't—Oh, dear. Someone should have told you. Yes, we're famous for our ghost. She seems like a kindly soul. Never harmed anyone."

"Does she sweep?" I asked.

Mrs. Travis nodded.

"Does she...does she sing?" asked Sam.

Mrs. Travis stopped and stared at Sam. "Well, now."

"Well, now," repeated a man from the doorway.

Ike Travis was tall and gray-headed, with a twisted frame. Under his dark mustache, he had a lightning smile: brilliant, gone so quickly you wondered if it had happened at all.

"Did you make pancake batter, Lucy, my love?" he asked.

"Of course."

"Would you rustle me up a stack of pancakes?"

"Company first," said Mrs. Travis. She raised her eyebrows at me and Sam.

"I'm not very hungry," Sam said.

"You're a growing child. Of course you're hungry. Eggs or pancakes?"

Sam frowned.

Ryllis had read somewhere that if you let a child eat when and what she wanted, she would be healthier, not so inclined to go anorexic or out of control. That phase in our child-rearing experimentation had lasted for a very aggravating month. Still, we did try to let Sam choose her food and decide how much. But Nick had said Sam was too skinny. God, I didn't know what to do. Ryllis would have known. If she hadn't known, she would have found a book at the library that explained everything, or called one of her friends and gotten a recommendation, or talked to a doctor. Something.

"Pancakes," Sam said.

"Good choice. Will pancakes do for you, too, Mr. Wilcox?"

"That would be great," I said.

Mrs. Travis went to the stove, where a nonstick frying pan already sizzled with melted butter. She ladled up some batter and dropped dollar-sized dollops into the hot butter. There was a satisfying hiss and a wonderful smell. "We've got good syrup here, too. Say, Ike, I was just telling them about our ghost."

Mr. Travis limped over and poured himself a mug of coffee. There was something wrong with the placement of his hips. I straightened the silverware at my place and watched Mrs. Travis flip the pancakes.

Ghosts. I had never believed in ghosts.

If there was one ghost, might there not be another?

"Who was she?" I asked.

"No one rightly knows." Mr. Travis pulled out a chair and lowered himself into it. "She's got to be an assistant lightkeeper's wife, doesn't she, if she died in this house? There was a period around the turn of the century when the keepers either didn't keep good logbooks or the records got lost, so we don't know who-all was on the job at the lighthouse. From the man who saw her, we get clothing details that make us think she's from around that time. She wore one of those pouter-pigeon suits, with the nipped waist and the pushed-up front, and a long A-line skirt. She had her hair piled up in a knot at the top of her head, like a Gibson girl."

"Who saw her?" asked Sam.

Mr. Travis pursed his lips. "Fella working on repairs in the attic. He was repairing the window. Saw a reflection. Thought it was his assistant, bringing him the hammer he'd asked for, but then he turned around and saw her, and his hair stood on end. The lady stood there, staring at him. At first, he thinks: Funny clothes—somebody from a play wandered up here—where'd she come from? She's staring at him and coming closer. He looks down and sees that the hem of her skirt is—"

"—It doesn't touch the ground," continued Mrs. Travis. "He can't see her feet. She's floating. She reaches for him, and he's out of there like someone lit a fire in his pants. Fell right out of the attic door, raced down the stairs, stopped just long enough to collect his assistant, and their pickup truck was screeching out of the driveway before we even knew what happened."

She set plates of pancakes in front of me and Sam, poured warm syrup from a pan on the stove into a little pitcher, and put that on the table where we could reach it. A plate with a stick of butter on it sat nearby.

The pancakes smelled great. I buttered and syruped my stack and ate, even though the story disturbed me more than I wanted to admit.

"We didn't know what happened until Bob came back to get his tools. Even then, he wouldn't come into the house," said Mr. Travis. "He asked me to go up in the attic and fetch his things, and he wouldn't tell us why until after I did it." He drank coffee. "He'd gone right home after he saw her that day, and he drew a picture of her. Showed it to us when he came back. Then he set it down on the porch for a minute, and it disappeared."

"Wasn't the first time things disappeared. Especially for this fella," said Mrs. Travis. She flipped more pancakes.

"The ghost didn't like him. Before she appeared in the attic, she kept moving his tools. He'd set them down and then reach for them, and they'd be gone. Sometimes he'd find them in another room. That didn't spook him enough to make him leave, though. It was only when she showed her face that he quit work on the project and hightailed it out of here."

"He left things in a real mess up in the attic," said Mrs. Travis. "We were working on some other things down here, and we didn't get up there to clean up right away. Then one night we heard sweeping on the ceiling."

"Whish, whish," whispered Mr. Travis.

"We knew the doors were all locked and we were the only people in the house. This was when we were fixing up the house to turn it into a B and B, before we even had any guests. We held each other tight. I don't think I closed my eyes all night, even though the sweeping stopped after about half an hour."

"In the morning, when it was light, I felt braver and went up to check it out," said Mr. Travis. "Dirt and mess all swept up into a neat little pile. Not a broom anywhere in that attic, I swear."

Sam reached under the table and slipped her hand into mine. Her fingers were icy. So were mine.

"We had some kids here one weekend who brought a Ouija board," said Mrs. Travis. "They tried to talk to the ghost. They told us later her name was Rue."

"Some people think she's looking for her little drowned child," Mr. Travis said. "Daughters of the head lightkeeper from the early years of last century said there was a little gravestone somewhere between the keepers' houses and the lighthouse, with the name Rose on it. It's all overgrown now, and nobody knows where it is. I have to say there's no reason to suspect a connection, but people like to put two and two together."

"Ike," said Mrs. Travis. "The girl here asked about singing."

Ike set down his coffee cup and licked his lips. "Singing," he said.

I set my fork on my plate. "A lullaby."

"You heard it too, Daddy?" Sam asked.

"When I went to get your quilt."

The Travises exchanged troubled glances.

"What?" I asked.

Mrs. Travis shook her head. "It's nothing."

"What?"

"Really. It's nothing. Leave it be."

"Not many hear her singing. Sometimes she screams or sobs," offered Mr. Travis. "I hate to hear her cry. It's just so sad.

More often she moves things around, no rhyme or reason, or leaves the cupboards open, even if we close them with latches the night before."

"I think she likes reading the labels on the boxes. We have so many strange foods now that they didn't have back in the old days."

"Where's the sense in that?" asked Mr. Travis.

"You come up with a better explanation."

I got the sense they were acting out parts in a play. The lines had the feel of a well-worn script, a soothing pattern of sound to pull one away from something one would rather not see.

"Have you been up to the light?" asked Mr. Travis.

I was glad he'd changed the subject. Sam looked pale. Her hand slipped out of mine, and she took a bite of soggy pancakes. "Not yet," I said.

"There's guided tours from noon to four. We've got some great volunteers who'll tell you about the light and its history."

"Daddy." Sam put down her silverware. "I'm done."

She had only eaten about half her pancakes. She had drunk a small glass of orange juice and some milk. Maybe it was enough. I finished off my pancakes and drank the rest of my coffee. "Thank you, Mrs. Travis. That was a great breakfast."

"You're welcome," said Mrs. Travis. "Bundle up, now, when you go out. It's damp this morning. Let us know if you need anything else."

"Thanks very much." I stood and picked up my dishes.

"Never mind. I'll take care of cleanup. Part of the service."

I put the dishes down again and took Sam's hand. We left the kitchen and headed up the stairs.

As we climbed, I felt a crawling sensation on the back of my head, as though someone watched me. I resisted the impulse to turn and glare. Had Nick known this was a haunted house? He couldn't have. How could he send me and Sam to a place where—?

The day was foggy and dark. Out the front window in Sam's room I saw that the tops of the trees along the coast disappeared into fog, as though dipped into skymilk. I made Sam put on a sweatshirt under her jacket, and talked her into wearing her rainboots and the wide-brimmed waterproof yellow hat she had grown up enough to think was too silly to wear anymore. "Nobody you know will see you," I said.

"Complete strangers will think I'm an idiot."

"So why should it matter? They'll never see you again."

She sighed noisily. Somehow the sound put heart into me. It was as close to a laugh as anything I had heard from her since Ama died.

We took our daypacks down to the guest kitchen. I washed apples, made PBJs, and filled water bottles. We loaded the supplies into our packs, then left for the day.

Near the top of the lighthouse tower, just below the level of the light, our guide talked about first-order Fresnel lenses, prisms, and the British clockworks that made the lens rotate. The clockworks had required winding every four hours, so the keepers would stay awake.

"The chains used to hang right down the center of the tower. There was this weight that dropped down. They had to hand-crank it back up. Now it's all electric. If the power fails, there's a sensor—" he pointed to a small square device that scanned the edge of a clockwork wheel as it rotated—"that alerts the Coast Guard station down the coast. We have a secondary system, an emergency lantern attached to the railing up here. Someone comes up to turn it on. Other than that, everything's automated now. Lighthouse keepers were phased out in the sixties, for the most part," the guide said.

"Why is the light running during the day?" Sam asked. From our vantage beside the gear assembly, we looked up inside the light. Two bulbs were in the center, one lit, the other present in case the first burned out. Housing them was a cage of glass: the many prisms that made up the Fresnel lens. It was like seeing the inside of a diamond.

"This machinery weighs several tons. To start and stop it takes more energy than just to leave it running."

I glanced out one of the tower windows. Below, the headland was covered by lawn, surrounded by white pipe railing
to keep people from falling over the cliffs. The red roofs of the
twin oilhouses were bright patches of color under the dark sky.
Waves frothed around the cliffs.

Amaryllis would have loved this place. She exulted even
in dark days, and she had loved high places and strange lights.

Sam stared up into the light, her eyes just like her mother's
had been. My throat burned.

"Next tour's waiting at the bottom of the stairs," said our
guide. He led us down the steel spiral staircase and waved us
out past a group of Asian tourists.

What were we supposed to do with our day? My mind
was a blank. We had explored the beach and toured the lighthouse. We could drive into town and wander around. Maybe
there was a movie playing, a matinee show.

Halfway along the road back to the keepers' house, Sam
grabbed my hand. She tugged me toward a muddy trail that
led up the headland into the spruce forest. "Let's have lunch in
the trees, Daddy."

Another thing Amaryllis would have suggested. She loved
paths that led to places she hadn't been. She always wanted to
explore.

I followed my daughter up the hill past branchless tree
trunks. All the trees were young—we had seen a historic picture from when the lighthouse and the keepers' houses were
first built, and the headland had been bare—the result of a fire
in the 1880s, before construction began. So, no tree here could
be much older than a hundred years, and they had grown in
thick, shading each other out so that all their greenery was
held in their tops, leaving the ground below needle-scattered
and dark. A gap here and there showed us slices of distance, a
gray sea under a paler gray sky, with a darker line where sea
met sky and clouds kissed water.

After we had climbed a ways, we came to a wide spot in
the path, a viewpoint where we could look down at the lighthouse between dark, lichen-draped evergreen branches. "Let's

eat here." Sam rummaged in her pack and pulled out her sit-upon, a tough piece of plastic big enough for her and her pack. She spread it on the ground and plopped down on it.

I got out my sit-upon and joined her. From this vantage we could see the red roof of the lighthouse tower, with its little red bulb at the tip, and above that a lightning rod. Beyond the light, an eternity of empty sea.

Mechanically I pulled lunch out of my pack.

"Wait, Dad. Don't eat yet. Look what I brought." Sam produced the two pennywhistles. She held the green one out to me.

I accepted it without thinking, put my fingers over the holes and lifted the mouthpiece to my lips. My embouchure formed around it, my breath flowed into it, and a tune came out, "Chinese Breakdown." I heard Amaryllis's voice, full of smile: "Let's have music everywhere we go! We need something really portable, for everywhere." So we had both learned pennywhistles, and Ama had also mastered harmonica. I could never get my tongue to behave correctly for that.

We had played wooden recorders and plastic recorders and stringed instruments, whistles and spoons and ocarinas. When we found an apartment where our neighbors didn't mind music, we had rented a piano even before we bought a TV. We had sung Samantha to sleep every night when she was a baby, and later, she sang with us. We had started with lullabies.

Sam played along with me on "Chinese Breakdown" for two measures. Then I lost the thread of tune and fell down into myself. Where was Amaryllis, with her quick ear for harmony? Gone. Breath leaked out of me, blurred the tune as my fingers lost their memories. I dropped the whistle.

Sam played a few more notes, then faltered to a stop. "What's wrong, Dad?"

"I'm sorry, Sam. I'm just not ready yet." I pulled my knees up against my chest. I was a terrible father. What was the matter with me? Here Sam was doing her best to cheer me up, and I kept falling into despair. What must she be feeling?

I could not force my hands to let go of my legs and pick up the pennywhistle again. "I'm sorry," I whispered.

She retrieved my pennywhistle and stuffed both of them into her pack. We ate lunch in silence.

That night we went to bed after another round of card games. Sam won most of them. I couldn't seem to remember what cards had been played. Sam looked pale and drawn and scrawny, the shadows under her eyes almost purple. I hugged her after she brushed her teeth. "If you get scared again tonight, come on in my room," I murmured.

She didn't answer. She hugged me back for a minute, then went into her room and shut the door. I retreated to my room and crawled under the featherbed, then lay for several hours staring up into the dark. Snap out of it, Reed.

Out of what?

This funk. Wake up.

Why?

I must have drifted off at some point. When the noise woke me, it was hours later.

Was it the wind?

No. It came from inside the house.

A scattering of driven rain struck my window, drowning out the sounds for a moment. The ceiling creaked.

Then I heard it again.

A pennywhistle, stumbling and fumbling, playing a tune I almost remembered.

A lullaby. The same one I had heard in Sam's room the night before.

Soft and soothing, the lullaby worked its magic. I felt drowsy and warm, ready, at last, for deep sleep. I drifted.

Reed. Get up. Go to Sam.

My eyes snapped open. Was that Amaryllis's voice? I sat up, pushed out of the warm blankets, pulled on my robe, and went across the hall to Sam's room.

I stood for a moment at the door, listening. The tune was steady and strong now.

I tapped on the door. "Sam?"

The melody faltered, then resumed.

"Sam." I grabbed the doorknob. It was freezing. I snatched

my hand away, then wrapped it in a fold of bathrobe and tried the doorknob again. It wouldn't turn.

The back of my neck prickled with cold. What was happening in that room? I pounded on the door. "Sam. Open the door! Sam!"

The tune kept playing. It was only music, but I felt a sense of something racing away from me. I rattled the knob. It turned, but the door was locked.

Only music! Music could do anything. Open up wounds you had hoped were closed, carry you to places old and new, summon shades you couldn't face because just thinking about them hurt too much. In the altered state of making music—

"Sam. Stop playing. Open the door."

The melody went on. I knew it was carrying my daughter away from me. She was on the other side of this door, and someone was piping her away, as surely as the Pied Piper had enticed the children away from Hamlin.

I had lost my wife already. If I lost my daughter too, it would crush me.

"Ama," I whispered. "Help me."

Sing to her, Reed.

I placed my palms flat on the door and listened to the pennywhistle play the lullaby. She made no mistakes. The music was smooth and true now.

"Alas," I sang, and coughed hesitation out of my throat. *Voice, I need you now.*

> *Alas, my love, you do me wrong*
> *To cast me off discourteously,*
> *For I have loved you so long,*
> *Delighting in your company.*

The lullaby turned thready, hesitant.

> *Greensleeves was my delight,*
> *Greensleeves was all my joy,*
> *Greensleeves was my heart of gold—*

The pennywhistle stopped.

> *And who but my lady Greensleeves?*

The lock turned. The door opened a crack. Sam rubbed her eyes and peered up at me. Her face was streaked with tears. "Daddy?"

I knelt and opened my arms. For a long moment I feared she would close the door again. I would reach out to stop it. I wouldn't let her be locked away from me. But had she gone so far away from me already that she wanted me to be on the other side of a door? Had I let her get so far away?

She opened the door and stumbled into my embrace. Storms of weeping shook her. I held her a long time while she cried, and thought about many things.

"She wanted me," Sam told me later. We sat side by side on the couch in the front parlor, cocoa mugs in our hands, and stared out at the night. "She's been looking and looking for her little girl. I knew she wanted me. She wanted to be my mother. And you didn't want to be my father anymore."

I put down my mug and pulled her into my arms. "I do. More than anything."

"No. Mom died, and you died too. You turned into a robot."

I hugged my daughter. "I've been so sad."

"Me too."

"I've been so sad I didn't notice how sad you were."

She slugged my shoulder with a fist. "Yeah."

"But I know now."

She settled, curled up against my chest. "Sometimes I want to remember Mom," she said. "Sometimes I want to do things we did with Mom. It makes me feel like she didn't totally disappear. Every time I tried that with you, though..."

"I know." I stroked her hair. "Remember last summer, when we stayed in the mountains?"

"And we found the eagle with the broken wing. We didn't know what to do. We got Mom. Mom said we should call the forest ranger. She always knew what to do." Sam sounded drowsy.

Sometimes I won't know what to do, I thought. And then I'll try to think what you would have done, Ama. Please come back that much.

Thank you.

THOMAS F. MONTELEONE

Lux et
Veritas

"You want me to do *what?*" said Carlo Duarte.

He was sitting in a booth in a bar'n'grill called the Coach's Place in White River Junction, Vermont. Two televisions displayed different college basketball games. Across from him was a woman dressed in black, and everything about her could be described by the word *indeterminate*.

Her age, for starters, thought Carlo. She didn't look old, per se, but her smooth, elliptical face was somehow endowed with a depth of wisdom, experience, and that sort of thing. And going right along with that ambiguous leitmotif, Carlo was not certain whether or not this woman was attractive or plain. Sometimes, when the light and shadows played their parts, and she turned her head a certain way, her features combined to be intriguing and interesting in ways that only the face of a woman can be. At others, she looked odd, homely, or downright scary.

Her style of dress was also hard to pin down, so to speak. Kind of a decadent *chic*-ness. Loose and flowing blouse and long skirt, all black, evocative of the pen-and-inks of Aubrey Beardsley. Add a scarf here, some rings and bracelets, and she had a "look" that got your attention—but for reasons that were ...well, indeterminate.

Same thing with her name. He was sure she'd given it to him when he'd called the number in the ad, and she'd said it again when they met for lunch, but damned if he could remember it. Ms. Stephanie...? Something like that. Well, it didn't matter, really. Either he'd remember it or she'd tell him again.

"Sir," she said in soft tones that still managed to convey her lack of patience with fools. "I made it quite clear. We're looking for a lighthouse keeper...on the White River. Are you interested or not?"

Carlo held up his hands in mock surrender. "Whoa. Yeah, of course I am. It would be perfect for me...but I never knew there was ever a lighthouse around here. Especially on the White River."

She gave him a patronizing and brief smile. "There hasn't been—till now. My...colleagues are building it as we speak."

"Oh, okay," said Carlo. "I understand. That's cool. When will it be ready?"

"Any time now..." The woman reached out and took both his hands in her own, and her touch was neither warm nor cold. "Tell me a little more about yourself. You said you're thirty-eight years old. Any relatives nearby? Wives? Ex-wives? Girlfriends, boyfriends? Any big commitments looming?"

Carlo withdrew his hands as he leaned back in the booth, placing them casually behind his head. "Well, like I said on the phone, I'm an artist. I do freelance illustration for some of the companies around here, but it's not a steady income. I'm trying to get enough paintings finished to get a gallery interested, but that takes time."

"And you think being a lightkeeper would afford you that time?"

"Yes, I do." He paused. "Why? Am I wrong?"

"No, not at all. You'll have all the time in the world. Your duties will still allow you time to paint. But you must never be distracted from your one primary responsibility—to keep the light burning."

"No problem," said Carlo.

"No distractions. Hence the questions about the other people in your life."

Carlo smiled, feeling a little self-conscious. "Never married. No girlfriends. It's not that I have trouble meeting them or anything like that, but most women don't have much patience for my lifestyle. I need to spend a lot of time alone... because of my work."

"Perfectly understandable," said the woman, standing up and reaching across the table to shake his hand. "I think you'll do just fine."

The lighthouse was located on the White River about twenty miles northwest of the "Junction," where it joined the Connecticut River on its journey south. Architecturally, it was similar to most New England lighthouses of present and past centuries. New Hampshire granite and lots of brick masonry gave it a classic substance and silhouette against the evening sky. The only thing that made it different from any other lighthouse was its location—about 150 miles from the seacoast.

Carlo Duarte thought about that anomaly. He had attempted to ask his interviewer about it, but she had said everything would be explained to him in the "fullness of time." There were other oddities about his employment arrangements, but they were all things he didn't even *want* to question. He would be paid each month *in cash*—a lot of cash. They didn't ask for a Social Security number, which meant no federal taxes or FICA deductions, and therefore no IRS; and absolutely no paperwork to fill out. That was copacetic with him; he believed paying and filing income taxes was voluntary under the law anyway.

Weird, yes. But a good deal as far as he was concerned.

So, in the meantime, after accepting the offer, he packed up all his painting gear in the old Chevy Blazer, with enough clothes and supplies to last at least a few weeks, and he drove up Route 4 past Royalton until he found the dirt road leading off toward the lighthouse. With his painterly eye, Carlo paused to absorb the scene as evening began to leach the colors off into twilight. Despite the incongruity of a lighthouse on the White River—especially at a point where the distance from bank to bank was less than two hundred yards and the depth of the channel couldn't be more than thirty feet—there was a feeling of *rightness* about it. Carlo couldn't articulate what he was feeling, but he just kind of *knew* everything was cool.

The inside of the lighthouse proved to be far more than he'd expected. The furnishings were warm and comfortable, the fixtures and appliances all state-of-the-art. Windows penetrated the space in so many places that every room was flooded with light. The effect was initially unsettling, because it seemed to expand the interior, warping the three-dimensional space of the tapered cylinder into a structure that was far larger on the inside than the outside.

A kind of architectural *gestalt,* thought Carlo.

Again he was forced to pause, to realize how quintessentially weird the whole set-up was...

It was like those scenes in the cheesy horror movies where you want to stand up and scream at the protagonist: *Don't go in there! Don't you hear the scary music?!*

He smiled to himself. Indeed, he *did* hear the discordant violins, but felt no sense of accompanying dread, no gut-level gnawing of fear. He knew he should be wary as hell of all the strangeness, but he rationalized it by telling himself he would keep bugging his employers to give him all the answers.

Entering the top floor of the structure, he found a space that resembled the deck of an air traffic control center—laminated built-in consoles, the obligatory computer, phone, and a couple of self-explanatory control panels, which he presumed linked up with the huge glass lens and lamp dominating the center of the space. It was all medium-high tech, and more than enough for what seemed like a job anybody could do in their sleep. Lying next to the keyboard was a thick, richly bound folio entitled *Procedures and Policies,* which ignited in him a brief moment when he expected all to be made clear to him.

Of course, he was wrong.

But he did learn how to turn the powerful lamp on and off, and how to synch up its rotation with the ever-changing celestial clock that marked off each new sunrise and sunset. The book was written in clear, precise language, and organized to such a Teutonic degree that it made him uncomfortable. Nobody, he thought, should be thinking in so orderly a fashion. Although he had to admit—after just a single reading and a dry run at the controls, he understood every nuance of responsibility and duty of the job. Technology and the whole tool-thing had largely eluded his interest until now, but after reading *Procedures and Policies*, he believed he could even field-strip the giant lamp into its components like a soldier with his weapon, then fix and gang-bang it back together again.

Not bad for somebody who spent most of his time worrying about running out of cadmium yellow or burnt sienna...

Several hours later, after he'd gotten everything stashed away in his living quarters, he was standing in front of a fresh canvas. He had chosen the room just below the top floor for his studio because he liked the placement of the windows, in terms of the kind of light admitted and the views afforded (both banks of the White River and the nearby peak of Mount Ascutney). He kind of liked the idea of seeing that familiar peak—the same one Maxfield Parrish always included in his electrically lush paintings. Then, just as he was about to make his first brush stroke, he heard a sound that lay somewhere between a buzz and a crackle (the huge bulb of the beacon bursting into heat and light), followed by the whine of the motors that would turn the lamp on its endless axis. Outside the tower, evening had surrendered to nightfall.

Smiling, Carlo felt a flood of job-satisfaction wash over his self-esteem centers. He'd set the timers, punched all the stacked commands into the systems, and waited for the semi-automation to take over. When it performed flawlessly, he felt good. The score was Carlo one, technology zero. Game over. Simple as that. The sensitive artist would no longer be intimidated and humbled by rampant science.

Again he checked his palette and prepared the initial dab of pigment, when it occurred to him to climb the wrought-iron circular staircase up to the lamp...just to see how things looked. As he laid down his tools, Carlo realized the day would soon come when he would probably cringe at the sound of the lamp firing up and the motors sliding into motion, but for the moment he was curious.

It was the artist in him, he thought. He needed to see what it *looked like*. That powerful beam sweeping out across the glassy surface and cutting through the blue aisle of night like a white-hot sword. He had to see it from the unique perspective of its *source*...

And he did.

Not surprisingly, it was a spectacular vantage point, and he never missed the hours that slipped past him as he sat first behind the thick glass, then later leaned on the railing outside, on the narrow gangway that encircled the beacon. Like a laser's lance stretched to the moon, the lamp's focused beam slowly turreted the Vermont river valley. Its sweep was canted down at an angle that scoured the woods and the wide, languid bends in the river.

Beautiful beyond imagining, but something else as well...

There was *power* here. At the apex of this solitary tower, he stood like a general looking down from the soaring prow of his war machine. So striking was the sensation, it made Carlo giddy. For the first time in his life he began to understand how it could happen...*why* it happened.

Power.

Hypnotic and utterly compelling.

Carlo liked it.

In fact, he liked the lighthouse-keeper gig in its entirety. He found himself anticipating the crackling ignition of the great filaments when the lamp would fire up. And when it did, he'd run up the staircase and watch, like a kid sneaking into a carnival tent, as the servo-motors cranked up the carousel of light and heat. He'd never felt happier in his life. The job had become an intoxicating elixir. As the weeks passed, he began spending more and more of the night hours just sitting up there, under the beacon's sweeping thrall, then doing more of his sleeping during the day.

Until he was doing all his sleeping while the sun was up.

Which meant he'd essentially *stopped* painting. Oddly enough, a month had slipped past before he even realized it. And when he was sitting at the lamp control console one evening, contemplating how long it had been since he'd attempted to create an image, he surprised himself by accepting that fact with absolute calm.

Not painting had always been simply unthinkable to him. It was something he'd done every day of his adult life, and it had become an organic part of his essence, his *Carlo-ness*. He'd always known nothing could stop him from painting. He'd been born to do it, and like the driven fools before him, the Monets and Renoirs and Van Goghs, he'd lived with the stink of turpentine under his nails.

Keeping his light kept him content. The passion to paint in order to feel *good* had been replaced; and it was okay with him.

And so it was at this point—when Carlo accepted the loss of his driving desire to paint—that he first saw the boat on its nightly crossing.

At first he was confused, because either it had been there all along and he'd been too obtuse to notice it, or it had just started a new nocturnal schedule—or else he was slipping off into the world of weird happenings.

The boat was not large, nor was it small. It appeared on the lighthouse shoreline at the deepest hour of the night, and there was no telling its color, name, or registration. Hard enough to even discern its "lines" (as the sailors used to say). The craft's silhouette against the lamplight that boiled off the water's surface appeared simple, uncluttered. A low, sweeping gunwale and no masts made it seem like it could be the hull of a submarine up for a look-see.

Hard to tell, thought Carlo.

He shook his head, smiled only a little bit. Like his employer, the boat's major characteristics were largely indeterminate—although each night (and he was seeing the boat every night now) he began to notice more details. Not that it was difficult to study the target—its passage to the antipodal dark shore proved glacially slow, mainly because of the boatman, who pushed the shallow barque along with a long, willowy pole. He could have been in the Louisiana bayou or a Venetian canal. Either way, his spindly, mechanical movements were unmistakable.

Then, one night, he noticed the boatman was not alone. Carlo could not imagine just not noticing such a detail; it must have somehow been kept from him till now. As he watched the boat pass through the sweep of the lamp's beam, he saw its open deck *teeming* with passengers. Hunched and huddled together, they formed an uncountable horde of silent souls.

Carlo suddenly understood more than he wanted to, more than he would ever want to *believe.*

Not that any of it made any sense...none at all.

He tried to kill time until the next payday—the next time he would have any contact with his employers, the next chance to ask a few questions. Hours slipped away with tar-pit slowness as he stood motionless in his studio, brush in hand, helpless to make it move. The elation and sense of completeness he'd previously experienced had left him, replaced by unquiet bewilderment. He could not create, nor could he make sense of the world of which he'd become a part.

"Remember what you said about 'the fullness of time'?" he said to her as she entered the lighthouse in her flowing skirts and blouse carrying her large, black shoulder bag.

Looking at him with a smile that looked like an afterthought. "Actually, I do..."

Carlo motioned to a small table in the kitchen, sat down opposite her, and folded his hands. He felt haggard and dazed. He'd been spending so much time alone with his thoughts, he was finding it difficult to conduct an interchange with another person.

"I think I understand what's going on here...but it—"

"Doesn't seem possible?"

"It's crazy!" he said, suddenly finding an anchor for his thoughts. "What the hell's going on out here? No pun intended!"

She smiled. "I understand your confusion. We knew you would catch on eventually."

Gesturing through the window toward the White River, he said: "Last time I checked, that's not the Cocytus...or is it the Styx?"

"Well, it is...and it isn't." She reached into her bag and placed a large parcel wrapped in brown paper on the table. "Here's your stipend."

Carlo tried to look directly into her eyes, found it difficult. "Please, don't distract me," he said. "It's bad for the job, I'm told."

"We are very happy with your work."

"I'll bet you are," said Carlo, forcing out a bark of mock-laughter. "But I think I need some answers."

"All right. You deserve them. I like you, Mr. Duarte."

"And your name, by the way; I kept thinking it was Stephanie or something like that, but..." Carlo paused to arrange his thoughts into a coherent sentence. "But...I either disremembered it, or you made me think it was something else...something other than what it is."

The woman with the ageless face nodded. "All right, that's close enough."

"Ms. Persephone, I presume."

She smiled.

"So, *why?* How? What do you need me for?"

"Have you ever heard any of those theories that talk about polar shifts, and the earth's crust slipping and sliding over the mantle? Any of that arcane geology?"

Carlo shrugged. "I guess I have. Never paid that much attention to it, though. Why? Are you telling me that things get moved around, like pieces on a chessboard?"

Persephone raised an eyebrow impishly. "The gods are capricious at times, especially Gaea. The process is more complicated than how you're putting it—although I am impressed with your perspicuity. There are cycles through which the world passes. All thing pass; everything changes. Right now, at this time and place, we need things to be *here.*"

"Okay; if I accept that as enough, what's with the light?"

She shrugged. "Obviously it is more than a light. It is like a key. It lights the path to the gates of Tartarus."

"So I'm a gatekeeper."

"After a fashion, yes. More like a twenty-four-hour repair-man."

Carlo stood, walked to the window that overlooked the banks of the White River. Evening was climbing the foothills of the Green Mountains. Everything looked so different, so benign, but it would change with the advancing darkness.

"Okay," he said. "So, like I asked you before—why me? Why now? I keep asking myself—what happened to the other guy? The guy before me?"

Persephone chuckled facetiously. "Don't ask. He had some grand ideas that he could be the new Prometheus..."

Carlo nodded. "So now he's got what—a bad liver?"

She shook her head and grimaced. "You could say that, yes."

"There's something else," said Carlo, returning to the table so he could sit facing her, as if this would somehow intensify the seriousness of what he wanted to say. "I'm not sure how to explain this, so I guess I'll just put it as plainly as possible: I haven't painted a thing since I've been here."

"I see..." she said, her gaze taking him in like a maelstrom.

"Something's been happening to me. Something's been... I don't know... *changing* me."

"You are so perceptive," she said with a sad little grin. "But you haven't caught on completely, have you?"

Carlo didn't like the sound of that. He gripped the edges of the table, reminding himself to keep control. "What're you talking about? What's happening to me?"

"You're becoming a demigod."

He looked at her and felt a furious tightening in his gut. "A *what?* What does that mean?"

Persephone leaned forward, reached for his hands, taking them into her own. It was, however, a touch with something missing. He imagined she'd done it to make him feel better, but it left him cold and wary. "I will assume you have noticed how . . . how *good* you feel since you've been working here? How healthy?"

"Yes, I have noticed. Go on."

"That's because you've become *immortal*—well, sort of..."

Carlo pulled his hands away from hers, ran his fingers through his hair. Her words didn't surprise him; not really. For the first time, he admitted to himself that maybe he'd suspected such a thing on some deeper, unconscious level. And yet, he couldn't actually accept what she said at face value either. The idea of living forever, while greatly appealing, also sounded silly—especially when you considered the little coda she'd added to the end.

"Ah...could we possibly get a little more explanation of the phrase 'well, sort of'?"

"As long as you are here," said Persephone, "as long as you stay in the lighthouse, you cannot die. Nothing can harm you."

"Okay, so what does that actually mean?" said Carlo, wondering if he already knew the answer to his next question, and needing only to hear her confirmation. "What does that have to do with me and my painting?"

Persephone half-lidded her eyes, shook her head so subtly he almost missed it. "Carlo, you are very intelligent. I think you know."

Standing up, he backed away from the table and walked to one of the windows. The vista of the river valley was now draped in the gray and purple mantles of twilight as he pondered her words. He *did* know, goddammit, and he'd kept thinking that if, somehow, he never spoke about it, never let his words make it real...then it wouldn't *be* real.

But it was.

The unspoken but implied second part of the corollary proffered by Persephone was elegant in its simplicity: As he'd become more godlike, then, he must, by definition, have become *less* human.

And that meant—what? Just about everything, when you took the time to think about it. It was no accident he'd lost his passion, his turbine-intensity to create, because that kind of energy came from the dark well of the soul. From a place where the essence of what it means to be mortal is heated and forged and tempered in that misshapen crucible of human experience.

Oh yeah, he knew, all right.

There'd probably been some piece of him, some micro-fragments of the collective unconscious that shot through him like gamma rays at the moment of his conception, that had *always* known on the intuitive level what was going on. Always known a weird transaction had been completed here. And Carlo felt so ashamed of himself. He'd always lived his life knowing there's no such thing as a free lunch; but this time, he'd bellied up to this particular trough, deluding himself that he was going to make it happen.

No way, baby, he thought as he turned back and looked at Pluto's main squeeze, sitting there like she was posing for Praxiteles.

"I want out," he said softly.

"Excuse me?"

"Don't act so surprised. Don't tell me there's no way out—I didn't sign any contract! No drop of blood, none of that Faustian crap here!"

Persephone stood and moved toward him, her long skirt imparting for an instant the illusion that she glided rather than walked. "No, none of that . . . You are correct."

Carlo exhaled, relieved at a very basic level. "So . . . what's next? Is this where you tell me that when I walk out of here . . . I'll die?"

She smiled. "You are an unusual man," she said. "I could grow to like you very much. I think I already have."

Backing away, he shook his head. "Uh-uh, we're not going there."

"No, I mean I admire you—in the classical sense. And you *will* die when you leave here, but not right away: in the right and due course of your life. You will be mortal again."

He exhaled again. More relief. She had this way of keeping the tension levels torqued way up there. Carlo was walking a metaphysical high-wire, and the subject of safety nets had never come up.

"Thanks," he said. "You've made me realize a few things about myself."

"You are most welcome." Persephone smiled, and for the time, allowed herself to look quite attractive.

"I guess I'd better gather up my things. I have this very strong hope I'll be needing them."

"You will," she said.

"Thanks. Thanks for everything. I hope you don't think I'm ungrateful, or anything like that. And I hope you understand why I have to go."

"I do," she said. "Probably more than you. Good-bye, Carlo Duarte."

Carlo nodded, began walking toward the stairs to his studio, then paused, turned to look back at her. "What about this...job? Do you think you'll have any trouble getting somebody else?"

Persephone considered the question for only an instant, her gold-green eyes flashing a look first to the window, which had become an oblong of shiny obsidian, then back to him. "No, but I will be a little more careful with the questions I ask."

Carlo paused. "Meaning...?"

"I will ask them if they are chasing any dreams."

Despite the swirled palette of emotions he currently felt, Carlo couldn't keep from smiling. "Most of them won't know what you're talking about. You'll have plenty of unimaginative pinheads to choose from."

Persephone chuckled. "I'll take that as both a curse and a blessing."

As Carlo put some miles between himself and the lighthouse, he could feel his mortality seeping back into him, invading the molecular structures of his cells like the metaphysical disease that it was. And it felt good. He slipped his *Disraeli Gears* CD into the deck; and sang along with Clapton, Bruce, and Baker as they rattled through "Tales of Brave Ulysses"—a fittingly Hellenistic reference to the latest chapter in his own life saga.

By the time the song had ended, he noted that the farther he drove, the less real the whole lightkeeper experience was becoming. In fact, the more he tried to concentrate on specifics, the more foggy and less distinct his mind images became.

Weird. Very weird.

His thoughts kept him from paying close attention to his driving, and more than a couple of times he'd kind of *snap* back to attention with his hands gripping the wheel on autopilot. He felt like an idiot, looking down the shafts of his headlights as they tried to find the tortured two-lane tar road. It made him wonder how the hell he'd gotten to this point on Route 4 without realizing it. Had he passed that quaint bastion of socialism they called the Vermont Law School yet?

Where was he?

State Route 4 through this rural part of Vermont twisted through endless curves as it struggled to follow the course of the White River. It was a bad road in daylight and downright treacherous at night. Everything tended to look the same until you were right on top of it.

It was just after he'd seen the signs for the town of Sharon and the Interstate that it started to rain.

Drops as big and heavy as bullfrogs. They spattered on the window like little bodies exploding with the suddenness of a mortar attack. Carlo kicked in the wipers, but not quickly enough. As he leaned close to the steering wheel, trying to see what lay beyond the smeared glass, he felt the Blazer's big tires lose purchase on an upcoming curve. Power-sliding toward the riverbank to his right, Carlo yanked the gearshift downward into second and buried the gas pedal.

It was a brilliant maneuver, which saved him from a launch into the dark water, but Carlo couldn't stop the lurching SUV from crossing the centerline at the blindest point of the next curve. That's why the driver of the Peterbilt truck and trailer didn't see him until the dark hull of the Blazer literally *exploded* over the grille and hood of the giant tractor.

Carlo vaguely remembered the shockwave of the impact, but could recall no sound. Nor did he have any memory of being thrown clear of the wreckage...but he must have been, because he was now picking himself up, pulling himself out of the soft, cloying mud of the riverbank. A cold nightwind laced through him as he turned away from it...

...to see the stark tower looming up before him. Its silhouette against the darker tapestry of the sky was hideously familiar, and its recognition vibrated deep into his soul like the idiot-hum of oblivion.

The sweeping beam of light passed over him, and as he acceded to Charon's gesture to come aboard, Carlo paused for a last glance at the lighthouse lamp. He wondered who might be the "unimaginative pinhead" staring down at him from beyond the fortress of its glass.

GARY A. BRAUNBECK

Captain Jim's Drunken Dream

*Water of life, water of chaos, water of
destruction—these the principal elements flow
and mingle in shifting patterns just as the
constellations change. There is a purpose to
this. I must endeavor to discover its secret.*
—From the journals of Ponce de Leon (1513)

If you take I-70 from Cedar Hill toward Buckeye Lake and
watch for the crossroad two miles straight ahead after you get
off the highway (it's marked by an eight-foot T post with a
sculpted iron noose dangling from it), this is the way to Hangman's Tavern, one of the most legendary watering holes in the
self-proclaimed "Land of Legend." The tavern has a story all its
own, one that the owner/bartender (who can play a mean harmonica despite a severely arthritic hand) will be more than
happy to tell you after closing time.

The Hangman, you see, is *the* place to go if you're looking
for good company, decent food, homemade brew, and, most of
all, stories. Everybody who comes here has got one—consider
it the cover charge. Some will break your heart; some will have
you doubled over with laughter; some will leave you shaking
your head in wonder; and some—a very exceptional few—will

leave you feeling a bit more wary about what lies hidden in the night outside.

But there is a particular story that everyone agrees should be the first one a newcomer is told, because, unlike some of the eye-rollers, groaners, and head-shaking shaggy-dogs spun here after the spirits have been released and everyone's inner bumpkin starts emerging, this one is sacred. This one no one embellishes; you'll hear it the same from the Hangman's owner as you will from a patron who's heard it only once.

More often than not, if you find yourself here on a Saturday night, the regulars will point you in my direction. "If you wanna hear the story of Captain Jim," they'll say, clapping a happy hand on your shoulder, "then *there's* the fellah you ought to be talking with."

There were a lot of people who witnessed *parts* of what happened before, during, and after the events of that night—the Cedar Hill *Ally* even ran a handful of articles about the episodes no one could fully explain—but I'm the only one who knows the whole thing. I was there. I saw it all.

That should count for something, shouldn't it?

First, though, you need to know how the Captain came to find himself here.

There once was a fifty-six-year-old merchant seaman named Jim Larousse who was traveling to San Francisco, where a possible job with a fishing fleet awaited him. He boarded a bus in Topeka, Kansas, and transferred to another in St. Louis. Between the two points he noticed that the final destination on his ticket was marked Los Angeles, not San Francisco. The L.A. route would take him south through Texas and Arizona, but he needed a northern route through the West to stop in Salt Lake City, so he could empty an old bank account to pay for the rest of his travels in case the job didn't come through. Jim explained the problem to the ticket agent in St. Louis, but nothing could be done until he reached Amarillo. Once there, he was given a new ticket on a different bus line going toward Denver. He got on the bus, assuming the bus lines would take care of his luggage, and slept until he reached Colorado.

The most important part of his trip was not getting the job but fulfilling a promise he'd made to his wife, Gloria, when she was in a hospice in Kansas, dying of cancer.

Gloria Larousse had only seen the sea three times in her life—one that was plagued by illnesses that left her unable to do much traveling (or anything else, for that matter)—and so depended on her husband to bring the sea home to her. Jim gladly filled her room with the sea's souvenirs, from multi-colored shells to oddly shaped bits of driftwood and stones, so long tossed by the tides that their surfaces were as smooth and clear as glass.

He made sure that at every voyage's end he brought home stories and keepsakes to fill his wife's days and dreams, always holding her hand and brushing back her thinning hair so her eyes were never far from his gaze—until it was time to pack up his sea bag, which had belonged to his father and his father before him, and head out on the waters again to find more treasures and tales for the woman who waited so faithfully.

Jim Larousse had promised Gloria that he would scatter her ashes in the Pacific Ocean.

Her ashes—sealed in a gold container because gold was her favorite color, the color of a true sunrise, she'd said—along with his personal records, rating slips, and recommendations from previous employers, were in his sea bag, which he'd been told was too large for a carry-on.

When Jim got off the bus in Denver, his sea bag was gone.

So were all of his work records.

His personal effects.

And his wife's ashes.

There was no way he could keep his promise to her.

He tried to locate the bag, to no avail. He called the main offices of both bus lines, but neither was able to track down his missing luggage. His problem had been passed on to the line's Lost and Found offices, and he gave them his new mailing address.

He used the money he got in Salt Lake City to buy a bus ticket to Ohio, where one of his cousins owned a restaurant. It left him nearly broke. His cousin gave him a job washing dishes for six dollars an hour, and that, at least, managed to pay for his cheap room at the Taft Hotel, as well as two meals a day.

Three times a week he would walk from the Taft to the Cedar Hill bus terminal, ticket stub in hand, to check for the bag. The bus lines had programmed his move to Ohio into their computers, so the bag—assuming it hadn't been lost completely, or stolen—would eventually find its way to Cedar Hill, if all went well.

Days became weeks; weeks became months. Five months and three weeks. Bus line officials informed Jim that if the bag did not turn up in another seven to ten days, odds were it never would.

And his promise to his wife would forever be a lie.

At least that's how he saw it.

The nights became sleepless, the days little more than bright blurs that kept him in motion until the sun set and it was time to walk again to the tiny bus depot to be either laughed at or treated with indifference, to take his place among the other denizens of the night streets who were lost but didn't know it, who were dying but couldn't feel it, who were all waiting for something they knew would never come but refused to admit it. His only comfort was the ticket stub in his pocket that told him not to lose hope. She was out there someplace, she had to be, and maybe she knew this wasn't his fault, that he was doing everything a good and loving husband was supposed to do, but that didn't stop him from wondering very late at night, when sleep wouldn't come, whether he'd made the promise to her because he loved her, or whether he'd done it to clear his conscience of all the things he'd wanted to say to her, all the things he'd wanted to do for her in life but never got around to.

Jim Larousse began to go a little mad. In conversation, he rarely talked of anything but the sea's smell and how his wife loved it—how its lingering scent on his clothes had brought the salt air to her, and helped her imagine that she could breathe it in deeply. How she would brag about how fine she felt listening to the breakers crash against the cliffs, or the clanging of the buoys, or the lonely keening of ships' horns sounding at midnight for the lighthouse keeper to show them the way. Jim himself had once been a lighthouse keeper, and when he wasn't talking about his wife or the smell of the sea, he talked about the majesty and nobility of the lighthouse, and those whose duty it was to stand watch over the waters.

If you talked with him often enough, and if he'd had enough Crown Royal to loosen his tongue sufficiently, he'd tell you where he kept his precious ticket stub when he wasn't waiting at the bus station; or how he built a small model clipper ship out of bits of found wood and tissue paper, some tiny struts, and a chunk of balsa out of which he carved the hull. He'd tell you about the model's display stand, and how he put it together using pieces of discarded crates dug out of the trash behind the restaurant, and the assortments of rocks and stones he used to create the faux cliffs.

He'd tell you about the small lighthouse he built from a model kit he bought for three dollars at a flea market, and how, on those nights when he's too tired to make the trek to the bus station, he'd take the ticket stub and place it atop one of the masts, amidst the yards, booms, and rigging, and how it looked like a mighty sail up there, bright in the beam of the lighthouse beacon, which keeps his ship on course, regardless of the weather.

"We were always gonna find us a lighthouse, Glory and me," he'd say. "There's dozens—hell, maybe even hundreds—of 'em abandoned all up and down both coasts. We were going to find one that needed fixing up—that way we'd get it for a song, you know? Something with a tower like a French castle, with a spiral staircase inside. Glory, she'd've liked that right down to the ground."

Then he'd take out the necklace he always carried, one that looked like something a child would make; seashells and little stones strung together, souvenirs from the sea cluttered together on a strand of knitting thread. Rumor has it that one night, some drunk tried to take that necklace from Captain Jim's hand—just to look at it, mind you, not to steal it. The guy left with a broken arm.

•   •   •

Haunting the Hangman only on a semi-regular basis, I'd heard about Captain Jim but had never actually met him. My visits to the tavern were restricted to Tuesdays and Thursdays, between five and eight P.M., depending on which shift Sheriff McGuire had assigned me that week. I'm a deputy, have been for the past six years. For a while, Joe—Sheriff McGuire—had assigned me only day shift, so I could be home in the evenings with my wife, Carol, who was expecting our first child. "I know it sounds old-fashioned and sexist as hell," he said to me, "but a man ought to be around to help out when his wife is in the family way . . . and I can't believe I said 'family way.' Tell anyone else, and I'll stick you with graveyard."

Carol miscarried halfway through her fourth month, and if things between us didn't exactly sour, she made it clear to me that it might be best if I took a later shift for a while. Since her sister was now staying with us (to keep Carol company; I guess there are some intimate sadnesses a woman can only speak of with other women), I asked Joe if I could have evening shift for a while, and he agreed. Which is how I came to be at the Hangman on the night I first met Captain Jim.

I'd finished around eleven-thirty, changed into my street clothes (yeah, we really call them that), and was just putting the keys into the ignition of my car when I realized that I didn't want to go home. Any other time, I'd feel terrible about that, but Carol and her sister would either be asleep already, or on their way, so my company wouldn't be missed.

I decided to head out to the Hangman. I'd never been there that late before. So off I went, only momentarily feeling a flash of irritation at my wife.

I don't purport to be an expert on the workings of the female psyche, but lately it seemed that Carol thought she was the only one in this marriage who felt the regret, the emptiness, the disappointment and grief at having lost a child. I'd tried to talk to her about it, but between the changes her body was going through and her sister constantly running interference, my existence in our home was superfluous. There were times I'd wanted to shout at the two of them that, yes, I knew Carol was in pain—but she wasn't the one who'd had to take apart the crib and box it up, along with the bassinet and blankets and bottles and baby clothes and everything else we'd bought, haul it all back to the store, and then stand there and try to smile and be pleasant while the sales clerk, who *knew*, couldn't keep the pity from her eyes...but saying things like that seemed selfish and hurtful. If the only way I could show her that I loved her and wanted to honor her feelings was to keep my distance and remain silent, then that is what I would do. There would be time to try again.

I walked into the tavern at five minutes to midnight. The place wasn't exactly packed, but there were more than enough people there to keep Grant, the owner, adequately happy.

The Hangman is long and narrow, bar on the right and small round tables on the left, a comfortably scuffed polished-wood dance floor in between, with a stage set against the far wall, and an ancient but functioning jukebox (whose selections leaned heavily toward old blues standards) off to the side. Gleaming brass horse rails braced the opposite wall and the bottom of the bar itself, while electric lanterns anchored on thick shelves just barely wide enough to hold them provided an air of twilight inside regardless of the time of day. The place smelled of cigarettes, pipe tobacco, beer, and popcorn, all of these scents mixing with the lemon oil Grant used to polish the bar. It smelled somehow safe and welcoming.

I took a seat at the far end of the bar—noting that more people than usual were clustered around the small area where darts were played—and ordered a Pepsi and a bowl of fresh popcorn. The Hangman serves the best popcorn in the world. Grant's father, from whom Grant inherited the tavern, had some secret recipe for flavoring the butter with subtle spices that turned each handful into an exotic taste of lands faraway. I'd once said that to Grant, who'd grinned at me and said, "So you turn wistful in middle age, and my popcorn is the catalyst for your flights of fancy. I can die a fulfilled human being."

Grant served me just as the cluster of dartboard enthusiasts burst out laughing, and someone I couldn't see shouted something in a tone of voice that suggested he was becoming agitated. I hoped no one started a ruckus tonight; I wasn't in the mood.

"How're you doing these days?" Grant asked, expertly flipping glasses upside-down and racking them overhead one-handed. Grant can do wonders with that one good hand of his.

"Could complain, but it wouldn't do any good."

"Carol still not talking to you?"

"Not much. I write memos and give them to her sister."

"Sorry, man."

"Thanks."

"Should I ask how goes the fight against the insidious forces of evil trying to overtake the streets of Cedar Hill, or do we just get to the intellectual highlight of the evening with the first round of 'Rock, Paper, Scissors'?"

I shook my head and laughed. "Do you always talk like a character from a Ray Bradbury story?"

"Actually, I was going for Rod Serling, but excuse me for trying to break the monotony with some crackling and literate conversation."

I lifted my glass and silently toasted him.

"Seriously, man, you okay?"

I shrugged. "Don't quite know what to do with myself at night lately."

"Well, now that you've finally gotten a taste of the nonstop fun and frolic that is the Hangman after dark, you could come here more often. It'd be nice if you actually bought a sandwich or something instead of just eating all my popcorn. You know, an impulse purchase to help keep me out of the poorhouse."

"Fine. Make me a BLT."

"Kitchen's closed."

"You're an evil man."

"Yeah, I get a lot of complaints about that."

The noise by the dartboard got louder, and Grant shouted, "Hey! Keep it civil, okay? You guys sound like an army in full rout."

Someone waved a placating hand. Grant finished racking the overhead glasses, massaged his arthritic hand, and leaned on the bar. "Tell you what—I'll see if I can whip up a club sandwich and fries for you if you'll do a favor for me."

"Make it onion rings instead of fries and you got a deal."

"Done." He gestured toward the crowd. "Captain Jim's here tonight, and he's in worse than his customary bad shape. I know he doesn't have enough to take a cab back to the Taft, and I'm sure as hell not gonna let him try to walk back to town, so do you think you could—"

"Sure thing. One less body in the drunk tank tonight." I craned to get a better look at the patrons sitting within the cluster, hoping to catch a glimpse of the legendary captain. "How the hell does he get around, anyway?"

"Most everybody knows Jim, so it's easy for him to bum rides out here. Usually I drive him back myself, but there's a Mitchum movie on Night Owl Theater at three that I want to catch, and my VCR's on strike."

"Which movie?"

"*Farewell, My Lovely.*"

"Ah, I understand completely."

Grant squeezed my arm. "I knew that if anyone would, it'd be you."

"I'm not sure whether that's a good thing or not."

"Let's call it a good thing, and we'll both sleep easier." He retreated to the kitchen. I ate two more handfuls of popcorn, then picked up my drink and walked over toward the Dartboard Brigade. Three guys dressed in denim and sporting John Deere hats were taking their turns, while another group of guys—some of whom I recognized as pump attendants from the truck stop—occupied two of the four tables in this area.

Captain Jim sat alone at the fourth table, two empty pitchers of beer, an empty mug, and three equally empty cocktail glasses spread out before him like an audience while he held court.

In his hand was a fourth glass, its ice melting into the Scotch, turning it the color of weak iced tea.

He wasn't so old as to be considered ancient—I knew he wasn't quite yet sixty—but the shriveled damage to his face was a testament to years of sea and sun. The perpetual twilight glow from the lanterns seemed a welcome companion to him; it hung about his shoulders almost exaltedly. He wore a small knitted wool cap whose edge was rolled tightly at the tops of his ears. He was mumbling to himself and gesturing with the glass in his hand. A bit of the liquor slopped over the side and spattered the tabletop. He pulled off his cap, revealing a head covered in thick, startlingly white hair. "I might be drunk," he said to himself, "but that's no excuse for untidiness." He used his cap to mop up the spill, stuffed it into one of the pockets of the tattered blue sailor's coat he wore, then sighed and stared down at the floor.

I've dealt with my share of drunks—the violent ones, the sloppy ones, the maudlin, pissy, angry, self-pitying ones—and over the years I've learned to place a barrier between them and my emotions. People are entitled to drink as little or as much as they want; I make no moral judgments. But when their drinking turns into public drunkenness and I have to step in, I find it's not advisable to let sympathy get in the way of performing one's duty. As a result, I've gotten really good at distancing myself when confronted with a drunk—which is why I was surprised at how quickly and how deeply I felt compassion for Captain Jim.

It was his voice more than anything else. His voice was the sound of an empty house when the door was opened, or an empty bed in the middle of the night, or an empty crib that never knew an occupant. It was dead leaves skittering across a cold autumn sidewalk; the low, mournful whistling of the wind as it passes through the branches of bare trees. It was a sound so completely, totally, irrevocably *alone* that hearing it just in a whisper's instant made you long for the warmth and safety of home and hearth; even if your presence there was superfluous, at least you weren't as alone as that sound.

I moved in closer, making it appear that I was intensely interested in the game of darts on which the participants' lives seemed to depend, but in truth I was drawn to Jim's voice as he talked to the floor and the table, the boards, empty pitchers, and glasses a captive audience.

"They say the first ones were probably built by the

Phoenicians or the Greeks. The port of Rodas was once guarded by a statue of Helios, *El Coloso*, they called him, standing taller than any of the ancient gods. Held a fire in his outstretched hand for all the ships to see. Egyptians had one in the port of Alexandria, built by Sostratos of Knidos, did'ya know that? Wouldn't lie to you. Sailors say its light can still be seen some nights, even though the structure's long gone. I've been there; I've been in all the places where the ghosts of the towers live, yessir. Along the Mediterranean coast where the Romans used to have them, the Atlantic coasts of Spain and France, up to the English Channel. You know, I once even stood at the top of the Tower of Hercules in La Coruña. It was built in the first century—A.D., that is—probably to guide Spanish ships sailing to Ireland. It's still there.

"In the beginning, they were all just piles of stones with wood fires burning at the top. Fires in towers, fires in the heart, all guiding you home. And to think it all started a night thousands of years ago when someone stood on the shore and looked out to the sea and thought, 'I'm going to build a tower whose firelight will be seen by those lonely travelers on the waters far away. Perhaps when they see it, they will come for a visit. A visit from the waters would be splendid.' All from a pile of stones."

He looked up at one of the empty pitchers on his table. "In the end, that's what they all go back to . . . just piles of stones scattered along the shore, waiting for the tide to come in and pull them into the water. But for a while—oh, Lord!—for a while, they stand there in majesty, don't they? We'd've been happy there, her tending the rooms, me tending to the lights and fog horn . . ."

He began to sway in his seat, and for a moment I thought he was going to fall off his chair, but he blinked, seemed to realize he was losing it, and quickly righted himself.

His gaze met mine. He lifted his glass in salute.

"Wouldn't happen to be from the bus station, would you?"

"Afraid not."

"Ah, well." He brought the glass to his lips and held it there, not drinking. "Doesn't hurt a fellow to ask." He downed the rest of the scotch in one quick swallow. "I know you." He grinned. "You're The Man, Johnny Law."

"You forgot 'the fuzz.'"

He waved that one away. "Dumbass nickname, that one."

I introduced myself and shook his hand. Even his grip felt lonely.

He patted down his pockets until he found a slightly crumpled cigarette pack from which he managed to pull one slightly crumpled cigarette. "Glory used to get on me something fierce about my smoking. I quit for a while. Then one day a few weeks ago, I just had a craving. You ever have that happen to you? Just wake up one morning and suddenly have a craving for something that you know isn't any damn good for you but you just got to have it?"

I shook my head.

"Well, you're young." He lit the cigarette, pulled on it, and let the smoke curl around his jaw as he slowly exhaled. "Ought to find yourself a vice of some sort. Keeps you sane when nothing answers the sound of your voice in the middle of the night."

I gestured at all the empties. "This your vice, is it?"

"I prefer to think of myself as an athlete in training. For the Olympic elbow-bending team."

"I'll have to remember that one."

He studied my face. "You here in an official capacity?"

"Yes and no."

"So I am doomed, after all."

"Still cheerful, I see," said Grant, coming up to the table and setting down a plate stacked with onion rings.

"Where's my club sandwich?" I said.

"I only got one hand, in case you haven't noticed." Then, to Jim: "I see you've met your ride home."

"Oh, I see. Too busy for your best customer tonight."

"Got a Mitchum movie tonight, Jim. Sorry. But you'll be safe with the deputy here. Can't afford to have anything happen to my best customer, can I? Who'd give the place a touch of color?"

"Is that what I am? Color?" He shook his head and looked

at me. "That's what happens when you live long enough. You get colorful."

"Great line. Strother Martin in *Butch Cassidy and the Sundance Kid*."

Jim looked at me, then at Grant. "I see you found another guy for your act. Allow me to offer my heartiest congratulations."

Grant laughed, squeezed Jim's shoulder affectionately, then retreated for my sandwich.

"I appreciate your kindness."

I shrugged. "My pleasure."

"I wouldn't be so quick with that one," he said.

It was close to two-thirty in the morning by the time I unlocked the door to Jim's room at the Taft. Despite the city's efforts to renovate the area in which the hotel was located, the Taft remained a depressing and slightly decrepit monolith of a building. In its heyday it had seen the likes of heavyweight boxing champions, famous artists, and three presidents; now it was just another in a long line of ruined places where the damaged, the despondent and the discarded, the lost and the shabby come when they reach the end of their rope and life offers no alternative but to crawl into the shadows of poverty and just give up.

"Nice room," I said to Jim as he turned on the only light, which hung down from a chain in the middle of the ceiling.

"Liar. But thank you."

Star and meteorological charts were scattered all around the room, which didn't surprise me (a sailor such as Jim would have an understandable interest in such things), but what threw me were the several opened books on physics and chaos theory math, all of them with dog-eared pages.

I handed him his key and was trying to come up with a courteous way to ask about the books, when I looked over at his bedside table and saw the model of the clipper ship, the ersatz beach, and the model lighthouse.

"That's quite something," I said.

"It's not done yet. I still need to finish carving out the figures." He looked at the display, then to me. "Myself and my Glory. Gonna show her the magic—Gloria, my wife."

"Yes, I know—I mean, I've heard about what—I mean—"

"It's all right. I realize that I am a popular subject of barroom conversation. Colorful character that I am."

"I meant no offense."

"I inferred none. Please, have a seat."

The only chair in the room was an old recliner whose stuffing had long since given up the ghost. I did not so much sit as sink. Jim reached into the pocket of his coat and removed a tarnished silver flask.

"A little nightcap, if you don't mind."

"Go right ahead."

He pulled down a couple of swallows from the bottle, sat on the edge of his bed, and stared at the display of ship and lighthouse.

"It looks almost as if you're recreating some sort of scene from a movie or book," I finally said.

"Close." Another swig. "It's part of my dream—the one that comes to me when I've had enough of this." He held up the flask. "If Glory was here, she'd tan my hide for partaking of the demon rum."

"I thought you drank Crown Royal."

"I was speaking in terms better suited to a colorful local character." Another sip, then he sat back against the chipped headboard. "So why isn't an upstanding fellow such as yourself home with his family?"

"I, um . . . had my shift changed recently, and I'm a little agitated nights. Makes my wife nervous, and I don't like to keep her awake."

"Ah."

"Really. She's not been very well lately, and I—" The rest of the words retreated back down my throat. There was no reason for me to explain anything to this man with the voice that sounded like a cold and sunless shore.

"So you've heard about my wife?" he asked.

"Some. I'm very sorry she was so sick for so long."

Before I could say anything else, he began telling me about Gloria.

He spoke as if he were composing a poem to be written down for the ages yet to come: the way she laughed, the delicate tapering of her fingers, the way she played rhapsodies on their piano. The frailness of body that could not cripple the strength of spirit; her temper, which could flare bright and hot as any sudden fire; the way she would always place one hand over her heart when she laughed while holding the other straight out (in case the mirth became too much and she died laughing). He described the softness of her breath against his neck at night, the velvet cradle of her hair, her sigh, her whisper, the way she always chewed on her lower lip when reading—all of this he wove into a rich tapestry before my mind's eye until, at last, I felt as if Gloria Larousse were sitting there in the room with us.

"You must miss her very much," I said when he finished.

"I do. She was the love I was meant to find. She was also grand company. Absolutely grand." He reached into another of his coat's pockets and removed the famous necklace. "See this stone in the center? This shiny black one?"

"Yes."

"I found this on the shore near the port of Rodas. An old, old, *old* man there swore up and down that this very stone was part of the rock that formed the flame the statue of Helios held above its head. He told me of a local legend that claimed if this stone were tossed into the waters by a true soul of the sea, it would light the way home.

"Gloria put this stone in the center of her necklace. There are thirty-three pieces strung together here, driftwood, shells, stones . . . thirty-three pieces from thirty-three different places around this globe. And in the center, Helios's magical flame. It's part of my dream, as well."

"The same one with the ship and the lighthouse?"

"Have I mentioned any other? No need to answer that, it was a rhetorical question."

"I figured."

"Bright fellow. How proud your wife must be."

I know he meant it in a good-natured, joking way, but something in it stung me.

To get my mind away from that particular dark corner, I asked: "So, what happens in this dream of yours, if you don't mind me asking?"

He rose from the bed and began pacing as he spoke, all the while rolling the necklace between his hands as if he were thinking of attempting a cat's cradle with it.

"At the very start, I'm standing on a beach in Florida. Glory always wanted to see Florida, so in my dream I've gone down there for her, and I'm at the *very spot* where Ponce de Leon landed in 1513, hoping it was the city of Bimini where he could find the fountain of youth; and as I'm standing there, I can see all the way to St. Augustine, overrun with the old and sick who wait in the salt air and sunshine for death to embrace them. I open my mouth to call out—don't know who I'm going to call out to or what I'm going to say, but it doesn't matter, because that's when the sea gives up its dead—and me, I'm pulled into the water. All of me becomes liquid, and I know the sea's secrets, and I watch...in my dream I watch as, off the coast of the Ile de la Seine, the Ship of the Dead appears, dropping clumps of viscera and isinglass, which drift in toward shore; by the banks of the Colorado River near an ancient Anasazi village, a decaying boat of cedar and horsehide drifts to land, and from it steps a ragged and bleeding woman who kneels by an undiscovered kiva, wailing a song of loss and misery in Urdu to the god Angwusnasomtaqa, praying that the Crow Mother will return her to her mate in the Netherworld; off Ballachulish in Argyllshire, a shipload of drowned crofters materializes, howling in the most dread-filled loneliness; a fisherman in Vancouver sees a mountainous trident emerge from the water, pierce through, then uproot an oak before it vanishes below the surface, creating waves so powerful they smash his small boat into splinters, but that's okay—you see, he drowns with a happy heart because he's seen a miracle, which is all he's ever wanted out of life; in icy hyperborean waters, another doomed vessel, captained by a German nobleman named Faulkenburg, races through the night with tongues of fire licking at its masthead; St. Brendan's Isle appears in the Atlantic—but for only a moment, just long enough for three Coelacanths to push off from shore and submerge into the waters; many miles away, the SS *Cotapaxi*, which vanished en route from Charleston to Havana in 1925, drifts out of the sea-mist, its crew, looking through hollow and algae-encrusted sockets where their eyes used to be, smile at one another, happy to be voyaging once again; then a kraken, the same one found by the Bishop of Midros, thunders out of its underwater cave long enough to snare two scuba divers in its mighty tentacles and drag them, shredded and screaming, back under the waves, while the *Raifuku Maru*—it was a Japanese freighter that vanished off the coast of Cuba the same year as the *Cotapaxi*—reappears just long enough for three crew members to throw themselves over the side because they're all diving for a baggage-claim ticket that's bobbed to the surface.

"And then I realize that all of it, all of them, *everything*, has moved in close to shore and is watching me. All of the fish in the sea, as well. All of them so near, trembling and staring up at me with their odd and cold eyes—because by now, you see, I'm me again, and I'm standing high above it all on a cliff, and I'm saying, 'Show me the magic.' And when I look down I see that it's not a cliff at all, but the observation deck of a lighthouse that, even as I am trying to understand how, is rising out of the ground like some great titan awakening from a thousand years of slumber. And before me the denizens of the sea make room for the great clipper ship that is coming toward my light. The ship moves in toward shore, and when it dares not come any closer, when the rocks below become too jagged and treacherous for its hull to chance, the fish swim beneath it and carry the ship on their backs as they crawl onto land. They bring the ship close, closer, until the crow's nest of its central mast is level with the lighthouse's observation deck. And she's there, my Glory, in the nest. Her hand reaches out toward me, and I try to take hold of her, to help her step over the rail and into my arms, and then..." He shrugged.

"You wake up."

"Nothing quite so anticlimactic. Then the Loch Ness Monster sticks its head above the surface, looks around, decides not to take part in this silliness, and submerges once again."

"You're kidding?"

"I'm kidding. The truth is, the dream just stops there. Her hand, so close to mine. At least, that's how it stopped last time." He pocketed the necklace and grabbed up the flask. "The thing is, in the last several weeks, the drunker I am when I fall asleep, the closer the ship comes, the nearer her hand. So I... well, I think you're a clever enough fellow to figure the rest out, aren't you?" He reached out and grabbed up one of the books on physics, flipped to a previously marked page, and asked: "You ever hear the term *syzygy*?"

"Can't say I have, no."

"Huh. You know they got themselves that weather lab over at Ohio State University?"

"Yeah...?"

"Well—and you can believe this or not—but I've been over there. Several times, in fact. Been over to the radio telescope, too. Damned impressive stuff."

"I'll bet."

He rubbed his eyes, seemed to consider something, then said: "I know folks think I'm crazy. I know they grin when they call me Captain Jim. And I know that you're probably gonna repeat this to everyone over at the Hangman and you'll all get a good laugh out of it, but I'm gonna tell you something I haven't told anyone else."

"Why haven't you told anyone else?"

He pointed to my hand. "Look at you. Young married fellow, shiny wedding ring on your hand, and here you are in a shabby-assed room with some crazy old man instead of on your way home to the wife. My guess is she don't much want you around these days. I know, I know—it's none of my business. I'm just guessing here...but I'm right, aren't I?"

"How did you—"

"It's the eyes."

"What? Something in a person's eyes tells you that they're having trouble at home?"

He grinned. "No. It's nothing *in* the eyes. It's something that's gone from them. You get old enough, you'll understand. Anyway, that's why I'm gonna tell you about…about what I'm gonna tell you. Right now, you and me, we're kinda the same in a way. We both of us love women who ain't there for us in one way or the other. I think you got a good face, a kind one. And I think maybe a young married fellow with a kind face and a wife that don't want him around will understand how I'm feeling—how I've *been* feeling for a long time now.

"I miss my Glory, like I said. But I got this here stone, you see, from Helios's fire, and I know more myths and tales about the sea than anyone you'll ever meet, and I've been over to the university. They laugh and grin at me over there, too…but they also indulge me. They show me how their expensive equipment works, and they humor a crazy old man when he asks them a crazy-old-man question.

"I have memorized the heavens, boy, the position of the stars, the movement of the planets, the timing of the constellations, the patterns of the tides, and the phases of the moon. I know a thing or two about meteorology. I've used compasses and barometers, sling psychrometers and aerovane indicators, light duration transmitters and radiosonde receivers. I can recite the variables of convection, tropopause, and jet stream patterns in my sleep. I can read any topography map you throw down in front of me, and predict with a 76 percent certainty the migration patterns of over two dozen species of birds. People think all I do is wash dishes, go to the bus station, and drink myself silly. But I've been *working*, boy, you understand? Studying things. Planning."

"For what?" I asked, genuinely interested; for a crazy old man, he was pretty compelling.

"Syzygy," he replied. "The moment that happens only once in a lifetime when all the planets in this galaxy are in perfect alignment. Know when that's gonna happen—well, okay, technically it's happening as we speak, the planets are all moving into position. But the alignment itself, the moment when high tide arrives and the moon reaches its zenith and the tidal forces vary in approximation with the inverse cube of the moon's distance from the Earth, *that's* gonna happen in less than twenty-four hours!"

I remembered having read something about that in the science section of last Sunday's paper (and only understanding every other word of the experts' explanations). I'd also showed it to Carol in hopes of sparking some sort of response from her, but—as usual—her sister Gina had waved me away with one of her You're-only-making-things-worse expressions.

"So it's happening tomorrow night," I said. "So?"

"I got... I got me this stone, see?"

"From Helios's flame, yes, I remember."

"Didn't you ever read anything about the gods of the sea when you were in school? How the alignment of the planets and the pattern of the tides and... and all the rest of it, how they can call the gods back to Earth?"

"I went to a Catholic school. The nuns weren't big on pluralizing the word *God*."

He closed his hand around the necklace. "I have kept part of Helios's light alive for him, and tomorrow night, he's gonna reward me. He's gonna show me the magic."

I felt so sorry for him. The loss of his wife, and the subsequent loss of her ashes, had truly driven him mad. I'd heard about how crazy he was, but I don't think I really believed it until that moment. Then the deputy in me came forward, and I started looking around the room for weapons—a gun, a knife—anything he might be able to use to hurt himself or others. The madness in his eyes actually scared me.

"I know that look," he said. "And you don't need to worry yourself. I'm not about to hurt myself or anyone else. I finally got something to look forward to. Why the hell would I want to shuffle off the old mortal coil *now?*"

I thanked him for the company and left for home.

As the fount and origin of life, water is naturally connected with woman; Aphrodite was born of the sea, the fountain is one of the emblems of the Virgin Mary, and in the Cabala, the Sefirah Binah is called the Mother, the Throne, the

Great Sea. Modern magic links it with Chaos and the stars. It has always been associated with the moon and with light, both of which are constantly altering because of their *flow*—changing shape, location, and purpose, as does anything that is intertwined with the core configuration of life. Some mythologies connect water and the moon with the depths of the mind, the unconscious, where the waters of Chaos are also the waters of potential life. "Perform no operation till all be made water," says the Book of Genesis; and so the vessel, the believer, this man of flesh and loneliness must himself be reduced to the liquid state of watery primeval Chaos before "philosophical mercury"—the miracle of physical existence from the sea—can surge forth to create a new material or condition. Or in the case of Captain Jim and the stone from Helios's fire, create both material and condition.

I have done much reading and thinking since the night when Captain Jim showed me the magic. I am wiser, I think, and I keep his story well. That should count for something, shouldn't it?

I walked through the back door of my home a little after four in the morning. I saw it leaning against the sugar bowl on the kitchen table.

The note was short and to the point, I'll give her that:

> *Gina asked me to fly back to Eugene with her. She thinks I might feel better if I got away from the house for a while. The walls closing in and all that. I'm sorry that we snuck out like we did, but Gina thought you might cause a scene. I do love you. I'll call you when we get in—just remember there's a three-hour time difference.*

I sat by the phone until ten-thirty. She didn't call. I knew Gina would convince her to wait until I left for work before dialing the number.

I was pulling out of the driveway at three-thirty when I heard the phone. The machine picked up on the third ring.

• • •

I wish I could tell you that my shift that night was so crammed full of auguries that a man would had to have been clinically brain-dead not to catch on, but in truth it was—for the most part—one of the most supremely dull shifts I'd ever worked. Traffic citations. Telling some kids to keep the noise of their party down to a loud roar. Keeping an eye out for a lost dog (which I found, safe and sound, much to the owner's relief). Writing it down would have bored the letters off a diary's page.

I kept thinking back to what Captain Jim had told me, and whenever he or his rantings crossed my mind (which was more and more frequently as the night wore on), I'd roll down the window of the cruiser—it was a wonderful, clear night, temperature holding steady at sixty-eight degrees—and look up at the stars. Forget what he said about chaos and the stars; to my mind, the heavens looked peaceful and all in order. Unlike my life. But that was for later, when I had to face a house devoid of voices, laughter, or the sounds of a child sleeping in its crib.

It was getting close to eleven-fifteen. I'd just checked the weather for the area—clear and warm, with zero percent chance of rain (straight from the National Weather Service, thank you very much)—when the radio squawked and the dispatcher told me to give Grant a call out at the Hangman. Official business. So I had no qualms about using the car phone.

"It's me, Grant."

"Oh, man, thanks for calling right back. Look, it's Jim. He's really—and I mean *really*—in bad shape."

"Drunk?"

"Hell, yes, but that isn't the problem. Drunk I can handle. He was going on about something called siz...sizee..."

"Syzygy?"

A pause. "How the hell'd you know that?"

"My still waters run deep. So what happened?"

"He was almost out of control, man. I threatened to throw him out—and you know I *never* do that. Bummed a ride from a trucker heading up by Buckeye Lake. They left here about ten minutes ago. I tried to get him to stay, but he was hellbent."

Something cold in my stomach. "Did he say *where* by the

lake he was going?" Creation of material and condition: I knew
what Grant was going to tell me before the fourth word was
out of his mouth.

"He asked the guy to drop him off near the fishing pier.
Said something about getting himself one of the boats and
rowing his ass to—"

"Cholera Island?"

"You got it."

"Son of a bitch!" I slammed down the phone, cussing myself up one side and down the other. All his talk of lighthouses.
All his talk of the sea and his dream and Glory and Helios's
light and the gods being called back to Earth by alignments
and patterns and—

—I hit the siren, fired up the visibar lights, and floored
the cruiser. A crazy old drunk in a rowboat in the middle of the
lake at midnight. Oh, yeah, no potential for disaster there.

In the early days of Cedar Hill, when the Welsh, Scotch,
and Irish immigrants worked alongside the Delaware and
Wyandot Indians to establish safe shipping lanes through
places such as Black Hand Gorge, the Narrows, and Buckeye
Lake, it was decided that a beacon of some sort needed to be
erected.

Two miles out from the shores of Buckeye Lake sits an isolated island that is perhaps ten, twelve miles in circumference.
Perfect for a lighthouse. Construction began in April of 1875,
but was halted in June that same year when a devastating epi-
demic of cholera swept through the county. People were dying
so fast and in such great numbers that bodies had to be collected in express wagons every eight hours. People were dying
faster than healthy men could be found to bury them. In a last,
desperate attempt to calm a rapidly panicking population, a
group of Delaware Indians—who would soon die from their
good deed—offered to take some of the rapidly accumulating
bodies across the water to the deserted island and bury them
by the tower's foundation. Something like five hundred bodies
were buried there, and remain under the soil to this day. About
a hundred years later, the island was purchased from the
county by the Licking Valley Boaters' Association. The founda-

tion was given a fresh layer of cement, and on top of it was built the Licking Valley Yacht and Boaters' Clubhouse—three stories of luxury and privacy where the members never stop to think that they're sitting on top of half a thousand dead bodies, or that their little paradise is called "Cholera Island" by the locals—most of whom will never set foot on its docks, let alone see the inside of the manorlike clubhouse.

Jim would have no trouble getting a rowboat from the pier—dozens of them were available year-round for the fishermen who rented the small bungalows. The waters of the lake were usually calm, but this late at night he might very well plow over some teenagers out for some midnight skinny-dipping.

I checked my watch. Given a steady speed of sixty-five to seventy, the trucker was probably dropping Jim off near the pier road right about now. Tack on another three minutes to walk up to the bungalows and docks, a minute or two more to untie one of the boats, climb in, and start rowing, and I had about five minutes. I'd make it.

And that's when the storm hit.

As simplistic and melodramatic as that may sound, it doesn't come close to conveying how suddenly, powerfully, and overwhelmingly *fast* the weather changed. One moment I'm flying up I-70 toward Buckeye Lake and it's a clear, warm, starry night outside, and the next second—and I am not exaggerating here, this oddity is documented if you care to check—the very next second, *WHAM!*—a downpour so torrential I couldn't see five feet in front of me. The wind hit the cruiser so hard (at forty-eight miles per hour, as it turned out), I almost went off the road. The rain became horizontal, and the thunder was so violent I thought for a moment someone had finally dropped the Bomb.

Perform no operation till all be made water.

It took me eleven minutes to make what should have been a three-minute drive. By the time I climbed out of the cruiser armed with the high-powered portable floodlight each sheriff's vehicle is equipped with, Jim was at least a quarter-mile out. I could see him because the emergency lights of both the lake's pier and the island's docks had automatically come on when the first power surge occurred. He was a shadow atop foam and fury, and there was nothing I could do in time to save him.

There was a break in the tumult of the storm, a moment of odd, displaced silence, and I heard something that might have been the sound of an empty-house voice crying out, *Show me the magic.*

The storm cracked and slashed and fractured and screamed. The water rose up into gigantic frothing fists that slammed against his pitifully small boat, but on he rowed. The snarling waves crashing over the pier hit me at my knees, more than once nearly knocking me over. Lightning splintered through the darkness, and the rain turned to hail that clattered and assailed anything it found waiting beneath.

All along the pier I could see curtains being pulled back inside the bungalows as frightened fishermen stared out at the insane man in the rowboat, struggling through a storm that wasn't supposed to be.

I grabbed onto a dock pole and held on, watching, helpless.

The water seemed to be pulsing, teeming with hundreds—*thousands*—of small objects. I managed to train the floodlight downward, and saw what at first appeared to be countless gray stones bouncing across the surface.

And then the wind eased up, as did the rain and hail, and I saw that they were not stones at all, but fish. Thousands of fish, all of them moving forward in deliberate, perfectly lined groups, synchronized swimmers, their cold eyes directed toward the crazy old man in the rowboat—

—Who, I saw now under the great flashes of lightning, was standing up, twirling something over his head. A last cry, and he released the necklace, which flew out, caught an updraft, sailed along like a majestic bird, and was swallowed by the water.

The fish, en masse, moved toward him.

The waters churned and the sky thundered.

The fish surrounded Jim's boat, seeming to cling to its sides, and through the mist and rain and waves guided him toward Cholera Island as a ship—a clipper ship, majestic and ghostly—moved through the fog and spray.

I stood there trembling. I had never seen a Wonder before.

Jim quickly ran to the base of the lighthouse, whose ghost was rising from the center of the clubhouse; the higher it rose, the more substantial its structure became, and the more spectral that of the Yacht and Boaters' Club.

I watched as Jim ran up the spiral stairs within, his shadow soaring by one of the small windows placed every seven feet straight up. I watched him emerge on the observation deck and turn on the great light. It was touched with gold on this night. His silhouette against it took my breath away.

As did the sight of the clipper ship moving in close to shore, then somehow seeming to float above the water, coming closer until the crow's nest of its central mast was mere feet from the rail where Jim stood.

I saw a thin and elegant woman reach out from the crow's nest, and I saw Jim reach toward her, and I whispered to the storm-ravaged night, "Show him the magic," and the woman took his hand and moved toward him, moved through the nest and rail that separated her from him, and in a moment that I will never forget, they held one another in the great light from the stone tower, so noble and patient and faithful.

Carol never came back from Oregon. I cannot honestly say I expected her to. There is some grief you can never recover from, and some people who will always remind you of that grief, no matter how much they love you and hope to make you smile again.

The mysterious storm that ripped through Cedar Hill and surrounding areas was a hot topic of discussion and debate for weeks; the National Weather Service radar had detected no storm activity anywhere near our area. There was—and remains—no rational explanation. We were hit by something that should not have been, but was, nonetheless.

The fish and the clipper ship and the lighthouse were gone with the dawn, of course. Wonders like that have no use for the analytic light of day. The sublime remains merely that, and always just out of reach.

And so the vessel, the believer, the man of flesh and loneliness was himself reduced to the liquid state of watery primeval Chaos before the miracle of physical existence from the sea surged forth, creating a new material and condition so he might hold in his arms the woman who was, is, and always shall be the love he was meant to find.

I think of Jim and his Glory every day. I don't know whether I find hope or sadness in these thoughts, but they keep me company.

A few months after all of this happened, I got a call from Andy Powell, who works days at the Cedar Hill bus terminal.

"I got something here you might be interested in," he said. It was Jim Larousse's sea bag. Inside was the container that held his Glory's ashes. I rented a boat and scattered them near the shore of Cholera Island. I kept the container. It's quite lovely. Grant displays it on one of the shelves behind the bar at the Hangman. Inside are dozens of seashells, bits of oddly shaped driftwood, and small stones so long tossed by the tides that their surfaces are as smooth and clear as glass.

You see, if you want a closer look at the model of the ship and the lighthouse—which sits alone on a high, bright shelf behind the bar, and which Jim gave to Grant on the last night any of us ever saw him—then the price is something for the "sea vase," as Grant has dubbed it.

If you give a shell or a tide-tossed stone, then Grant will gently take down the model, and you can marvel at its craftsmanship and the love in the faces of the two figures, one who stands atop the lighthouse, the other, a woman, in the crow's nest of the ship.

"What's the story behind this?" you might very well ask.

That's when the regulars will point you in my direction. "If you wanna hear the story of Captain Jim," they'll say, clapping a happy hand on your shoulder, "then *there's* the fellah you ought to be talking with."

And that's true. I was there. I saw it. I know the truth

about Captain Jim's drunken dream. And even if my own life never amounts to more than a footnote somewhere—even if I never find a woman who will love me as Glory loved her Jim, even if the sound of my voice becomes more like an empty room or dead leaves skittering across the autumn streets—I will always have his story, and I will always tell it well.

That should count for something, shouldn't it?

CONTRIBUTORS

Rick Hautala has had more than twenty books published, including the million-copy international bestseller *Nightstone*. Nearly seventy-five of his short stories have appeared in national and international anthologies and magazines. His media tie-in novel, *Poltergeist: The Legacy—The Hidden Saint* was published in 1999, and four other novels came out in 2001

A graduate of the University of Maine, with a Master of Arts in Renaissance Literature, Hautala is married and lives in southern Maine with his family. He has served terms as vice president and trustee for the Horror Writers Association.

Jane Lindskold spent her summers on Chesapeake Bay, where she learned to appreciate the constancy of lighthouses. These days she lives in New Mexico, a state so dry that the tiny pond in her yard attracts migrating birds. Her more recent novels include *Changer* and *Legends Walking*.

Brendan DuBois is the award-winning author of short stories and novels. His short fiction has appeared in *Playboy, Ellery Queen's Mystery Magazine, Alfred Hitchcock's Mystery Magazine, Mary Higgins Clark Mystery Magazine,* and numerous anthologies. He has received the Shamus Award from the

Private Eye Writers of America for one of his short stories, and has been nominated three times for an Edgar Allan Poe Award by the Mystery Writers of America.

He's also the author of the Lewis Cole mystery series. His most recent novel, *Resurrection Day*, is a suspense thriller that received the Sidewise Award for best alternative history novel of 1999. He lives in New Hampshire with his wife, Mona.

Ed Gorman has been called "One of the most original crime writers around" by *Kirkus Reviews* and "A powerful storyteller" by the *Los Angeles Times*. He works in horror and westerns as well as crime and writes many excellent short stories. To date there have been six Gorman collections. He is probably best known for his Sam McCain series, set in the small-town Iowa of the 1950s. He has also written a number of thrillers, including *The Marilyn Tapes* and *Black River Falls,* with the latest being *The Poker Club*.

Billie Sue Mosiman has published eight suspense novels, garnering an Edgar Award nomination for *Night Cruise* and a Stoker Award nomination for *Widow*. Always active as a short story writer, she has seen her work selected for various magazines and anthologies. She has also co-edited several anthologies. Her most recent work is the novel *Red Moon Rising*. She lives in Midway Texas.

Kristine Kathryn Rusch has been nominated for several dozen fiction awards, and her short work has been reprinted in six *Year's Best* collections. She has published twenty novels under her own name and has sold forty-one total, including pseudonymous books. Her novels have been published in seven languages and have spent several weeks on the *USA Today* and *Wall Street Journal* bestseller lists. She has written a number of Star Trek novels with her husband,

Dean Wesley Smith, and is the former editor of *The Magazine of Fantasy and Science Fiction*, winning a Hugo for her work there. Before that, she and Smith started and ran Pulphouse Publishing, a science fiction and mystery press in Eugene.

She lives and works on the Oregon Coast.

Matthew Costello was known primarily as a horror writer and author of bestselling computer games until the late 1990s, when he began collaborating with F. Paul Wilson on bestselling mainstream science fiction. Costello is primarily a character-driven writer. Whatever else is going on in the story, Costello is letting you know about his people.

A.J. Matthews's first novel, *The White Room*, was published in 2001. He is a semi-retired junior high school English teacher who lives in southern Maine with his wife and two sons. This is his first published short story and his first collaborative work with Matthew Costello. When not writing or reading, he is usually found asleep on the couch.

In her twenty-five years as a writer, editor, and publishing consultant, **Janet Berliner** has worked with such authors as Peter S. Beagle, David Copperfield, Michael Crichton, and Joyce Carol Oates. Among her most recent books are *David Copperfield's Beyond Imagination*, an anthology that she created and edited, and *Children of the Dusk*, the final book of the Madagasacar Manifesto series, coauthored with George Guthridge. Currently Janet divides her time between Las Vegas, where she lives and works, and Grenada, West Indies, where her heart is.

Yvonne Navarro is an award-winning Chicago area novelist whose work was first published in 1984. Since then she's had twelve novels, a reference dictionary, and over seventy short stories published. Her writing has been nominated for the Bram Stoker Award several times and she won the CWIP Award for Excellence in Adult Fiction in 1997. She's the owner of Dusty Stacks Bookstore and also studies martial arts. Sometimes she'd like to chuck it all and run off to Arizona.

Nina Kiriki Hoffman has been writing for almost twenty years and has sold almost two hundred stories, two short-story collections, novels, a young-adult novel with Tad Williams, a Star Trek novel with Kristine Kathryn Rusch and Dean Wesley Smith, three R.L. Stine's Ghosts of Fear Street volumes, and one Sweet Valley Junior High book. She has cats.

Thomas F. Monteleone has been a professional writer since 1972. He has published more than a hundred short stories, many of which have appeared in best-of-the-year compilations. He is the editor of six anthologies, including the highly acclaimed Borderlands series, edited with his wife, Elizabeth. Of his twenty novels, *The Blood of the Lamb* received the 1993 Bram Stoker Award, and the *New York Times* Notable Book of the Year Award. His books and stories have been translated into twelve foreign languages.

Monteleone lives in Grantham, New Hampshire.

Gary A. Braunbeck is the author of several short story collections. His first solo novel, *The Indifference of Heaven*, was recently released by Obsidian Books, as was his Dark Matter novel, *In Hollow Houses*. He lives in Columbus, Ohio, and has, to date, sold nearly two hundred short stories. His fiction, to quote *Publisher's Weekly*, "stirs the mind as it chills the marrow."

Visit our web site at
www.downeastbooks.com,
or call (800)766-1670 for a free catalog,
to read more about these
and other fine books:

*LIGHTHOUSES FROM ALOFT: 51 Scenic
New England Lights,* aerial photos by Charles Feil

*LIGHTHOUSE IN MY LIFE: The Story of a
Maine Lightkeeper's Family,* by Philmore Wass

LIGHTHOUSES OF MAINE
by Bill Caldwell

*LIGHTHOUSE HORRORS: Tales of Adventure,
Suspense, and the Supernatural*
stories by Bradbury, Kipling, Poe, and others

*GHOSTS OF BOSTON TOWN: Three Centuries of
True Hauntings,* by Holly Nadler

*HAUNTED ISLAND: True Ghost Stories from
Martha's Vineyard,* by Holly Nadler

*NANTUCKET HAUNTINGS: 21 Firsthand
Encounters with the Supernatural,* by Blue Balliett

MAINE GHOSTS AND LEGENDS
by Thomas Verde

GHOSTS ON THE COAST OF MAINE
by Carol Olivieri Schulte

continued next page…

THE DEAD OF WINTER, by David Crossman.
Murder mystery set on a Maine island

SOMETHING IN THE WATER, by Peter Scott.
Adventure novel with a supernatural touch
set on the Maine coast in WWII.

For younger readers:

LIGHTHOUSE LULLABY
by Kelly Paul Briggs (ages 3–5)

THE LITTLEST LIGHTHOUSE
by Ruth Sargent, ill. by Marion Litchfield
(ages 4–7)

CAPTAIN'S CASTAWAY
LIGHTHOUSE DOG TO THE RESCUE
SIRIUS, THE DOG STAR

3 stories by Angeli Perrow, ill. by Emily Harris
True-life adventures of lighthouse children
and their loyal dogs (ages 5–9)

THE SECRET OF THE MISSING GRAVE
THE MYSTERY OF THE BLACK MORIAH

2 novels by David Crossman featuring intrepid
13-year-old boy and girl on a Maine island
(ages 10 and up)